Kup

Kup
A man, an era, a city

Irv Kupcinet's Autobiography
with Paul Neimark

Bonus Books, Chicago

92   91   90   89   88   5   4   3   2   1

Library of Congress Catalog Card Number: 88-71005

International Standard Book Number: 0-933893-70-1

Bonus Books, Inc.
160 East Illinois Street
Chicago, Illinois 60611

Printed in the United States of America

To the future—Jerry, Susan, Kari and David.
To the past—in memory of Karyn.
And to the cast of thousands who filled Kup's Column.

Contents

1

1943

The Japanese were being driven from Guadalcanal. The Germans from Tunisia. Mussolini from Italy. Roosevelt, Churchill and Stalin met in Teheran.

Upton Sinclair's *Dragon's Teeth* won the Pulitzer Prize.

Polio killed more than a thousand people in the United States, but penicillin was first used by the public.

Ted Lawson's book, *Thirty Seconds Over Tokyo*, and Wendell Wilkie's *One World* were the talk of the literary world.

Oklahoma was still the rage on Broadway. "Mairzy Doats," "I'll Be Seeing You," and "Oh What a Beautiful Mornin'" were on everybody's lips.

Shoe, meat, silk stocking and sugar rationing began.

The zoot suit (with the reet pleat) was popular among the hepcats.

And turf fans were enshrining "Count Fleet," which won the Triple Crown—Kentucky Derby, Pimlico Preakness and the Belmont.

Those were some of the events which seemed noteworthy in 1943. One not noteworthy event was the birth of Kup's Column in the *Chicago Times* on January 23.

Yet over the following 45 years, the column enabled me to know people and get enough stories—many of which I'll be telling here for the first time—to fill a book. . .shelf.

I've known nine presidents. One gave me a laminated White House card. On the back was scrawled OPEN SESAME, and he proved it by revealing to me why he made one of the most controversial decisions in history. One gave me a vision of Camelot, though that knight in shining armor proved as human as the rest of us. I was among the first to know of his involvement—and his brother's—with Marilyn Monroe. I knew of another president, many years before he took office, firing a gun in anger at an actress he was dating. (Would the course of history have been changed for better or for worse if he'd been a better shot?)

The column gave me an unforgettable audience with a Pope (during which I had the most embarrassing moment of my life) and a unique meeting in a hotel room with the U.S. Senator who wanted to be king. In his hotel room I found the blank piece of paper which exposed him as a fraud.

From pilgrimages to Israel both before and after it became a State to crashing the "coronation" of the Queen of England, from boardrooms to bedrooms to locker rooms, the column took me behind the scenes and to the inside of the majority of major happenings in the worlds of politics, entertainment, art, sports and big business.

But the column was just as much about big "little people" as Popes and Presidents. And what I left out was often as important as what I put in. For example, when movie queen Veronica Lake (whose blonde-hair-over-one-eye coiffeur was the national rage) and Gary Cooper came to Chicago to sell war bonds, I accompanied them around town. It was obvious that the diminutive sexpot had the hots for the six-foot, three-inch Coop. Finally, when no one else was around, Veronica looked Coop straight in the eye and said: "Do you want to fuck me?"

I recall that particular moment because it was the first time I'd ever heard a big name actress use *the* four-letter word. I left it out of the column.

On the other hand, I did print the daily drama, the tale of one city whose blood pressure I've been taking for 45 years. The long-time-no-see Capone brother, Jimmy, made my column after being missing for 33 years. I spotted him in a Cicero nightspot. Ditto for another member of the Capone mob (you can't use the name because he fronts as a respected businessman, see, chum?). He was as handy with a BB gun as he was with a sub-machine gun. During the wartime meat shortage, he simply went out the back door of his Southwest Side home and peppered away at sparrows for his main course.

When I found out that Louis Sprenzel had hand-printed 54 letters to a man he didn't know, I ran the story. Every one of the letters, using the lewdest terms, were death threats. They were written to President Franklin Roosevelt. And when the Chicago Bar Association refused membership to Negro attorneys, with the "explanation" that the CBA was a social club and not a professional organization, I itemed:

> If the CBA *is* a social organization, the members have some adjusting to do with Uncle Sam's Internal Revenue Department, since most were under the impression they belonged to a professional organization and deducted their annual dues on their tax returns. For 3,000 members, a 25% penalty at 6% interest for the last six years should give Uncle Sam a windfall in six figures. . . .

Equally as typical of Chicago was a one-eyed, limping woebegone dog of obscure parentage aptly named Rags. Adopted by the railroad men of the I.C. switchyards off Randolph, he lived in one of the many shacks in the yards between the lake and Michigan Avenue. His favorite pastime was riding the cabs of the switch engines. One dark night that summer, Rags was in his usual position beside the engineer. Suddenly, with a wild yelp, he jumped from the slowly moving locomotive, darted to the adjoining track and stood guard over the prostrate form of a man lying across the rails. A few hundred yards away another switch engine was bearing down on the unconscious body. Rags' excited barking was recognized by the oncoming engineer, who slowed down to see what was wrong, then stopped just in time. *Kup's Column* showed appreciation of Rags by telling of his heroic rescue. It got national attention and Rags barked on coast-to-coast radio.

There was a war story in every American home. Yet, if the war touched everybody and everything, the essential fabric of American life remained. The ritzy, for-blue-bloods-only Shore Acres Country Club (as hard to get into as Fort Knox) shut down, but the shows—and the games—still went on. Heavyweight Champ Joe Louis won another fight, against Buddy Baer. The Yanks won another World Series, against the Cards. And Charlie Chaplin made another anti-Semitic remark.

Mme. Litvinov, the wife of the former Russian Ambassador, was in Washington entertaining a few friends, including Chaplin, before leaving for home. Charlie chilled the conversation by declaring, "Despite all those rumors, there's not one drop of Jewish blood flowing through my veins." To which Mme. Litvinov quickly bon mot-ed, "Such a shame, Mr. Chaplin, such a shame!"

Ira Gershwin told me about not being able to find some lyrics he'd written for a new show—until his wife told him that the maid had complained to her: "Can't Mr. Ira go down to his office instead of scribbling around on all these pieces of paper I keep having to throw away?"

Frank Sinatra was having trouble with his radio sponsor and was contacted by an executive of a large vitamin concern. "We're interested in putting you on the air to advertise our vitamins," the executive told Swoonatra, who at 120 pounds was the teenage rage. "Me?" asked the amazed Frankie. "I'm underweight and the public thinks I'm anemic." The vitamin exec informed Frank that they were launching a "before-and-after" campaign and wanted him as an example of *before*.

And Errol Flynn, the new Romeo of the screen, was sued for statutory rape by underage Peggy LaRue. It didn't hurt Errol's career, since it fit to a T his Don Juan image that made him admired by men and adored by women. The fact that Flynn was a raging bisexual—in fact, would have sex with anything on two legs (and that might be an understatement)—was a well-kept secret. Miss LaRue, by the way, was cast at the time in *The Arabian Nights* as one of the seven virgins.

Hollywood had a heart, too, though. When Jimmy Cagney came through Chicago for the bond calvalcade, he told me that the great love of Clark Gable's life, Carole Lombard (who soon after was killed in a wartime plane crash), had his vote for the "most real person" in tinsel town. "She was one of the few stars who never forgot the so-called little people on the lot," Cagney said. "There was one time when an electrician was fired. He needed the job badly for his family and Carole knew it. She was negotiating with the studio at the time and put a rider in the contract that the electrician had to be rehired."

In Chicago, Danny Thomas, who was in his 132nd week at the 5100 Club after starting on trial there for 10 days, revealed his one superstition to me. Just before the Russians started their drive against the Nazis, he started to sing his side-splitting "Berchtesgaden Choo-Choo," the song about a German soldier who was fed up with fighting the Russians. "The Russians have been doing so good ever since I started singing that song," he said, "that I'm afraid to stop now. I'm going to keep singing it until they get to Berlin. But after I get them that far, they'll be on their own."

Victor Mature, the actor-Coast Guardsman, was doing a swell job for the Treasury Department on the bond drive, but not making any friends for himself or the movie industry with his after-hours shenanigans. His latest major engagement was in front of the Ambassador one dawning—when he one-two'd a Near North Side society gal.

On a more philosophical note, the writings of Professor Apostolos Makrakis, the "Modern Socrates," well-known in his native Greece, were recently published in America through the efforts of one Gus Andronis. Also born in Greece, Andronis read extensively, and lived frugally. He was able to enlist the aid of two translators so he could convince Putnam's in New York to put out two volumes of Makrakis' philosophy. I was able to get this scoop because I saw him several times a week at the famous nightclub, Chez Paree. . . where he was a waiter.

The very first month that I began the column, the Gail Marks Memorial Foundation wrote and asked what I thought would be the most worthy charity to which they could give funds. I in turn asked my readers, and the hundreds and hundreds of letters I received in the following few days alone stunningly revealed to me how many truly worthwhile humanitarian organizations Chicago had. And how much unknown suffering.

I didn't ignore a single request after that. A private who was stationed at Virginia Beach as a supply sergeant wrote and asked if we could get games for their rec room. A lieutenant in another part of the country wondered if we could possibly find a radio for them. Readers sent games and radios.

When my editor, Russ Stewart, asked me to come over to his office on the second Monday in January of 1943, he had something a little different in mind than what Kup's Column turned out to be. I had been writing a sports column, ending it with a bunch of brief "people" items. Walter Winchell's gossip column was the hottest thing in print, and everyone was trying to compete with him. I was no exception, but I widened the scope of the column. I did use his three dot technique, however, to separate items. A funny story about that—I didn't know at the outset that PR people picked up items from one column and sent them as exclusives to columnists in other cities. One day a previous item of mine appeared on Walter Winchell's page. When I saw Winchell's column with my exclusive in it, I used a note in my column chastising the great W.W. for stealing material. A few days later I received this terse note: "Kup—please return my three dots—W.W."

It was an always turbulent, sometimes tragic, often triumphant year. For Kup's Column, it was a beginning.

2

Pre-"Kup"

I guess I have to be an item in my own column and briefly tell you something about the first twenty years of my life. One of my earliest memories dates back to my pre-school days, when I was so small and shy that I would hide when company came to the house. Apparently I overcame the shyness, but not the smallness, by the time I was graduated from Nathaniel Pope grammar school. I was elected president of my class, but I was still too short to wear long pants. It was embarrassing to deliver the class commencement speech as the only boy still clad in knickerbockers.

I was the last of four children born to Anna and Max Kupcinet. We were poor (but so was just about everybody else) and lived above a grocery store at 16th and Kedzie, a typical ethnically mixed Chicago neighborhood. There were two bedrooms with one bed in each for a family of six. My oldest brother Ben worked nights as a newspaper pressman. By the time he went to sleep, everyone but my mother was out of the house. He was nearly 20 years older than I and on the road much of the time, so I actually didn't even get to know him until I was 14 or so. My sister Sophie slept with my mother in one room. My brother Joe and my father and I shared the other bed, usually with me in the middle. My father was an early riser—3 a.m. to get started on his job as a bakery truck driver.

One of my earliest recollections is rising at that hour during the summer to help my father deliver bread. He'd gently nudge me and, if I didn't awaken, put his mouth to my ear and whisper, "Irv..." It sounded like a trumpet to me. I'd throw on my clothes and in 10 minutes we'd be on the road. My brother Joe had worked with my father before me. They had to walk over to a big barn on South Wabash because Pa was delivering then with a horse and wagon.

We worked until late in the afternoon with only one break—the high-light of the day at about 8 a.m.—when we stopped for coffee and dough-nuts. It might seem like a tough summer vacation for a grade school kid, but I never thought about it. Working with my father gave me a chance, about the only chance I had, to get to know him. He *never* had a vacation from his back-breaking schedule. I remember coming home from grammar school one day and seeing him slumped in a chair, bandaged nearly from head to foot.

"What happened, Pa?" I cried, rushing over to him. It turned out that his truck had stalled on the tracks and had been hit by a train—he was lucky to be alive. He went to work the next day. It was no surprise later on when he died younger than he should have—in his fifties.

The only brush I had with death as a kid was when I was five, crossing the street at Kedzie and Carlisle. I saw a penny, raced to pick it up and the next thing I remember was finding myself trapped, terrified and bloody, underneath a streetcar.

Fortunately, the old, high-built "Toonerville Trolley," which had col-lided with my head and screeched to a stop on top of me, had just enough clearance for one small Kupcinet. It seemed like a million years until I saw two hands reaching under. . . and finally pulling me out. They were the hands of the tailor on the corner. He closed his shop and carried me home. The doctor came over and stitched me up on the kitchen table.

Between regular school and religious school, working with my father in the summers and helping my mother around the house the rest of the year, there wasn't much time to get into any other trouble. Spare moments were consumed by softball and football. When I was six, seven, eight, I played football one-on-one on the sidewalk against Louie Reindeau, then my best friend. We had to make two squares to get a first down—and we'd just wind up and plunge against—and we hoped through—each other. We didn't have enough money for a real football, so we pretended we were car-rying one. It made the confrontation even more intense—no one could fumble.

I graduated to softball with the older boys, usually in an empty lot at 15th and Albany. Whenever possible, we'd go out right after dinner and play until we couldn't see the ball anymore. There were eighteen or nine-teen of us, and a few were guys in their twenties—Philly Brezinsky, and somebody called Knuckles who always wore gloves (because his fingers were short)—and I had to go all out to keep up. Even though I was the smallest kid in my class and didn't shoot up to six-foot, one-inch and two hundred pounds until much later, somehow I was able to hit homers and play a pretty fair first base.

That was about it. I really don't remember birthdays or holidays. We didn't do much celebrating. I never saw a turkey on Thanksgiving. My mother was Orthodox and kept two sets of dishes. My father really *was* orthodox—an orthodox White Sox fan. From as far back as I can recall, there was a big Sox banner on a hall wall.

Once in a great while on a Sunday afternoon, we'd take the double-decker bus which cost 10 cents and, in good weather, allowed you to sit on top out in the open to visit our rich relatives. They lived on the North Side, which was the cream of the city in those days. It was a treat for me, but not for my parents. My father's sister had married a wealthy real estate tycoon and they looked down on us. Max and Anna Kupcinet knew we were in a different social strata and felt very uncomfortable. There were a few other relatives around town, but we never saw much of them. As the years passed, the relatives all drifted farther and farther apart, while my own family of six seemed to grow closer.

My interest in journalism began early. I wish I could say it began in fourth grade with Miss Herman, a small, dark and beautiful teacher at the Pope School. I had a crush on her. In eighth grade as class president, I wrote the valedictory speech for my class—and got my first taste of rejection as a writer. My teacher, Mrs. Post, a rough-and-tough battle-ax in her sixties, made me rewrite the whole thing. But it was my first day at Harrison High School that set my course in life. The get-acquainted tour for freshmen led us to the student printing shop next to Mrs. Josi's journalism class. There the editorial staff was putting the weekly *Harrison Herald* to bed. I was fascinated. Students could actually write, edit and print their own newspaper!

I decided then and there that I'd be a newspaperman. My enthusiasm was so obvious that it caught Mrs. Josi's attention and she invited me to be the first freshman to enter journalism class.

My mother and father insisted that all their kids go through high school, which was unusual in those days. As I look back at my high school days, I realize they were a precursor to my adult life. It was a heady experience, including my start in journalism (working on the *Harrison Herald* for four years as sportswriter, sports editor, editor and editor emeritus), playing football for four years, starring in the school play, *It Pays to Advertise* (during which I naturally fell in love with my leading lady, pretty red-haired Ruth Heller), participating in a dozen or more extracurricular activities and, then, being elected class president in my senior year (which called for me to deliver a graduation speech with the inevitable, "We who are the future of the country...."). Somehow, I managed to maintain a B-plus average in my studies. I returned to Harrison a few times in later life to speak to the journalism class and to the student body. And some years ago, Benny Goodman, who reached the heights in the jazz world, and I were honored together as prominent alumni.

My brother Joe and I went through college as well. Some days, though, I learned more on the way home from high school. To get to Harrison, I had to walk through Douglas Park, which was largely a Polish area. The Jews and Poles were always at each other's throats and you literally had to fight your way to and from school every day and run fast when you weren't fighting. The many different ethnic groups in our neighborhood got along remarkably well, but kids will be kids and, being so small for my age then, I was beaten up regularly. Davy Miller, a well-known fight referee, had a restaurant nearby which became a gathering place for the tough Jews who would go into hiding in the park waiting for the Poles.

But maybe the most important part of my education took place when I was playing hooky. Those few times when we'd visited our relatives, I'd gotten a glimpse of downtown and even a youngster could tell that *here* was the center of everything. Sometimes it took me months, but whenever I could save up fifty cents, I'd take a day off from school and take the bus to the heart of the city. It was always a miracle.

I'd see a movie at the Chicago Theatre, then walk for miles, trying to take in everything I could. There was always more. About the time I was graduating high school, a bridge was being built across the river at Wabash Avenue. Later on, I'd come to know that bridge as well as any part of Chicago, walking across it each day to the newspaper where I've worked for more than fifty years. Chicago is multi-faceted, with so many diverse kinds of people, yet that bridge somehow through the years came to mean something to me which made everything come together. It was more than metal and mortar connecting two parts of the city. It was a kind of statement that, no matter where you came from, you could get to the other side. I was a happy kid from a loving home, but you couldn't see the part of the city that never sleeps from the back of a bakery truck. And, without ever burning the bridge to my old neighborhood, I was going to find a way to reach the other side of the river and achieve my goal in life: To make a hundred dollars a week as a sportswriter.

After high school, I took a year off to earn enough money for college. I worked for the Pullman Company cleaning railroad cars at $17.50 a week. There were hundreds of car cleaners, and I was the only white, and the youngest. I picked up on the way the blacks spoke, and somewhat on the way they thought. It gave me an understanding of the black experience that few people had in those days and served me well later in life. In fact, I got along better with them than they sometimes got along with each other. There was one knife fight, I recall, where one man cut another's belly clean open. It was the ugliest scene I had ever witnessed—actually seeing someone's insides. I didn't know what to do, but a few of the fellows to whom I'd grown close simply came over and walled me off from the fight so I'd have no chance to become involved.

I had one apparent fault—falling asleep on the job. After all, they were *sleeping* cars, weren't they? One day, while I was taking a nap, the boss looked in on me before my buddies could warn me. I was fired. Fortunately, I'd saved enough money to go to Northwestern, where I played football and studied journalism before transferring in my sophomore year to the University of North Dakota.

My decision to transfer from Northwestern to the University of North Dakota was based on my twin loves of journalism and football. In my sophomore year at Northwestern, I was selected as a "demonstrator" at the coaches' clinic conducted by Northwestern coach Dick Hanley. One of the coaches attending the clinic was C. A. "Jack" West of North Dakota. He decided to do some recruiting, and he singled me out as a potential transfer. My football future at Northwestern was clouded because of a fist fight I had with Hanley's younger brother, Lee, who was a regular on the varsity. During a scrimmage we became entangled because of the way I had blocked him on a play. That led to the fight. After that Dick Hanley indicated my chances of playing for him were slim, even though I was good enough to be a demonstrator for his clinic. I was definitely vulnerable when West started painting a glowing picture of the University of North Dakota.

Knowing of my interest in journalism, West offered me the job as director of athletic publicity at the school. That was enticing enough to help me make the decision to attend the University of North Dakota in Grand Forks, North Dakota.

I knew it would be a culture shock—from Chicago's West Side to a tiny town of 25,000 people. But I enjoyed every minute of it. My salary as athletic publicist was—get this—$25 a month. But remember this was the depth of the Depression. And so desperate were conditions in North Dakota that the state legislature passed a bill which limited pay to any college faculty member, including the football coach, to $1900 a year. That gives you an idea how difficult were the Depression days.

But for me it was an exciting experience. I had a tiny office in which I handled sports publicity. My job brought me into contact with sports writers around the country. I also wrote sports for the student paper, conducted a sports show on the local radio station, which added a few more dollars to my income, and, of course, played quarterback on the football team (known as the "Fighting Sioux," as might be expected in that region).

I found living in Grand Forks a fascinating experience. I made lasting friends with many of the townspeople, who were more than hospitable to a college football player. The winters were something else. I recall asking about the weather when I first arrived. The inevitable answer was that "it gets cold, but it's dry cold so you won't mind it too much." Dry or wet, 40 below zero, with howling winds that swept the prairie state, could shiver your timbers. Suffice to say, I survived, shivering.

After my college days I played professionally with the Philadelphia Eagles for a short time. It was 1935 and pro football—especially the Eagles—was undergoing tough financial times. Bert Bell, owner of the team (who later became National Football League Commissioner) figured if he got a player whose name made news, that would bolster box office receipts. So he recruited "Alabama" Pitts, the number one football star of a leading educational institution. No other team thought of signing the talented Pitts, because the institution was...Sing Sing Prison.

A few days before the first game of the season, Bell called a meeting and announced the acquisition of Pitts, sketching his career for us and asking that we treat him as we would any other player. He did add that if Pitts became the box office attraction he hoped, that would benefit everyone. The meeting broke up and I was about to leave when Bell motioned me aside. "Kup, I have a special assignment for *you*," he said. "You have the honor of being Alabama's roommate. Sleep well." And with that, Bert walked away.

As it turned out, I did sleep well. When Alabama was quiet, he was quiet—and he was quiet with me. He seldom talked at all. Maybe it was a result of being in prison, or possibly he felt unsure of himself being put into a group of college men. In any event, after the publicity of his signing had faded, his 165 pounds didn't measure up and he was released. Several years later he became noisy again, I guess, and was killed in a saloon fight.

To many people, it might seem glamorous to make the pros. But I was always a pretty good athlete and what I really wanted to do was make the pros not as a jock, but as a journalist. So when an injury conveniently ended my career, I wasn't unhappy in the least. I wouldn't have stayed in football much longer even without the injury. I wanted to be a newspaperman.

In 1935, the *Chicago Times* hired me at $32.50 a week as a sportswriter.

My first assignment was to cover the Chicago Bears—the beginning of a love affair now in its sixth decade. I quickly became very close to George Halas, a founder of the NFL and Bears owner/coach, more of which I'll discuss later.

Early in my sportswriting career I got myself into some other hot water that made the headlines. In 1938 I was in Tampa covering spring training. The biggest star there—physically as well as talent-wise—was that mauler of the English language, Dizzy Dean. Diz didn't have any great veneration for the press. He also had a habit of giving three contradictory stories to three different reporters on the same day. When I cornered him with it years later, he drawled, "Waaal, I *like* you newspaper fellows. And I think each one of you ought to have his own special story. So I give *everybody* a scoop!"

This particular day in 1938, though, the mauling was going to be physical, and the scoop real. I was standing around the lobby of the Tampa Terrace with a friend, Jack Miley of the *New York Daily News*, who had written some critical stories about Dean. When the elevator door opened, out walked Dizzy and his wife Pat. She spotted Miley and shrieked to Dizzy: "There's that fat S.O.B. who's been writing those terrible things about you!" Dizzy left his wife's side and rushed over to Miley, spewing epithets with the speed of a Dean fast ball. When they were face-to-face, the exchange became even more heated. Dizzy towered over Miley, who was short and stout. At that moment, some 18 members of Dean's team had just finished an exhibition game and entered the hotel, cleats slung over their shoulders so as not to damage the floor of the lobby. They came right over, joined in the argument and one player took his cleats and damaged Miley's head.

Fists started flying around. I figured I'd better punch someone, too, and the only guy bigger than I was Dizzy. So I slugged him. It made all the front pages. Later on, we patched it up and were buddies until his death in 1974.

But the one event in my early years—really in all my years—that stands out in bold relief is my marriage. To write a chapter on it would be to make it less, because Essee is in *every* chapter of this book. Often, she's a more important part of many chapters than I.

I met this gorgeous redhead in 1935. She was then several years younger than I. Today she's about half my age and still gorgeous.

Of course, I've always had a weakness for redheads. But none of it meant much until I returned to Northwestern in '35 on a visit and happened to meet Esther "Essee" Solomon, an undergraduate. She's given me happiness, love, a lot of laughs and sometimes a lot of trouble. She's given me some of my best scoops, too. Once when I was out of town getting a story, she wrote my column. I put a stop to that. She was too good.

At the time I met Essee, she was going with the captain of the Northwestern football team. In fact, she had brought him home to meet her father, a well-to-do businessman who nevertheless made his kids work in the Near North Side drugstore he owned. Her dad hit the ceiling because Essee's beau wasn't Jewish and Jews weren't supposed to date non-Jews in those days. Of course, that only made her more determined. But after we got to know each other, it was as Clark Gable (who later turned out to be Essee's favorite actor friend) said to Joan Crawford in *Strange Cargo*: "It looks like it's you and me, Babe, and what can *we* do about it?"

After graduation from Northwestern, Essee worked part-time at Michael Reese Hospital doing mental testing. She said she married me because she always gave her boyfriends Rorschach tests and I turned out the most normal. I proposed to her at a hockey game I was covering. She got hit with a puck shortly thereafter, so she still doesn't remember what I said. It was something romantic like, "I suppose we're going to get married." She had to spend the next couple of days telling several other guys that she wasn't going to marry them, and on Dec. 11, 1938, Mr. and Mrs. Joseph D. Solomon of 14 Elm Street announced the engagement of their daughter, Esther Joan, to Irv Kupcinet, son of Mrs. Anna Kupcinet of 3150 W. Ainslie. Her mother made the wedding dinner a white tie affair for three hundred at the Belmont Hotel—about 6 from my side and about 294 from Essee's. Our honeymoon was spent covering spring baseball training in Florida.

Neither one of us would tell you we haven't had our problems. Many days, marriage makes one-on-one tackle football on a cement sidewalk seem like a picnic. Yet, like very few couples, through my work and Essee's multi-talents, we've had the opportunity to "see it all," as she puts it. And we've seen it together.

As far as *I* am concerned, the honeymoon isn't over.

3

Harry S Truman

I met Harry Truman while he was still a senator. We hit it off instantly. When he became vice president in '44 and, of course, president the following year, the White House was always open to me. When he was vice president, with an office in the Senate building, he gave me a laminated card, on the back of which he wrote, "Kup, you're entitled to admission. The front and back door is always open."

During the seven years he was president, Truman gave me many an item. Most were merely fascinating footnotes to history, yet at least one was of lasting significance. And one special event in late 1952 had no historical worth, but it was worth a lot to me. Eisenhower had been elected president over Stevenson, but Harry Truman was still occupying the White House and he invited my family for a "presidential tour" before he moved out. Our little party was made up of Essee, my eleven-year-old daughter Cookie, eight-year-old son Jerry, and seven-year-old Barbara Nellis, the daughter of former Chicagoan Joe Nellis then practicing law in Washington. We began with a tour given by guide Paul Yost. After a short while he received a signal from a Secret Service man which meant, Yost whispered to me, "that the *real* White House guide will be along in a minute."

A few seconds later, President Truman and his daughter descended the spiral staircase from their second floor living quarters. The president was in a jovial mood that day, greeting us by poking fun at the White House furnishings: "Be seated and be uncomfortable." Truman began by going over some highlights of White House history. He talked so naturally that from the first moment, the kids forgot they were in the presence of the president. They felt more like a favorite uncle was telling them some exciting stories. When Truman brought up the presidential portraits, the kids got an extra treat. The president and Margaret led the way until we stood before the picture of the tenth president. "John Tyler and I are distantly related," Truman said. "But I never liked him because, after he was president, he supported his native Virginia in seceding from the Union during the Civil War when the whole nation's future was at stake."

"I agree with Daddy," Margaret laughed. "But for an entirely different reason. See that nose of Tyler's? That's known as the Truman nose! *I've* got it and I *don't* like it."

"It's a lovely nose, Margaret," the president protested.

"You remind me of Governor Stevenson, Daddy," Margaret replied. "I told him the same thing and he said I had a nice nose, too. Well, it's a nice nose—for President Tyler. But not for a woman."

We walked on from room to room. Suddenly, the president halted and pointed to a corner of the ceiling. "Just above that corner on the second floor," he said, "is my bathtub. So this is the room I would have tumbled into if they hadn't rebuilt the White House before it fell apart completely."

Inevitably, the subject of politics came up. "I have a confession to make," our precocious daughter said to the president. "I was for Eisenhower in the last election."

"Ah," smiled the president, "another woman taken in by the glamor of a uniform and hero worship!" Then, in a serious tone, he added, "Well, you stick to your beliefs. And let's all pray that Eisenhower proves a good president. He doesn't have an easy time ahead of him."

Cookie had more questions, of course. One was that she'd heard Truman say he'd be happy to leave the White House. "Why would anyone want to leave this magnificent place?" she asked him.

"Young lady," he answered, "are you familiar with Joliet in your own state?" Truman was referring to our "leading" prison. "If you're not," Truman went on, "ask your mommy or daddy. They have guards down there— guards who don't leave the prisoners alone for a minute. Well, it's almost the same for me. I have guards here, too, and they never leave me alone for a single minute. You know what I'd like to do, Cookie? I'd like to get out and have some fun—and get away with it!"

As we were leaving, we passed through the doorway of the main reception room. Before Truman, the official seal of the president had been inlaid in the floor of the White House foyer. Visitors unknowingly stepped on it upon entering. Truman had the seal lifted from the floor and placed over the doorway. And he redid the seal. The eagle, instead of facing the warlike arrows in his left claw, now faced the olive branch of peace in his right. "Now," Truman told us, "we have an eagle of peace, not war."

That was a rare day. Yet there were many memorable meetings with Truman before that. To others, he was full of surprises. But inside the man was an unflappable stability. He made decisions as important as those of Roosevelt and Lincoln. He changed the course of history. But history never changed Harry S Truman.

Maybe F.D.R.'s most important decision, in fact, was unexpectedly to dump Vice President Wallace and substitute Truman. F.D.R. knew he was ill, the country was in a war. No less than the steadiest, surest hand would be needed at the helm . . . as well as a good campaigner who could reach the average American.

People felt they could walk up to Harry Truman and shoot the breeze with him like the guy next door. They sensed he was one of them, and he was. A few days before the '44 election, I remember Truman coming into Chicago. On the train with him was Ed McKim, one of Truman's closest friends and an Omaha insurance exec who served under Truman in World War I. Before they began the coast-to-coast trip, Harry said to McKim: "We're going to have trouble with our laundry, Ed. We can send our shirts out whenever we reach a large city and have them forwarded. But as far as handkerchiefs and socks go, well, remember our war days? We washed them ourselves then, and we'll have to wash them ourselves now." McKim agreed, but made a private deal to have a porter do his personal laundry. Not Truman. Every night he did his own washing.

A few days later, Harry Truman was vice president of the United States. A few months later, he would be president. Yet just as the senator never forgot he had been a humble haberdasher, the president never wanted to forget that he had been a senator. Shortly before Roosevelt died, Truman was presiding over the Senate but, as vice president, had no voice in the debate that was raging on the floor. He turned to Brian McMahon of Connecticut and exclaimed, "Damn, I miss my seat in the Senate! I wish I could get into this argument."

"Maybe some day you will have your say," McMahon replied prophetically.

Several hours later, the debate ended and Truman left the Senate floor. He went to his office and wrote a letter to his mother. It was 4:30 p.m., Apr. 12, 1945. Just as he signed it, he received an urgent message to come to the White House to meet with Mrs. Roosevelt. F.D.R. was dead. Harry S Truman was now president of the United States.

Truman never mailed that letter to his mother. Instead, after the ceremonies on the White House portico, he phoned the 92-year-old woman in Grandview, Missouri. "Mama," he told her excitedly, "you're talking to the president of the United States."

"I know *all* about it," she replied unexcitedly. "I just heard it on the radio. Now, Harry, I want you to *behave* yourself!"

There is no doubt that the first source of Truman's unsurpassable strength was his mother, Mrs. Martha Truman. Until her death in 1947, she wrote her son regularly, sometimes disagreeing with him, and unflinchingly "giving me a piece of her mind," as Harry put it. If Truman had a *sense* of history, his mother had *seen* history. She could recall the Civil War, when the notorious Lane Raiders of Lawrence, Kansas, who were northern sympathizers, swept into her home-town in a border state and ransacked hundreds of homes. Because of this, she remained a Dixie loyalist throughout her life—even refusing to admit that the North won the war. When her son Harry was campaigning for the vice presidency, he telephoned her and mentioned that he had a speaking engagement in Lawrence. "Do you have to go to that dreadful town?" she asked indignantly.

"I do, Mama," he said.

"Well, Harry, if you *must*, while you're there, see if you can find the silverware those damn northerners stole from my parents!"

By the same token, President Truman got a kick out of teasing his mother about her southern sentiments. In May of 1947, for instance, he okayed the purchase of a large painting for the White House. Titled "The Peacemakers," it showed President Lincoln conferring with Generals Grant and Sherman following the North's victory in the Civil War. "I have only one problem with this painting," the President told me. "Where in hell am I going to hide it when my mother comes to the White House?"

Only a few dozen women have had the privilege of bearing a son who became president. None was less impressed with that fact than Martha Truman. Harry's wife was cut from the same enduring cloth as his mother. Unlike Martha, though, Bess established a record for maintaining a discreet silence and staying in the background. When she was asked to pose for an official portrait to be hung in the White House along with the portraits of the other First Ladies, she recoiled from the suggestion. Finally, Harry gained her consent by saying, "All right, Bess, no one can make you pose for the portrait if you don't want to. What I'll have to do is to dig up one of your real old pictures and have them hang that in the White House." Mrs. Truman posed for the portrait.

After Truman left the White House, no one was happier than Bess. She had never liked the social obligations, nor much else about it. In 1953, she allowed a rare, very brief press conference.

"Do you miss living in Washington?" one reporter asked.

"I wouldn't say so."

"Well, is there anything that you miss in Washington?"

"Yes," she answered curtly. "I especially do *not* miss the White House!"

But though Mrs. Truman was regarded as a person who remained in the extreme background publicly, it was an erroneous characterization to say she played no part in White House decisions. Like Martha, she was a woman of strong opinions who sat down with Harry each night for a no-holds-barred discussion. He often referred to Bess, in fact, as "my boss."

Unlike Nancy Reagan, Bess Truman exercised her influence on the president in private, never in public. Her strong-willed opinions on presidential matters were strictly between them, never to be revealed to outsiders or the press.

I came to know Margaret quite well. Whenever she came through Chicago on the train, the president would call and say, "Kup, be sure and take my little girl to the Pump Room for lunch and make sure she gets back safe on the train." He always referred to her in those days as "my little girl."

And Margaret loved the Pump Room. "I think I'll make all my future trips from Independence back to New York or Washington through Chicago," she told me after her first visit. "You have a wonderful city and the Pump Room is delightful. Where have I been all these years?"

Through the years, there was an interesting oddity about my lunches at the Pump Room with Margaret. When she was merely the daughter of the president of the United States, we were seated at the second-ranking booth: Number Eleven. After she starred on TV with Jimmy Durante, she was escorted to the glory seat: *Booth Number One.* "How come," I asked the late Phil Boddy, maître d' of the Pump Room, "you sat us at Number One this time?" He replied: "Before, she was only the president's daughter. Now she's a star."

Her father was glued to the radio on Mar. 7, 1947, when she made her singing debut with the Detroit Symphony Orchestra on ABC. And when some of the reviews were negative, the president instantly fired off letters of invective, as he did in that famous letter to the *Washington Post* music critic, Paul Hume.

Tallulah Bankhead, probably the least likely person in show business to be embarrassed, told me red-faced of a faux pas she made with the president over Margaret. Miss Bankhead was then starring in NBC's "The Big Show" and was in her dressing room when a messenger informed her: "The president is on the phone for you." Margaret Truman had been one of the guests on the show, and Tallulah figured a prankster was at work and ignored the call.

"It's *really* the president," insisted the messenger.

"Oh, then it must be the president of NBC," poo-pooed Miss Bankhead, who then picked up the phone and challenged in her gravelly voice, "What do *you* want, Mr. McConnell, dahling?"

Needless to say, it was President Truman himself who, in typical fatherly fashion, had phoned to thank Miss B. for the splendid treatment accorded his "baby." After almost falling off her chair, Tallulah quickly recovered her composure and told Truman, "Dahling, it was so wonderful of you to take the time to call." Truman then said that as he listened to the show, he recalled the time he sat next to Miss Bankhead's father, the former Speaker of the House, William Bankhead, while Tallulah was performing in a Washington theater. "With curtain call after curtain call for you, I watched your father wipe away tears from his eyes. And that's what I was doing tonight, Tallulah," Truman said, "when Margaret received all that wonderful applause."

At the same time, she had the family knack for poking fun at her father's protectiveness. When I phoned Margaret in July of 1955 to give her the scoop that in its next issue a major magazine's poll would announce she was "the girl who would make the ideal wife for Liberace," she let out a howl from New York that could be heard clear to Independence, Missouri. But then she quickly hit the ball back into the other court, saying: "Kup, please tell whoever is responsible for the honor that I'm deeply flattered, but one piano player in the family is enough."

When it came to humor—one of his greatest strengths—Harry Truman could both dish it out and take it. Margaret sang at the White House Correspondents annual dinner, for example, where the president was the guest of honor. It was in March of 1948, and just about everybody doubted that Truman would be re-elected in the fall. "Well, if I'm here next year," he said, "*I'll* do the singing." In 1953, after he left office, there was a report floating around that Margaret would enter politics as a candidate for Congress. "I'm against that," Truman told me with a twinkle in his eyes.

"But know what I told Margaret? I said I'd help her if she wanted to run. But I also told her that if any of her opponents criticized her—I'd write 'em a nasty letter! *That* changed her mind."

Unlike Bess, Harry Truman had no reluctance about posing for pictures or paintings. It was part of an American tradition, and he liked it and used the time to relax. The one that bears the best likeness to him was done by John Slavin—but was slashed while on exhibit at the Smithsonian Institution. As soon as Slavin heard about the incident, he was horrified and phoned the president to ask to have the painting repaired.

"Do you mean there won't be any signs of damage?" Truman asked. Slavin assured him there wouldn't.

"Well, I've always said I'm pretty fortunate as presidents go," Truman laughed. "Lincoln and McKinley were assassinated, Roosevelt was shot at, I was only slashed, didn't feel a thing and now you say you can make me as good as new."

In 1949, the nation's leading cartoonists launched a coast-to-coast bond drive tour by calling on President Truman to be sketched while he worked. A White House aide told them Truman had agreed, but that they could only stay 10 minutes. Harry Truman was so fascinated by the drawings, however, that he allowed them almost an hour. One of the cartoonists was Rube Goldberg, whose drawings in the *New York Sun* during the '48 campaign were bitterly derogatory.

"I hope you realize, Mr. President," Goldberg tried to conciliate, "that there was nothing personal in the cartoons I drew about you."

Truman smiled. "To the contrary," he replied. "I have one of them hanging on the White House wall."

"You *do?*"

The president ushered him over to the one Rube Goldberg cartoon hanging on a wall of cartoons in the White House. It consisted of a huge blank space with this caption: RUBE GOLDBERG REGRETS...and ran the day after Truman won the election.

Prime Minister Churchill provided Truman with a hearty laugh, too, at their very first meeting in Potsdam. Churchill revealed to Truman his experiments with the "miracle harbors" which enabled the Allies to supply the Normandy beachheads immediately after D Day. When plans for the harbors, which played a crucial role in America's victory in Europe, were completed after two years, all the tiny models of the originals were sent to the Prime Minister for approval. They arrived before Churchill sailed for Canada and were placed aboard the ship. And then, as Truman howled, Churchill confided how he stripped naked and, in the privacy of his stateroom, played with the models in the bathtub!

If Churchill's toy boats were pivotal against the Nazis, it was President Truman's agonizing decision to drop the atom bomb on Japan that totally ended the War. He hoped and believed—and so far he has been right—that those bombings of Hiroshima and Nagasaki would preclude any future use of atomic weapons in warfare. Once he made the decision, Truman never looked back.

I asked Truman about his decision to drop the bomb on Japan and wondered, as some authorities had pointed out, if it wouldn't have been better to summon the Japanese to an isolated and outlying island for a demonstration of the holocaust of an atomic explosion. He replied that possibility had been discussed, but at that time nobody knew for sure that the bomb would work. "What," he continued, "if we gave the demonstration...and the bomb didn't work?"

People from all walks of life were able to joke with Truman and feel he was one of them because he was that rarity in the 20th century: A president who wasn't rich. A month after assuming the presidency, he was studying a pile of important papers and documents, many top-secret, when his secretary interrupted to hand him an envelope.

"Another important document?" asked the president, ripping it open. Then, answering his own question, he exclaimed: "Gosh, I'll say it is—it's my paycheck!"

Scheduling a Truman address to the nation over national radio in late October of 1945 says much about the man. When it was announced that the speech would be aired at 9 p.m., this automatically meant that the Bob Hope Show would be cancelled. Hugh Davis of Foote, Cone and Belding, the ad firm that handled advertising for Bob's program, rushed to Washington.

"Why does it have to be at nine o'clock on October 30th?" he argued vehemently. "The Bob Hope Show is the most popular show on radio. You've got to change it."

But the president's advisors wouldn't be swerved. They were convinced that precisely because almost everyone listened to Hope that it would be the best time for Truman's speech. "But," the president's chief advisor confided to Davis, "if it's any consolation, when we told the president the time we had scheduled the speech, he felt the same way you did. He said to tell you he'd rather listen to Bob Hope tonight, too."

If Harry Truman enjoyed himself more in the White House than possibly any other president, he also was capable of unsurpassed seriousness.

A seeming country bumpkin who was probably our least impressive president in appearance, Harry Truman had the most self-confidence of any of the nine men I've known who occupied the White House. He was thrust upon the American public and the world in the shadow of one of the genuine giants of the 20th century, Franklin Roosevelt. Yet without hesitation or hindsight, he made decisions such as dropping the atom bomb, recognizing the State of Israel over protests by the State and Defense departments, and firing the most popular military man of the era, General Douglas MacArthur.

When he was a county judge in Missouri, Truman had charge of vast state funds for road-building—generally the most un-kosher of pork barrel projects. One day, political boss Tom Pendergast dropped in with several contractors. "Harry," said Pendergast, "here are a couple of men I'd like you to meet." They shook hands and then the most powerful contractor said to Truman: "You know how we operate in this state. You've got a lot of paving contracts to let. We'll take charge of them in the usual manner." Truman exploded: "The hell you will! Those contracts are going to the lowest legitimate bidders and that's *that*. Now, out!" Pendergast turned to the contractors as they were leaving and remarked, "I *told* you he's the contrariest cuss you'll ever meet."

Not that Truman didn't have his faults. He had a hair-trigger temper, for one. His most famous flare-up was over critic Paul Hume's rap of Margaret's singing. The ultra-vitriolic letter he wrote to Hume embarrassed even Margaret, who defended Hume as "a splendid music critic who has every right to express his views." But because of Harry's fume over Hume, the White House staff tried like hell to keep away from him the *London Times'* review of Margaret, which read: "Her singing is much like Harry's piano playing—both of the corn belt variety." One White House insider told me, "If he sees that, he'll stop the Marshall Plan in England for sure!" The president called columnist Drew Pearson a son of a bitch publicly and, when Secretary of Defense Louis Johnson said something minor but ill-advised to reporters, the president excoriated him in front of his peers at the close of a Cabinet meeting with: "*You* leave by the secret exit, because you've got hoof-in-mouth disease!"

Yet he was big enough to admit his mistakes. He openly apologized to the *New York Times'* Arthur Krock for saying Krock's interview with him "came out of the air." And when Truman introduced Lincoln scholar Ralph Newman (who helped Truman catalogue the books for the Harry S Truman Library) at a dinner, the president mistakenly introduced him as a Pulitzer Prize winner. The following morning, reporters were all over Tru-

man. "When did Newman win the Pulitzer Prize?" they asked sarcasti-
cally.

"Last night," Truman replied. "*I* gave it to him!"

Despite his powerful leadership and unique ability to communicate
with people in all walks of life, when it came time for re-election, Truman
was still looked upon as "the accidental president." His Republican opponent, Tom Dewey, was considered a shoo-in. The Gallup Poll had Truman
being overwhelmed. Even Eleanor Roosevelt, before sailing for England in
spring of 1948, confided that she couldn't possibly support Truman. Her
son had come out for Eisenhower the week before. Yet when Truman
came to the Blackstone Hotel a few days before the election, he confided
to me: "You'll see the reddest-faced pollsters on November 3rd that this
country has ever known." John Jarecki, an IRS collector, happened to be
standing nearby. Truman turned to him and said, "Say, do I owe you any
money?"

The night of the election, he retreated to his home in Independence
to await the returns. Among his "must" reading that night was this newspaper editorial I had once sent him:

> The president didn't have a chance. For three years in office, he had been a
> bungler. It was time, people were saying, for a change. The president had
> gotten along badly with Congress. His nomination at the convention had
> been bitterly opposed. Why keep a president who had proved so incompe-
> tent, whose re-election seemed impossible. He meant well, but a president
> of more capacity was required. An imposing list of great men within his
> own party opposed his nomination. Some objected so strenuously that they
> formed a third party and adopted a platform which sizzled with antipathy
> to the president.

The editorial was written in 1864, about Abraham Lincoln.

Truman went to bed early that night, slept like a baby and, when he
awoke, was still president of the United States. Everywhere but in the in-
famous headline of the *Chicago Tribune*'s early edition: DEWEY WINS.
Truman chuckled over it as he ate his favorite breakfast—strawberries.
When he opened his mail, there was a one-word wire from Bob Hope:
UNPACK!

Truman's inauguration, the first to be televised, was a gas. "Well," he
said, grinning, "this is the first time I've got *both* bosses along with me."
Truman had called Vice President Barkley "boss" as far back as their early
days in the Senate. "And Mrs. Truman—hell, she's been my boss as far
back as I can remember. When they tell me what to do, I *do* it. Sometimes." Septuagenarian Barkley, by the way, gave a practical demonstra-

tion at the Inaugural Ball of his eye for pretty girls by flirting with a stunning redhead—my wife. "Some newspapermen certainly get more than they deserve," Barkley winked at me. Truman stayed up until three o'clock in the morning at the ball and, for the first time in years, slept until "the middle of the morning" the next day—7 instead of 5 a.m.

During that second term, the public grudgingly but inexorably began to recognize Harry Truman for what he was. Truman's prompt and decisive action in ordering U.S. planes and ships in planning the defense of South Korea "saved the United Nations from extinction," according to UN head Trygve Lie. Yet he sent no more than troops, fully resisting any thought of dropping The Bomb. General MacArthur, however, had other ideas and possibly Truman's most controversial decision was to fire him. He gave me one of my biggest scoops there.

It was on my TV show "At Random" in December of 1960 that I asked Truman what so many others had: Why really did you fire Mac-Arthur? This was our exchange:

"Was there any pressure on you to release the A-bomb again in the Korean conflict?"

"Yes, from MacArthur. He wanted to do that."

"MacArthur *did?*"

"Oh, yes, he wanted to bomb not only Korea, but China, eastern Russia and everything else! That's the only weapon we had that he thought they would understand."

"Was that the main reason you recalled him?"

"That, and for disobedience of orders. He was in private contact with the Republican minority leader in the House of Representatives, Joe Martin, and had been warned repeatedly that the Commander in Chief was. . .the Commander in Chief."

"Why didn't you mention any of this in your memoirs, Mr. Truman?"

"I didn't want to do MacArthur any damage. But when you asked the question point-blank, I decided to answer it."

The next day, General MacArthur labeled what Truman said as "completely fake," and the press once again got on Harry's case. I phoned him. "No further comment, Kup," he said. "History will take care of itself."

Following the General's death in 1964, Bob Considine released a hitherto unpublished interview with MacArthur. In it, the General said: "I would have dropped 30 to 50 atomic bombs on the enemy's air bases and depots strung across the neck of Manchuria." A year later, the former President met with a small group of us at the Sheraton Blackstone in Chicago.

"Looks like you've been vindicated on MacArthur," I told Truman.

"When history gets all the facts, Kup," he replied, "they'll agree that my only mistake was that I should have fired him sooner. I had Generals Marshall and Omar Bradley, among others, study the records of MacArthur's conduct. They came to the same conclusion I did. I was very patient with MacArthur." Afterward, Truman was to make a speech at the Executives' Club. The questions were shown to him beforehand. One was about MacArthur. "Put *that* on the *top* of the pile," Truman said.

Truman also gained in stature during his second term because it had become plain that this plain man was popular with the people. The countless little things he had done so spontaneously for so long had begun to form a geometrically growing chain of support from one end of the country to the other. When he had come to town as senator in 1944, for instance, Chicago policemen Eddie Egan and Johnny Payton were assigned to him. Later, when Truman sat down to eat dinner at the Tavern Club on Michigan Boulevard, Egan and Payton moved away. "We'll eat at another table," Egan said.

"Oh, no, you won't," exclaimed Truman. "You'll sit right here!" The waiter had to reset the table.

"What a regular guy," Egan later said to me.

Harry Truman never forgot a friend and was hardly ever late for an appointment. On Apr. 10, 1945, two of his oldest pals from Missouri arrived in the Capitol and called the vice president. "I'm tied up with appointments until Thursday night," Truman explained, "but I'll join you in your suite then and we'll have a real old-fashioned time." Thursday night at the appointed time, they were waiting for Truman, but he didn't show. About 20 minutes later, the phone rang. It was Colonel Harry Vaughan, Truman's military aide, who informed them that Truman might be late. Keenly disappointed, because Harry had never done anything like this before, they decided to idle away the time by listening to the radio. They turned it on, and heard Harry Truman being sworn in as President of the United States. Less than an hour later, he phoned them. "Have you heard the news?" They said that they had. "Then you understand," Truman said, "that this one time I won't be able to make it."

A few weeks later, President Truman was able to persuade an old high school chum, Charlie Ross, to become his press secretary. The instant they shook hands on it, Harry suggested that they call their favorite teacher in Independence, Miss Tillie Brown, so she would be the first to know of the reunion of her two pupils. Ross broke down and cried during the talk with "Miss Tillie" and, as usual, Truman took over.

"Little" things...such as the time Truman, walking on the White House grounds, looked through the fence and saw some youngsters playing ball. A typical sports fan, Truman stopped and watched them. After a minute, all the youngsters and a number of spectators detected the president and rushed over to the fence. The Secret Service agents—maybe Truman's only real "boss"—also rushed over and insisted that the president return to his office. "I will," he said, "if someone gets me my World War I field glasses right away." The glasses were gotten, and from a window in the White House, Harry Truman continued to watch the kids play ball.

"Little" things...like throwing out the policy of not allowing White House employees to attend performances by celebrities there...like inviting the wives and children of newspapermen to join him so that the reporters and photographers could be with their families on Christmas Day ...like the time nine nuns from a convent in Pensacola sought in vain to see the president when he was visiting the area. They were rebuffed at every turn. Dean of the White House press corps Merriman Smith happened to hear about it and went right to Truman. "Why, of course, I'd be *glad* to meet them!" Truman responded and walked over at once to where the nuns were standing. Sister Superior Paschal, her voice choked with emotion, was hardly able to tell Truman that they merely wanted to touch his hand. He shook hands with each, then chatted with them at length.

And then there were the Fultz quadruplets—identical four-year-old black girls from North Carolina, who were brought to Washington by the editor of *Ebony* magazine in the hopes of getting a national celebrity to pose with the youngsters. But *Ebony* never dreamed that Truman would turn out to be that celebrity. The quads were rebuffed at every turn. Finally, on their last day in the Capitol, *Ebony* editor Herb Nipson decided he could at least show them Blair House. As they pulled up in front, Truman was emerging with the Secret Service detail for his morning stroll. He stopped in his tracks when he spotted the identical quads, walked over, knelt beside them and said softly, "My, but you are *pretty* girls." The *Ebony* photographer euphorically snapped a picture and the next day it was in every paper in the U.S. Naturally, Truman's critics said it was staged. With almost any other politician, it might have been. With Truman, such events were daily occurrences.

One key to Truman's accessibility and bonding with Americans was his love of walking. Six times daily, he briskly crossed busy Pennsylvania Avenue going back and forth between the White House and Blair House. Once or twice a day, he simply went for long walks for the sake of walking. Secret Service agents who accompanied him sometimes couldn't keep up. A number of newsmen also found it next to impossible rising as early as Truman and keeping pace with him, so one suggested they hire a taxi and follow him in comfort. "Oh, no," Truman vetoed. "Anybody who gets up early and takes long walks will live to a ripe old age. And I want you boys around for a long, long time."

Daughter Margaret once told me how she tried to convince her dad to give up his early morning walks. After all, Puerto Rican fanatics had attempted to shoot their way into Blair House in an effort to assassinate the president. "Know what he said?" Margaret told me. "No assassin in his right mind would get up at 5:30 in the morning to shoot a president!"

One of my more humorous incidents with Mr. Truman occurred when he came to Chicago as former president to deliver a speech. Russ Stewart, then managing editor of the *Chicago Times* and my dear friend on the newspaper, and I met him at the hotel and accompanied him to his suite. "Let's strike a blow for liberty," he said—his way of asking us to have a drink. When the time came for him to make his speech downstairs, he turned to us. "Now you two fellows are in charge. Handle the phone calls or anything until I get back."

No sooner had he left than the phone rang. I answered it and recognized the voice at the other end, without letting on. It was a Chicago agent who wanted to talk to Margaret about making an appearance. Immediately, I adopted the president's nasal twang, which wasn't difficult after all those years of being with him. "I'm the president and I want you to stay away from my daughter, you son of a bitch!" I shouted. "Don't be calling and bothering her anymore. You get me?"

He got me. When Truman came back, we told him about it and he had a bigger laugh than we did. The next day the agent was all over town, proudly proclaiming how the president had blown up at him and called him a son of a bitch. I didn't want to spoil his story, hence never told him that it was I, not Truman, he had been speaking to.

We are in the fourth decade since Truman left office and his ascendancy continues. He is now thought by many to be one of a handful of truly great American presidents. In 1961, I wrote:

How will history rate Truman? Much higher, I think, than most of his contemporaries. Harry's greatest hero was Andrew Jackson, but I believe this forceful, forthright man of Independence will ultimately be ranked above his hero. History faced Truman with harder decisions than most presidents. There were many who despised him because he never looked like a president—but he acted like one and is certain to be ranked among the great chief executives in our history. With unshakable faith in his fellow citizens, he demystified the job of president, was always out in the open for all to see and understand. Would that his successors will heed that lesson.

Yet the best assessment of Truman may have come from Adlai Stevenson: "Harry Truman proved the genius of American democracy," Stevenson observed, "that it can produce a plain citizen who, when the times demand, can scale the lonely heights. We honor him, we love him because, more than any other American of his time, he justified and renewed our faith in ourselves."

Give 'em hell, Harry!

4

First Pilgrimages to Israel

As I write this Israel, conceived in liberty and born in bloodshed, is 40 years old. It's been 40 years of a helter-skelter existence that no nation, less dedicated, could have survived. And my thoughts go back to July 31, 1947, when I joined a group of prominent Chicagoans on what the press described as a "Mission of Mercy." Purpose: To explore the conditions in what was then Palestine—one year before it became Israel—and the displaced persons camps in Europe. We'd then report back for a Jewish fund-raising campaign. The eight-man commission consisted of movie mogul John Balaban, head of what was then a giant movie chain, Balaban & Katz; Attorney Abe Pritzker, patriarch of one of the nation's wealthiest families; Nathan Cummings, art patron and business entrepreneur; Leon Caine, a steel executive; William Hollander, advertising and publicity chief of the B and K theater chain; Harry I. Hoffman, president of J.S. Hoffman Food Co.; Eli Rock, a representative of the Joint Distribution committee, major beneficiary of the United Jewish Appeal; and this reporter.

We reached Palestine's Lydda (now Ben Gurion) Airport on the morning of August 3rd, after a day's rest in Shannon, Ireland. The instant that I got off the plane, I had an overwhelming impulse to get down on my hands and knees and kiss the ground.

Traveling with us from Shannon to Palestine was, among others, Major Alfred Joseph Patrick O'Shaughnessy, director of a displaced person camp at Adriatica, Italy. O'Shaughnessy, a retired major in the British army, painted a DP picture even more bleak than most of us had contemplated. "The Jews in my camp are at the lowest ebb of civilization," he told us. "I have three thousand of them and believe me all but a few are going to die there unless some country comes to their aid. They have lost all hope of ever leaving the camp alive. Their morale is gone absolutely and they walk around as if waiting for death to claim them."

The next day our team traveled to the Negev, the southernmost province of Palestine, to visit two *kibbutzim*, or communal farms. There the Jewish refugees were transforming incredibly arid regions of the desert into areas of incredibly productive crops. At Revivim, barely three years old and operated by only thirty men and eight women, I saw the only cannery in the world located in the middle of a desert. Fish caught in the Dead Sea by the British/Arab commission were sent to Revivim in refrigerated trucks. There, led by 30-year-old Youssef Hepner, who was brought to Palestine by his parents from Germany in 1933 when Hitler took power, they were trimmed and canned. It was a rare and, as things turned out, quixotic example of how British, Arabs and Jews could on occasion work together.

After our four-day tour of Palestine, we flew to Rome where I saw my first European DP camp—and saw the horrors of war magnified by the hopeless hours of waiting for people who have no place to go. At Camp Cinecitti, formerly a movie studio built by Mussolini, I was told a typical story by Leon Preisler, a red-haired 26 year old. His mother, father, two sisters and three brothers were put to death by Nazis. His wife's mother, father and two sisters also were slain, but one younger sister survived. Because he was strong and young, the Nazis permitted Leon to live by doing heavy labor in the concentration camp. His wife, not so strong, soon succumbed to the Nazi's torturous tasks and brutality. Now he and his wife's younger sister were the sole survivors of the two families.

Leon drifted from camp to camp. Then, for two and a half months, he wandered away from the camps, totally alone in the world, scavenging for food at Lubeck, near Berlin. There, liberated persecutees had gathered in hopes of finding members of their families. And there Leon Preisler found his sister-in-law. They fell in love, married, had a child. They had no choice but to live again in DP camps, shifting from one to another to another. Unlike most other displaced Jews, the Preislers wanted to go not to Palestine, but to America. Mrs. Preisler even had a relative in Chicago, Helena Schwimmer of 2023 S. Harding. The odds were overwhelming against their ever making it. Maybe, somehow, they did.

After leaving the DP camps in Italy, our flying Mission of Mercy paused in Prague, Czechoslovakia. There we saw a tiny plot of ground measuring 25 by 15 feet where the ashen remains of 9,000 Czechoslovakian Jews cremated during the Nazi reign of terror are buried. Czechoslovakia's Jewish population of 360,000 was all but wiped out by the Germans.

From Prague, we traveled to Warsaw. Here death and degradation were burned most painfully into my mind and my senses. There, in the ghetto, I could actually still smell the stench of human bodies after four years. Fifty thousand Jews had been slain in the reprisal against their 1943 uprising. They had been forced from their ghetto homes, bombed from the air and blasted from the ground until an island of bodies a mile and a half square had been completely leveled. After our day's survey, it was a relief to leave Warsaw. I desperately wanted to hear just one story with a happy ending and after seeing the horrors of DP camps in Italy, Czechoslovakia and Poland. Frankfurt, Germany gave it to me.

Larry Lubetsky was 16 when the Nazis came to his native town of Kavnas in Lithuania. As with practically every story I had heard, the Nazis eventually got around to forming lines—one made up of younger, stronger people to be used temporarily for heavy labor, the other marked for death. Larry Lubetsky's family was lucky. Though his father's sister and her daughter were put in the death march, Larry's mother, father, brother and himself were waved into the line on the left. Soon after, the family was split up. Larry's mother was shipped to Danzig, while he, his father and brother went to Dachau.

One day, a strange and unusual thing happened. While hard at labor, Larry was suddenly summoned by an SS colonel, who said: "I will return at 6 p.m. Go to my quarters and have them *clean*."

Larry hurried to the colonel's quarters. He worked even harder than he had outside, knowing that if the SS officer found one speck of dust and took offense, Larry might be put to death. At a few minutes before six, having gone over the place several times, Larry took the liberty of relaxing for a moment against the door—he dared not even sit down—and waited for the colonel to return. Six p.m. passed and became seven . . . then eight . . . then nine!

The worry that Larry had felt at a few minutes after 6 had now become a cold panic. He couldn't stay. He couldn't leave. If some other officer walked into the colonel's quarters and saw him there, the first reaction would be to shoot and ask questions later, since what else would a slave laborer be doing but ransacking the quarters of an officer? If Larry left, he had next to no chance of getting back to his barracks alive from what was off limits.

Lubetsky's panic fused with his hatred of the camp to give birth to a daring plan. As fate would have it, the SS colonel was about Larry's size. Quickly, he took the officer's second uniform from the closet, went into the bathroom and tried it on. It fit. He hid his own disheveled clothing and, a few moments later, emerged from the colonel's quarters, saluting and barking a few Heil Hitlers as he made for the camp exit.

And then he was out!

For three days and nights he walked, hiding every time he heard a noise. On the fourth day, Larry recognized American tanks in the distance. He raced toward the sound of freedom. There were some tense hours during which Lubetsky had to convince the U. S. soldiers that his story about the colonel's uniform he wore was true. Finally, he convinced them. Larry Lubetsky was safe and free. But what of other members of his family?

They had all survived—the only such family we encountered. His mother, after a year at Danzig and other concentration camps, had been rescued, rejoining her husband and two sons. What's more, Larry's childhood sweetheart, Reva, had escaped from a concentration camp where her entire family was slaughtered, and made her way across the borders to West Berlin after hearing Larry was there. They were married as soon as possible.

But one happy ending was not enough. The most pitiful army the world had ever known was on what seemed a never-ending, torturous march across Europe. Without the fanfare of drums and bugles, often without food, this march of drained men and women and shoeless children swept eastward and southward across the face of a continent. They were soldiers without weapons—except the one weapon of a determination that knew no continental barriers—waging a daily war of survival so that someday they could reach Palestine.

Stonewalling them at virtually every turn were the Arabs and the British. The Arabs, culturally opposed to the Jews for centuries, overwhelmingly outnumbered the several hundred thousand displaced Jews in the Middle East. If a small minority, such as the Arab I interviewed, were willing to live side by side with the Jews in Palestine, they didn't dare say it. As for the British, the mandated landlord of the Promised Land, Palestine was the most tender of many sore spots in a once far-flung empire. Thus, they contended that permitting unlimited immigration would offend the Arabs (and offending the Arabs might endanger the powerful

British interests in the Suez Canal, causing them to lose precious oil reserves). Though the British Empire had shrunk, the unorganized, penniless displaced Jews were totally shackled by England's political, military and legal might.

So the Jews went underground.

It required long hours and vows of silence to discover and be shown the underground railroad. Operated by young men whose lives constantly hung in the balance, it was not unlike the one a century before in our own country that moved slaves from South to North. This railroad illegally moved slaves of a different kind across the borders of Europe down to the Mediterranean seacoast where equally illegal ships awaited their human cargoes for the "Palestine Run." Only 150 could be taken at a time, sometimes as few as 50. At best, they traveled part of the way to the seacoast in trucks. For most, it was a forced march on foot, sometimes crawling on their bellies with sunken stomachs in the dark of night without food or rest toward border guards. Infants were carried in their parents' arms, teenagers who in America would be shouting for Frank Sinatra's autograph knew that to cough, to cry, even to whimper, might mean to be discovered and lose everything.

A handful of children had reached the ships shortly after I arrived. They had left Warsaw in 1945 accompanied by a single adult, Dr. Joseph Bat. Their destination: Rome. Time and again along the way, he came upon other orphaned children, drifting aimlessly. They begged and pleaded to go with him. How could he say no? Their parents, all their relatives, had been murdered or died in concentration camps.

Eventually, the handful of youngsters had grown almost to 200. But as one month became another, one season turned into the next, the total shortened to 100, then 50, then less. The nearly two years on the road had taken their toll. Joseph Bat watched with a breaking heart as five- and ten-year-old faces were lined with decades of age and teenage bodies shriveled when they should have been sprouting to a healthy maturity. Most of all, he watched scores of youngsters die, his own medical expertise helpless to save them. But, finally, he saw some reach the ships.

The ships were old hulks, from 5,000 to 10,000 tons. Living conditions on them, if you can call them that, were even worse than the DP camps. Built to handle 500 people, they'd take 1,500 or 2,000. There was no food aboard except what was scrounged before leaving. There was no mess hall—people lived there. There wasn't room to turn around. Sanitary conditions were the worst imaginable. If the voyage was a rough one, as many are in the Mediterranean, people vomited where they stood.

The ships hugged the coastline for as long as possible, hoping to avoid British detection. The odds were fifty to one against making it. But fifty to one looked good after eight years of hell.

And even for those who made it to Palestine, the war was not over. British agents were constantly seeking the identity of those who arrived by illegal ships. Many were discovered, jailed and deported. Their final victory against insurmountable obstacles was thus turned into a crushing defeat. But for these few hundred thousand who escaped the fate of their six million slaughtered brethren, just the chance of reaching Palestine was infinitely better than wandering hopelessly from camp to camp.

Authorities in one camp I saw distributed a sparse amount of canned goods which some of the Jews shrewdly sold on the black market to raise money for their pilgrimage. It was discovered, and the authorities began issuing the food in already opened, bacteria-filled cans. The Jews then somehow set up their own makeshift welding plant in a hidden part of the camp to seal the cans as good as new. Though these people who once had homes and clothes and autos now were forced to live like animals, they never lost their resourcefulness. And as long as there was a Palestine, there would be hope.

In March of 1949, I made my second trip to Israel, which after becoming an independent state in 1948, won a bitter war with the Arabs. I was part of a delegation making a ten-day study of conditions there.

With 36 other Americans, I left the last of a typical Chicago winter behind and first found myself in Paris for one evening. Something is always going on in Paris, of course. That evening it was a big bash given by 20th Century-Fox annually to commemorate George Washington. The place was packed with American and French dignitaries—yet none got more attention than I with my tan jacket and bright red tie at a formal affair. I was easily the "outstanding" person at the dinner. And the most embarrassed. But who would pack a tux on a mission to the primitive farms of Israel? But I did remember to bring along a $25,000 check from Walter Winchell for cancer research to present to the Weizmann Institute, then headed by Abba Eban.

Next morning I was in Marseilles, looking out at the Mediterranean and, more importantly, at the focal point for the greatest mass exodus in history. Not even the biblical flight of the Jews from Egypt compared with the flight of the modern Jews from Europe through the Mediterranean to Palestine.

Things had changed. Tens of thousands of Jews were in one stage or another of migrating to Israel from Europe. More thousands of Jews in

Moslem-dominated North African countries were also on the move toward the Promised Land. Now, eight new ships, including the once presidential yacht Mayflower, regularly and openly went to and from Israel, each time carrying an average of 10,000 people to the world's newest state. The horrors and homelessness of the past would never be forgotten, but now, for the first time, there was a future.

Madame Lena Kirchler was another heroic figure. After the war, she spent thousands of hours bringing orphaned youngsters from the Warsaw ghetto to a haven in France. She found a number of the children simply wandering about the ghettos and forests like stray animals. They had no names, no records and, of course, no families.

I spent most of the next three weeks in Israel. First we went to Tel Aviv. As we landed, I said two prayers. The first was for the Holy Land. The second was for the plane—which was forced to land under Israel's wartime blackout. There, I met Israel's first president, Chaim Weizmann. I remember Weizmann's words as he admired the statue of George Washington we presented him, "How old was Washington when he became president?" I told him "only 46." "I'm an old man of 74 years" he sighed, "and I have so little time to accomplish so much." And, in Jerusalem, Chief Rabbi Dr. Isaac Halevi Herzog reminded me of Barry Fitzgerald. He had been stationed in Dublin as chief rabbi of Ireland for 18 years and still had a thick Irish brogue. Yet I was as impressed with the average Israeli soldier and citizen as I was with the heads of state.

In Haifa, for example, I asked Capt. Baruch Newmark about Israel's stunning defeat of the Arab states. In sports parlance, it was clearly the upset of the 1948 season. "I can probably answer you best by telling you of my own experience," he said tersely. "I was in the thick of battle and they told me my 16-year-old son had been killed fighting in Jerusalem. There was a moment when I wanted to die. But after that moment, I fought even harder. I felt that were we to win, he would live on somehow. Then, other youngsters would be able to live out their full lives."

One of those youngsters was Mildred Goldberg, at 14 pressed into service by the Israelis to penetrate Arab lines by running messages. When the Arabs stormed Notre Dame Gate leading to the Jerusalem, Israeli forces were caught shorthanded. A crucial message for help to Capt. Newmark was entrusted to Mildred. Somehow, she made it—after being struck by mortar fragments. She arrived at the Captain's headquarters covered with blood, one hand almost severed. "For you, Captain," she whispered, handing him the message. Then she passed out. She was immediately taken to a hospital where her left hand was amputated, but her life saved.

And Newmark's forces arrived just in time to stem the tide of one of the most ferocious Arab attacks of the war.

In March of 1949, of course, the war was over. A new yet joyful battle was being waged: To build a life from scratch in an arid land. The Parsons family was one of many engaged in that struggle.

It was 5:30 a.m. in Tel Aviv, the first rays of sunshine barely beginning to dance on the Mediterranean, when the Parsons, along with 450 other members of their communal farm, awoke. A graduate of Boston University, Ed Parsons had developed an enviable law practice, owned a beautiful home. His wife and their children had all the comforts of upper middle class urban America. Yet they pulled up their roots and left for Palestine. The children were now healthier and happier and, Ed and his wife felt, were getting a better education living in Kfar Blum kibbutz.

But I knew there were two sides to every story. The Jews had won the war and were prospering by leaps and bounds. Yet what of the 500,000 refugee Arabs who had to flee Israel?

In almost two weeks of looking at the State of Israel from top to bottom, the only Moslem I had seen was an Arabian horse—mounted by a Jewish policeman. So I decided to spend the last few days in Arab territory, Acre on the Mediterranean. I got there by way of Safad on the northern Palestinian border (taken from the Arabs early in the war). I stopped at the town of Tiberius on the Sea of Galilee, a beautiful body of water surrounded by mountains. It was here that Jesus spent many of his years as an evangelist and, according to the New Testament, performed the miracles of walking on the sea, turning water into wine for a wedding feast, and filling the twelve apostles' nets with fish.

From Tiberius to Safad is only 50-some miles. But by truck it was more than a two-hour drive almost straight up the Galilee Mountains some 3,000 feet. There was no other way it could have been reached except through the narrow road of hairpin curves with nary a safety rail. The night I went, the cold heavy rain meant one missed hairpin and our small group would have been toppling a few thousand feet down the rocky mountainside. After the first couple of hundred feet up, though, I stopped worrying. What difference did it make whether we fell 250 or 2,500 feet?

The temperature was 20 degrees above zero when I reached Safad. I made my way hastily to the Heralia Hotel, eager for food, drink and, above all, warmth. I got the food and drink, but no warmth. Only three days earlier the hotel had been released by the military for civilian use. No stoves, the ordinary means for providing heat in this ancient capital, were available. It was as cold inside as outside. I ate dinner in a heavy coat, handling the food as best I could with gloves. The next day, after a chilly night where even this champion sleeper had trouble dozing off for more than a few moments at a time because of the bitter cold, we arrived in Acre.

Once an important Moslem city with a population of 25,000 or so, it had become a ghost town of less than 3,000 Arabs living under the rule of Israeli occupation forces. Sitting on the Mediterranean's edge, Acre was a typical fortress town ringed with thick walls constructed by the Turks, its rulers of centuries ago. In fact, there still stood one of the cannons used by the Turkish forces against Napoleon's ill-fated effort to capture the Middle East. Now, I saw a handful of barefooted, bearded Arab fishermen mending their nets and repairing their boats as they plied the trade of their ancestors with hardly a change.

Shortly after 6 p.m. on March 18, I found an Arab, in the proverbial marketplace, who could speak English and who was willing to speak it to me. Ruhi Jarrar, 34, told me in halting but distinct English, "We are not happy here. The food is all right, we are getting it from the Red Cross. We are not being mistreated. But we have no work. We were promised jobs by the Jews, and not one of us has a job."

Jarrar, the father of five, had "only" one wife. "Democracy is fine, I suppose," he said. "But the most important thing to a man is to have a job." The Israeli government had given the Arab children schools, textbooks printed in Arabic, and free lessons for adults in Hebrew. But a sense of purpose and self-respect to a vanquished homeless people was another matter.

The last question I asked Jarrar was whether he thought Arabs and Jews could live side by side peacefully in Israel. "I will try," he answered slowly. "I have my doubts." I had my doubts, too.

After 22 days and 15,000 miles, I returned to my desk on March 22. Over the next few weeks, a lot of people asked me what I thought of the new Israel and the Middle East situation in general. Quite a few also wanted to know what they thought of Chicago over there. I had tried to tell the Israelis that Chicago was now a seat of culture and learning. But it was to no avail. To the rest of the world, we were all still gangsters. The *pièce de résistance* took place on my last day in Tel Aviv, where I heard an Israeli officer use the word "tsk-caw-go."

"What does that *mean?*" I asked.

"Heavily armed," he replied.

Be it ever so humble. . . .

5

The World's Most Exclusive Event

Everything was booming in the 1950s, not just babies. America was prosperous and partying, and so were Essee and I.

When we first got married, we took a little apartment at 10 West Elm for $60 a month. It took Essee a year and a half to get pregnant (I told her it was because she couldn't make up her mind with whom) and our daughter Cookie was born nine months later. Three and a half years after that, our son Jerry was born. I was in New York covering a story at the time, and another columnist scooped me on the birth of my son. We had moved to 2918 Pine Grove when Cookie was six months old. It was big enough for the four of us, but not for all the visiting celebrities we were beginning to entertain almost nightly. So, shortly before 1950, we moved to what became Essee's favorite place at 442 Wellington. It had two master bedrooms, six and a half baths, seventeen closets, two maids' rooms, and a hallway that was a sixteenth of a mile long. At one of our parties, even Orson Welles was inconspicuous.

In the 1950s, to get to L.A. or New York, you had to go through Chicago because rail was the main mode of travel. Virtually every big name who came through Chicago came to 442 Wellington—not only from show biz, but the worlds of politics and art, business and sports. Some, as when Frank Sinatra brought Ava Gardner to our home, came to get away from everyone. Some came for fun—Essee threw parties that were unequalled, where the antics of the famous were sometimes unbelievable.

But before revealing all that, I've got to tell you about the world's most exclusive party.

And how I crashed it.

On May 27, 1953, The Kups TWA-ed their way over the Atlantic for the coronation of Queen Elizabeth. My friend Nick the Greek and my bookmaking buddies would once have laid odds of a thousand-to-one— against what I was going to try and pull off.

When Princess Elizabeth made her entrance into the world in April of 1926, the chances were next to nil that she'd ever succeed to England's throne. Her illustrious uncle, the Prince of Wales, was, at the sprightly age of 33, next in line to become King. Who could imagine that someday he'd sacrifice that for love. Well, if Queen Bess could beat the odds and be crowned England's monarch, maybe a brash reporter from the Midwest could beat the odds, too, and scoop the world on her coronation.

London, of course, was somewhat off my beat at that time. So for several days before leaving I boned up on our cousins across the sea. Before my own Queen Essee and I ever boarded the plane, we had gone through about a dozen books about London in general and about the coronation ceremony in particular. Probably the most useful piece was Richard Joseph's *Your Trip to Britain*, sent along by Judy Garland and her hubby, Sid Luft. The book showed considerable regard for the American visiting England on a tight budget, and I circled every reference for my wife's attention. Essee, however, made her own separate list from the book, jotting down all the names and addresses of the leading fashion designers in Paris, only an hour from London by air.

The TWA flight was, Essee told me, serene and beautiful. As usual, I fell asleep almost as soon as we left the ground. I had a good excuse this time, though. I had gone without sleep for two days before leaving while emceeing the 24 hour Cerebral Palsy Telethon. I had this recurrent dream for the entire flight of waving to youngsters.

Once we landed, it didn't take long to see that London was completely consumed with its coronation. Even Chicago with the Bears in the championship game or New Orleans at Mardi Gras time weren't in the same league. Everywhere you looked, there were huge placards bearing two giant initials: E. R.

Elizabeth Regina.

The adoration for the Queen-to-be, in fact, was virtually so unanimous that it was startling. About the only dissent came from *The London Daily Worker*. The communist paper showed its disapproval of the last of

the world's great monarchies by omitting almost all mention of the festiv-
ities. By the same token, the other side of the coin of British devotion to
their new monarch was a coolness, veddy un-British in its obviousness, toward their former King. In America, there was sympathy for the Duke of
Windsor, who gave up his throne "for the woman I love." But not in England.

The British also treated Charlie Chaplin as a kind of Benedict
Arnold, because he had retained his British citizenship all the years he'd
made out like a fat cat in the United States. One London editor told me
about the stories on Chaplin running at that time in the British press.
"He's a genius and we recognize him for it, but he never gave England a
thought when he was living in America and compiling a fortune by making movies. You can keep him." The British were similarly incensed about
Anthony Eden's going to Boston for his upcoming operation. "A blow on
the nose to British surgery," one headline read.

Other than that, only a handful of stories not about the coronation
took up any space in the British mind or on the pages of their 11 dailies,
including the one with the largest circulation, the Mirror. U.S. Ambassador to Italy Claire Booth Luce was a topic for a couple of days because of
the story of her arrival at a hotel in northern Italy, exhausted after a long,
dusty drive. The concierge asked her to register, and the imperious Ms.
Luce told him to get the name from her suitcases. The next morning she
discovered that she was registered as Signora Guaranteed Raw Cowhide.

Then there were a couple of other American "ambassadors," not necessarily of good will, Senator Joe McCarthy and Gregg Sherwood Dodge.
The British made no secret of their feeling that President Eisenhower
should "crown" Joe McCarthy. The minute I got off the plane, in fact,
British reporters were asking me about Joe before I could ask them about
Bess. I ducked the question and hustled Essee into a taxi. There was no
escape, though. The cockney cabbie recognized us as Americans and
blurted: "What you going to do about that bloke, McCarthy? E's a tough
one." When we got out of the cab and entered the Savoy, an Indian in the
lobby walked over and inquired in impeccable English, "May I ask, sir, if
it's true that your Senator McCarthy wants to be President of America?"

Gregg Sherwood Dodge caused a page one stir by choosing coronation time to pay a visit to husband Horace's modest 103-room English
mansion, which was only a stone's throw from the Queen's castle. She was
the fifth wife acquired by the multi-multi-million-dollar auto heir. Wearing a $75,000 engagement ring set to shame by a wedding band with 28
diamonds, she captivated the London press with such bon mots as, "I'm

thrilled over our new English home. It's so much roomier than our three houses back in the States."

Ironically, my fate would be intertwined with both Gregg and Joe. I had first interviewed her back in Chicago when she was a struggling showgirl who had just come from "sleeping two in a bed" in Beloit, Wisconsin. Little did I know that a few years later, Gregg would become one of the two hugest *Oops!* of my career and Senator Joe an even bigger scoop than the one I was hoping to pull off for the coronation.

Of course, London even without a coronation is something to behold. The football and cricket seasons were at their height. British football isn't the kind played by the Chicago Bears, of course. It's soccer—drawing larger crowds than the World Series and more betting than the Kentucky Derby. Cricket matches, the quintessential British game, are played from noon to 6 p.m. and have been known to last several days, four o'clock tea notwithstanding. On Sunday morning, there was Hyde Park, where the soapbox orators never take a break. Except for those few moments of local color, I spent almost all my waking hours looking for royalty or stories about royalty. Essee and I attended the gala opening of Noel Coward's Cafe de Paris in hopes that some of the royal family might be there. The only royalty there was Humphrey Bogart and Lauren Bacall. We mingled with the crowds at MGM's timely release of *Young Bess* (the life of Queen Elizabeth I) and *Henry VIII* at the Old Vic Theatre. We bumped into a homesick Alan Ladd, whose movie commitments in London had kept him away from the States longer than he liked, but no bluebloods.

At night, I dolled up in black tie and tux and made the rounds of the coronation parties. In fact, I engaged in a little game with Earl Wilson, the New York columnist, to see who could attend more parties. Not a day passed during our London stay that Earl and I didn't run into each other at least four times. The contest ended up a tie, because each of us attended *all* the parties. Earl delivered a low blow after I left, though. He waited for me to get out of town (which wasn't easy), and then gave a party in honor of himself which put him one up for the freeloading championship of the world.

My game plan in covering the coronation was somehow to weasel my way into the day-before dress rehearsal, from which the press was banned, and thus be able to file a column describing the sacrosanct ceremony before any of my fellow ink-stained wretches. But how to crash such a splendiferous setting?

My big break came when I ran into an old Chicago friend, prominent businessman and art collector Nathan Cummings, who had impressive ties in Great Britain as well as the United States. Lo and behold, he proudly showed me his invitation to the dress rehearsal and bells started to ring! "Mind if I accompany you to Westminster Abbey?" I asked. Good old Nate didn't know it, but he was to be my shield in crashing the world's most exclusive party.

British royalty, not incidentally, is covered by the press far differently than we cover the President here. The Queen was never followed by a dozen photographers or hundreds of reporters. And that's everyday coverage. At the coronation, the photographer chosen to cover Westminster Abbey had to operate out of sight, inside the pillars of the Abbey itself, literally sealed for five hours, shooting through small openings. Thirty-one reporters, in white tie and tails, after being checked assiduously for their credentials, were allowed inside the Abbey at a distance. I wasn't one of them, of course. No matter—I didn't want to file the same story as other reporters who were watching first-hand or on TV. It was the dress rehearsal or nothing.

The possibility of crashing that final dress rehearsal had already been described by the London press as "an impossibility." Scotland Yard, the military police, the London bobbies and empire troops surrounded Westminster Abbey around the clock. Guards on the inside checked identification cards issued to the relative handful of people invited.

The event began at 9:30 a.m. and was to take more than three hours. All the invitees had been instructed to be at the Abbey by eight o'clock. I got there at 7:30, watched a colorful procession into the Abbey of church dignitaries, royalty and celebrities. Field Marshal Montgomery was among the first, the Archbishop of Canterbury among the last, with the Duchess of Norfolk who was pinch-hitting for the Queen.

As a kid from Chicago's West Side, I had slipped past quite a few Andy Frain ushers to see Bears, Cubs and Sox games. But this would be the supreme test.

The early going at the entrance to the Abbey was comparatively easy. I stayed so close to Cummings that we practically were in lockstep. He showed his credentials to the guards and I walked right behind him as if we were one. The ploy worked until we approached the final security detail, where in the crush of the crowd, Cummings and I became separated. To get by the last guard, I quickly flashed my Chicago press card, which had an official look. There was an instant when I thought the guard was going to stop me, but he didn't. I still can't quite believe he waved me on, but then security wasn't comparable to that needed in today's terror-stricken world. It was a crashing experience. And a minute later I managed to squeeze myself into a choir balcony pew with Field Marshall Montgomery and a couple of peers and peresses who stared at the strange companion who had joined them. I recognized Montgomery, but not the others in the pew, which I'm sure was mutual. Now I was looking straight down on the throne as the rehearsal began.

There were many highlights in the ceremony, beginning with the *recognition*. The Archbishop, accompanied by the Lord Chancellor, Lord Great Chamberlain and Lord High Constable, made his way to the east side of the "theatre" and said to the audience: "Sirs, I here present unto you Queen Elizabeth, your undoubted Queen. Wherefore all you who are come this day to do your homage and service, are you willing to do same?" It pretty much meant, "Do you take Elizabeth to be your lawfully wedded Queen?" And the nobility in that section of the Abbey answered as one: "God save Queen Elizabeth." This ceremony was then repeated to the west, north and south.

Next came the *anointing*. The "Queen" removed her crimson robe and seated herself in King Edward's chair. Four knights held a canopy of gold cloth above her head while the Archbishop of Canterbury, with holy oil held in a gold spoon, made the sign of the cross first on the palms of both her hands, on her breast, and finally on the crown of her head. Assisted by the Mistress of Robes, she then donned the supertunica, an unparalleled tapestry of gold. Some 40 minutes later, during the *delivery of the orb*, she changed gowns once again. This time the "robe royal" was draped about her.

The supreme moment was the actual crowning. While the Queen was still sitting in King Edward's chair, which was directly in front of the throne, the Dean of Westminster brought the crown to the Archbishop of Canterbury...who placed it ever so gently (it weighs six pounds)...on the head of the Queen. And as he did, the entire Abbey chanted, "God save the Queen."

Still, there were a few thrills left. The Queen was then guided to the throne. Homage was paid to her first by the Archbishop of Canterbury, who ascended the throne and knelt before her. Simultaneously, the other bishops in the Abbey knelt. When the Archbishop rose and walked away, the Queen's husband ascended the throne, knelt before her and promised "to become your liege man of life and limb, and of earthly worship, and faith and truth I will bear unto you, to live and die, against all manner of folks." He then kissed her on the right cheek. The dozens of others who followed repeated the ritual, with one exception—they only got the left hand.

Finally, communion was given. The Queen stepped down from the throne, joined by her husband, and they knelt together in prayer like any married couple. Even with stand-ins, it was stirring.

When it was over, I bid tallyho to Field Marshal Montgomery and all the royalty who thought they knew me, hurried back to the hotel room, hit the typewriter, and filed the story.

Twenty-two hours and 40-some minutes before it happened.

The next day, the day of the actual coronation, I saw the greatest gathering of prominent personalities in my lifetime, from heads of governments to millionaires from America, sultans from distant lands, to Hollywood stars.

Two million people lined the procession route. A few hours before the coronation, a carpet of humanity stretched from Buckingham Palace as far as the eye could see. Countless people lined the streets in what can only be described as a combination of our own presidential inauguration, the Fourth of July and New Year's Eve. They were assembled in vast numbers in front of leading hotels, cafes, theaters—all waiting for the moment when the parade passed by and they could gain one glimpse of the Queen.

Yet, despite the unparalleled numbers of people within a small area, what struck me most about the crowd was how orderly it was. Woven together by classic British patience and good manners, the hundreds and hundreds of thousands seemed to move together as one, ever ebbing and flowing, never pushing and shoving. Double-decker buses and cars lined up for miles, yet you hardly heard a single horn. When traffic did finally manage to creep along, autos always stopped to give pedestrians the right of way.

Thousands had camped out for nights in the streets of London along the parade route just for a momentary glimpse of their pretty, young new monarch as she rode by in her golden carriage, drawn by eight horses. I spent the night before talking to some of them. There was Percy Laverick, for example, who had traveled two hundred miles to London from his home in Manchester. I found him huddled under his "waterproof" in Trafalgar Square. He had been sleeping on the sidewalk during the torrential downpour an hour before. When I asked him if it was worth it, he stared at me in amazement.

"I want to see my Queen. She's *somebody*, you know. I want to take part in the *coronation*. There probably will never be *another* in my lifetime."

John Rackham of Suffolk, nearly a hundred miles from London, was wrapped in a blanket, munching a sandwich brought from home to sustain him through the wait for the parade. "I want to be able to tell my children I saw the Queen in her golden carriage," he explained. "I'll be able to talk about this for the rest of my days." Closer to Buckingham Palace were Cecilia Elton and her sister Peggy, wearing hats reading "Liz is a whiz" and "Bess is best." "Ever since Grandmother used to tell us stories of King George V's coronation," said Cecilia, "we've been hoping someday to see someone become King or Queen." Peggy confided that it had taken both their savings for three years to make the trip. Their grandmother's one piece of advice as the girls left: "Pick your spot in the gutter and don't move for anybody."

A few yards down on the curbside was Elizabeth Livingstone of London, sitting with a bundled child in her arms. I wondered out loud if that wasn't a horrible ordeal for the child. "'Tis that and I'm sorry," she answered. "But I made up my mind to see Queen Elizabeth wearing the crown and I wouldn't miss it for anything in the world. I could not find a baby sitter, so the two of us will have to spend the night here on the curbstone." Next to Elizabeth were three teenage girls, happily singing in the rain. Why were they here? "You mean *not* be here and miss the Queen?" exclaimed the first. "Don't be silly, man!" said the second. "Be *home* during the coronation?" Home was the Isle of Wight in the English Channel.

We talked to many others. One of the last was Keith Whitfield who had come down from Glasgow. He didn't answer right away when I asked my question. Then, after a few seconds, he said: "Come to think of it, I must be nutty." Then he added, "Maybe we are all nutty—but the Queen means so *much* to us."

The next morning I sat and watched the actual coronation on TV with Danny Thomas and Josephine Baker, among others, in the Picadilly Circus offices of London theatrical agent Sir Lew Grade. Queen Elizabeth was officially crowned at 12:33 p.m. London time. When Prince Philip appeared on the screen, Danny remarked: "That could have been *me*—politics, you know, old boy."

Naturally, there were a couple of things I didn't have in my story. There was the moment at the actual coronation when the Archbishop of Canterbury held aloft the crown of St. Edward for that brief second before placing it on the Queen's head—and like any woman, Elizabeth's hand shot up to her hair to make sure it hadn't been mussed. There was the bittersweet smile, gentle and yet etched in emotional bronze, on Queen Mother Elizabeth's face as she watched her daughter being crowned. . . revealing a mother's joy and a wife's sadness, for the coronation was made possible by the death of her husband, King George. There was the tremendous suspense and awe in the eyes of young Prince Charles. Would he wear that crown some day?

It had occurred to me fleetingly that some unforeseen event could have occurred before or during the ceremony to turn my story into an *Oops!* I'm sure the faint of heart would have worried about the Archbishop having a heart attack the night before or the Queen coming down with a bad case of laryngitis and not being able to recite the ritual. I honestly didn't give it any thought. You don't cancel a coronation.

That night there were hundreds of parties, and hundreds of thousands of dollars' worth of fireworks were exploded. The multi-colored explosions in the sky, along with the millions of dollars of decorations which were constructed and painted up until the eleventh hour, temporarily turned the usual outer dull gray of London into the most brightly colored city in the world.

Before returning home, I flew to gay Paree for a day. As always, we bumped into Chicagoans. Don Duncan, the yo-yo and parking meter tycoon, was there. Don lived at the Ambassador East half the year and Palm Springs (where his home was one of the show places) the other half, now was in Paris on business—talking to city authorities about installing parking meters. There was Henry Crown, the famed Chicago industrialist, about to leave with his wife Gladys for the Riviera and who was good enough to leave his chauffeured-driven Cadillac behind for us. We made the rounds, and I was able to cull a final but small humorous item. At a party given for leading Chicago banker Edward Beninghoven, Ed stole the show at the club owned by famed singer Patichou. With five other men, he rolled up his trousers to the knees and imitated a ballet dancer, exhibiting an unusually shapely pair of legs. I put it in the final column which I wrote 12,000 feet in the air somewhere over the Atlantic, knowing Ed's fellow bankers back on LaSalle Street would get a few chuckles.

The two-week marathon was over. For once, my own good Queen Essee, a white-knuckle flier, was almost too exhausted to worry. I feel perfectly at home 12,000 feet in the air, agreeing with Bob Hope that "if you're flying, it's nice to be in a plane." I fell asleep a few thousand miles from home, visions of royalty still dancing in my head.

6

Other Early "Unforgettables"

There were, of course, other memorable men and women I met during the early days of my column.

One was a tall, polished, well-read man who usually made a point by quoting poetry or literature. His name was Nick Dondolas, known to the world as the most famous gambler of his time: Nick the Greek.

Nick shied away from all publicity. For years, he refused to let Hollywood do his life story and, if a reporter appeared, The Greek would change the conversation from gambling to philosophy as smoothly as he'd bluff a pair of deuces into winning a $10,000 poker pot.

One of Nick's late night hangouts in Hollywood was the long-gone Dave's Blue Room. A fine eating place, it was one of the few to stay open until the wee hours. The movie industry with its early-to-bed and early-to-rise hours had made Los Angeles a 12 o'clock town. Dave's Blue Room was an exception. And it was there that I first met Nick, and where I often ran into him on the Coast. We were both night people and loved the post-midnight hours. One time a fellow named "Wichita Bob" Carnahan was the prime topic of conversation because he'd gambled for 36 straight hours in Reno. I asked Nick if he'd ever gambled for a longer stretch. "I don't really keep records of such things," he answered. "But I did shoot dice in New York once for six days and six nights." I let out a whistle that lasted for about six seconds.

I think Nick was willing to open up to me because of the friendship that developed over the long hours we sat in Dave's, sipping coffee and discussing everything from Plato to poker. And I think he sensed that I knew him for what he was—a very classy gentleman who happened to make his living as a gambler. His reputation was spotless, which is remarkable in view of the characters with whom he mingled in plying his trade. His word was his bond, as shown by the fact that he could walk into any gambling casino in the country and obtain any amount of credit.

There were many stories about the huge sums that Nick won, so maybe the most interesting are the few where he lost.

Nick would never tell a complimentary story about himself. But one of his close friends related a tale which demonstrated how much The Greek was universally respected. It happened at a high-stakes poker game in New York City. Suddenly, the place was held up. One of the gamblers made a false move and was shot dead. As the leader of the robbers passed The Greek on his way out, he stopped, doffed his hat and said, "Sorry, Nick."

Nick did tell me the story about a famous Turkish gambler who came all the way to Chicago to play cards with him. "I want to see for myself if you're really that good," the Turk said, displaying a bankroll of $25,000. Within a few hours, Nick had it all. But the good-natured Greek staked the Turk to another $25,000, and this time the visitor won $150,000 from Nick. That's when Nick decided to quit. The Turk made a request before departing: He asked for a picture of Nick, and The Greek obliged. On arriving home, the Turk purchased a huge mansion with his winnings and hung the picture of Nick, enlarged to six square feet, in the reception room. Beneath it, he kept candles constantly lit to "The God of Gambling."

Probably the time Nick got nicked the most was when he was awaiting a ship in New York that would take him overseas to his native Greece on a vacation. Departure was a few days off, so naturally he got into a dice game. Within a short time, he was a cool half million dollars to the good. Nick left the game and joined some friends for a late snack at Lindy's. There he was told an old friend had joined the dice game and would love to see Nick. The Greek returned—and lost $1,600,000!

He had to sell some real estate in Chicago to pay off, but pay off he always did. Hand out he always did, too. Nick was the gambling profession's softest touch. Fortunately, he won enough to cover his generosity. Nick was that rarest of all bets—a million-to-one shot that came through.

Then there was Elizabeth Meriwether Gilmer, better known to the

American public as Dorothy Dix. Really the first American advice-to-the-lovelorn expert, she wrote a column until she was almost 90. And she may have been a lot more savvy and witty than those who followed in her footsteps. Later on, I'll tell you an Ann Landers story, for example, that you'll find hard to believe. But I can tell you a good one about Ann's equally famous twin sister, Abigail Van Buren (of "Dear Abby" renown), right now.

When I wangled an exclusive interview with Miss Dix in the late 1940s, she told me of a young woman who wrote t her and said that she had gone out with a man she'd only met the day before. She asked, "Do you think I did anything wrong?" Miss Dix answered, "Probably, my dear, probably."

Many years later, Abby ran a letter from a young lady who wrote and said that she had been out with a man she'd just met and simply asked, "Do you think I did anything wrong?" "Probably, my dear, probably," Abby answered amusedly.

What didn't amuse Abby was when I pointed out in my column that that same question and answer had appeared in Dorothy Dix's column some 20 years before. As a matter of fact, Miss Dix was famous for the line.

The unflappable, ladylike Abby was furious. She told me that I had to be mistaken and what I could do with my mistake. What I'd intended was really only a little fun-poking, but now it became an issue of accuracy. I immediately dispatched to Abby my interview with Miss Dix. But Dear Abby was furious over what she considered an impugning of her reputation. I haven't heard from her since, while Ann Landers has been and continues to be one of my dearest friends.

I met with Miss Dix the first week of 1947. She lived in New Orleans. Essee and I were there for the New Year's Day Sugar Bowl weekend. The hardest part was locating Miss Dix, somewhat of a recluse, especially in her old age. Although she made a practice of not giving interviews, for some reason she decided to make an exception in the case of a Chicago reporter who wouldn't take no for an answer.

My couple of hours with this animated octogenarian were special. Born just a couple of years after President Lincoln was assassinated, she had a unique view of how times had changed. "They decidedly have," she told me. "I can recall many years ago when girls would write to ask if it was proper for them to help a gentleman on with his coat. Now they write to ask if it would be permissible for them to go on a weekend trip with their boyfriends." She predicted that things would go even further than that—though I wonder if even Miss Dix wouldn't be surprised at today's morality.

Dorothy had two secretaries to help her answer every one of the almost two thousand letters a week which she received. If a letter had a self-addressed, stamped envelope enclosed, it was answered the same day. The others took two days. She had been married only once, and widowed for many years. Where did she get the name Dorothy Dix? "I just took it on the spur of the moment, when one of my editors suggested that Elizabeth Meriwether Gilmer was a little long. I always liked the name Dorothy, so I took it. As for Dix, my colored nanny always used to call her husband 'Mr. Dix.' I liked the alliteration. I've been offered huge sums of money for the name," she told me, "but I prefer that when I die, Dorothy Dix goes with me."

During World War II, Dorothy was flooded with letters from servicemen with love problems. "I think the pin-up pictures that decorated their quarters were the single biggest reason for their troubles," she told me. "The boys began to imagine that their girls back home all looked like Hedy Lamarr, Betty Grable and Rita Hayworth. I told them pretty much the same thing: 'Either take down the pin-up pictures or, once you get home, wait until you've forgotten what Rita Hayworth and Betty Grable look like before you take any rash steps with your wife or girlfriend.'"

What letter seeking advice did Miss Dix remember most? "Naturally, I'll never forget a lot of them. But I do recall one I didn't print. It was from a young girl who'd been married only a few weeks when she and her husband separated. Now she wanted a divorce. She wrote to me, not for advice about that, though, but to ask me to help her with another little problem she had. She couldn't remember her husband's name!"

And then there was Ben (King of the Hoboes) Benson.

I always maintained a strict open-door policy in my office. Anyone, from wanted criminals to unwanted presidential candidates, could walk in. And they did, often. Ben was a regular. Though in the late 1940s he represented a small, ever-diminishing segment of society, the professional hobo, I felt his philosophy was actually on the rise. Ben's home territory was Chicago's own West Madison Street, but his reputation was national. He dropped into my office one hot Saturday in July of 1946, I recall, to talk about whether he should run for re-election as President of the Hoboes of America at their upcoming convention in Britt, Iowa. "I want to retire, Kup," he told me, "but they won't let me. Once I announced I wouldn't run again, this movement started up to draft me." Although soft-spoken, it was plain that to Ben the presidency of the H.O.A. was equal in importance to that of the presidency of the U.S.A. Part of the reason he was soft-spoken, however, may have been because he didn't have a single tooth in his mouth.

Ben was thinking about retirement because he'd just reached his 62nd birthday. "Even if I'm re-elected," (which he was), he told me, "I'm going to California [by thumb and by boxcar] and rest up. You know, I've traveled a lot of miles in my life." My own estimate is that the figure was 50,000 plus. The amazing thing is that Ben never paid a penny to get from one place to another. Just for the hell of it, I asked him how he'd finance his semi-retirement. He just grinned and shrugged. After all those years of living off the cuff, he wasn't going to start worrying. The closest Ben ever came to working, he related, was sketching passersby for a nickel or a dime. He took a pencil and pad of paper from my desk and, to prove that point, quickly dashed off a portrait of me at the typewriter. I recognized the typewriter.

Ben was accompanied that day by another West Madison Street denizen known as Bozo, who in contrast to Benson was rather handsome and sophisticated, sporting a goatee and long sideburns, with clear steel-blue eyes and a rapid staccato voice that put most radio commentators to shame. If he had one weakness as a hobo, it was that he didn't drink. Still, he was genuine, admitting he never took baths. "If you have a job to do," he asked me, "and you had to choose between hiring a hobo or a white-collar worker, which would you pick?"

Before I could answer, he told me. "The hobo, of course! Here's why: A hobo hates work, so he'll find some way of finishing the job in a few minutes. You people call that an efficiency expert."

Bozo backed up this bit of philosophy with painful hard experience. He actually had worked for a day or two as a migratory worker picking cherries. He even paid his income tax and always carried an old withered refund check of $1.35 from the government. The check was made out to Harry Clark, Bozo's pre-hobo name, and obviously times had not been hard enough for him to see fit to cash it.

I felt as if I should offer these two gentlemen something for their visit. All I had was a pack of cigarettes, a habit which I abandoned for cigars shortly thereafter. Who knows—a small influence on my quitting cigarettes may have been that both hoboes waved away the pack instantly. Then Bozo pulled an expensive Havana out of his pocket, no doubt panhandled from a LaSalle Street stockbroker. "Never smoke anything but these," he commented.

Afraid that if I spent much more time with Ben and Bozo I'd end up a hobo myself, I asked a final question: With the war over and the economy starting to boom, what did they see for America—and hoboes in particular—in the future?

"Things are pretty tough right now," said Ben without blinking. "I just walked down Skid Row, and you see hundreds of homeless. If things were good for us throughout the country, they'd be on the road. But right now, we've got to stick in the big cities."

"But hell," added Bozo, "things will improve. Soon there's bound to be another Depression, and we hoboes will be okay again."

I bade them farewell. "Don't work too hard," I jibed. But just the mention of the word *work* brought Ben back into first gear. "Don't *you* work too hard, Kup," he exclaimed. "Hard work—that's what killed my old man. But it ain't gonna kill *me*. My philosophy is to eat more, sleep more, and do less. Personally, I don't have much time for work anyway. I need all my time to develop my inner self."

Brief memories of others that bless or burn: Artur Rubenstein, the most celebrated concert pianist of the day, who told me of his visit to William Perlberg, the 20th Century-Fox producer. Rubenstein admitted to Perlberg that he had recently read the spicy bestseller *Forever Amber* after he noticed the huge number of persons reading it on his tours around the country. "Personally, I didn't enjoy it," said the pianist. "How could any dope buy such a story for the movies?"

"I have a little secret for you, Mr. Rubenstein," Perlberg answered. "I am the dope who bought the story for the movies." Rubenstein was a bit embarrassed, but unmoved in his opinion. "And I'll tell you why," Perlberg went on. "Because great men like you took time to read it."

There were the Quiz Kids, led by 12-year-old math whiz Joel Kupperman and American history whiz Harve Fischman. When the Kids were doing an extensive bond-selling tour, Joel Kupperman was punished by his mother for being naughty and was ordered by her to remain in their Fort Wayne, Indiana, hotel room. Harve and another Quiz Kid, Richard Williams, decided to come to Joel's rescue. They composed a series of notes reading, "I'm being held captive in Room 835 by a fiend. Help before it's too late!" and dropped them from their hotel window. Then they watched the passersby below pick up the pieces of paper and, horrified expressions crossing their faces, rush into the hotel. Soon the manager and security were banging on the door to Room 835 . . . where they found Kupperman quietly engaged in a game of gin rummy with his mother.

There was Lila Leeds, who served time in jail, along with Robert Mitchum, when caught smoking marijuana at a Hollywood party. Later, she came to Chicago to start over. I found out that a couple of shakedown experts were planning to plant some more pot in her hotel suite or her dressing room at the Rialto Theater, where she was appearing—and was able to warn her in time.

There was a little-known announcer on a Chicago variety show I hosted sponsored by William A. Lewis (whose slogan was "Where the models buy their clothes") when TV was in its infancy. His name was Myron Wallace, but you know him better as Mike Wallace.

There was Babe Ruth, given a "Babe Ruth Day" on Apr. 27, 1947, by baseball Commissioner Happy Chandler at the suggestion first made in my column. After the game, I talked by phone at his home to Ruth, who was dying of throat cancer. "Six innings would have been enough, Kup," he rasped poignantly.

There was Jim Thorpe, possibly the greatest athlete of all time, earning Christmas money working in Chicago's Merchandise Mart Post Office.

And millionaire businessman Henry C. Lytton, who celebrated his 100th birthday by requesting that the newspaper photographers "take no close-ups—because they make me look old!"

And there was John Sengstacke, publisher of Chicago's black paper, The Chicago Defender, who, along with 29 other prominent black leaders, was invited to The Chicago Tribune's 100th Anniversary dinner at the Stevens Hotel. When Sengstacke saw that the blacks had been segregated in three tables of 10 each at the end of the room, he promptly turned around and walked out, followed by the other 29. This was long before the Civil Rights Movement, but it was symptomatic of the zeal burning then in the breasts of many blacks.

And...many others. But, to paraphrase Sinatra's famous song, too numerous to mention.

7

Oops!

When you write six columns a week for 45 years, you may occasionally misspell a name, get an address wrong or simply louse up the facts.

The greatest protection any newspaper writer has is his copy desk. I've had some good copy editors through the years to whom I'm truly indebted. Without them, this chapter would have been a lot longer. Still, some goofs inevitably saw the light of day, and I decided early on to acknowledge them immediately with a light touch that began with: *Oops! Sorry....*

In December of 1957, for example, I called handsome Tony Marvin (the "Ed McMahon" to Arthur Godfrey, famous radio and TV host), "one of TV's most eligible bachelors."

The next voice I heard belonged to Mrs. Tony Marvin.

When former Miss America Bess Myerson co-hosted the telecast of that pageant about a decade later, I itemed that she wore the same gown she did the year before. I should have known that Bess wouldn't be caught dead with the same dress two years running (she'd actually worn the gown for Miss America TV commercials earlier that summer). However, her own more recent *Oops!* puts mine to shame.

On occasion, I even changed history. Writing about Harry Truman's inauguration, I included a "fact" regarding McKinley's inauguration in 1902. After numerous calls and letters, I corrected the date to 1900. After more calls and letters, I finally inaugurated him in 1901. After that, I still received one letter from W. G. Sturdivant of 7755 N. Haskins: "You say

President McKinley's inauguration was in 1901. That's wrong. It was Mar. 4, 1897. I was there." I printed W. G.'s letter, but this time I *didn't* have to say *Oops!* Sturdivant was there for McKinley's *first* inauguration.

The corrections of my oopses almost always came from my readers. Certainly, I didn't hear from McKinley. However, when I made actress Gloria Swanson a sprightly 55 instead of a youthful 53, I *did* hear from *her.*

All in all, I've had less than my share because, whatever else, I've always been pretty meticulous in verifying what I wrote. My two biggest oopses were not in the column, but trying to get news for the column. Fortunately, they occurred fairly early in the game—about 10 years apart, in L.A. and Rome—and now are almost painless, even humorous memories.

In 1949, while making my second pilgrimage to Israel, through one part luck and 99 parts chutzpah, I was able to gain a private audience with Pope Pius XII. I arrived at the Vatican too late to be fully briefed on the nuances in meeting the Pope. When the rich golden peal of a tiny bell told me it was time to go in, I wondered how I should greet His Holiness. Should I genuflect and kiss the Pope's ring or, as a non-Catholic, simply shake hands? Speak first or wait for him to begin? What should we talk about? All I'd been told was: "Wear a conservative suit, don't be late and, remember, you can't quote the Pope in your column. And don't talk politics."

Pope Pius emerged from his study and made his way to me, dressed in a long white flowing robe with a white shawl and white skullcap. The moment I saw him, I felt at ease and, as he approached, I instinctively reached out my hand. He understood, grasped it in both of his...and held it during most of the conversation. In spite of his 73 years and apocalyptic responsibilities, the eyes behind his glasses sparkled as he spoke. His skin was clear and firm, his energy seemed incredible.

He asked where I came from and, when I answered, exclaimed that Chicago was very dear to his heart. I brought up the names of two members of the hierarchy with whom I knew he was familiar, Samuel Cardinal Stritch and Bishop Bernard Sheil, and he asked me to send his greetings to them. He asked why I was overseas and I explained that I was traveling with a delegation of Americans interested in the plight of displaced Jews in Europe. He replied that he was greatly impressed with the new state of Israel, and would bless our delegation. He understood and spoke perfect English, and was aware of the problems of displaced persons in general and Jews in particular. His tone was genuinely warm and friendly, and I don't think I've ever met a person who radiated more patience, under-standing and sympathy.

Naturally, I ignored the instructions about politics and congratulated His Holiness on his fight against communism. He didn't say anything—but he did nod his head with great meaning. The audience terminated by his signaling to one of his secretaries, who slipped a small package into the Pope's hand. His Holiness then handed it to me—a medallion which bears his likeness. We shook hands again, the special audience was over, and I went out the nearest door.

Unfortunately, it was the *wrong* door. Suddenly, I was in a giant red velvet room filled to capacity with 1,500 people...all of whom began to genuflect at my entrance! I realized something was askew. I whirled around—there stood His Holiness behind *me*. I had preceded the Pope be-fore the general audience!

Dying from embarrassment, I looked right and left, spotted a door at the other end of the hall and made a beeline for it. I was never so glad to close a door behind me.

When I got home, I confided the incident to Essee, who asked if it wasn't unbearably embarrassing to have all those people genuflect for me.

"I just figured they read the column over there," I answered noncha-lantly.

But it *was*...embarrassing as hell.

Yet the biggest *Oops!* of all was when I went out to Hollywood to watch the filming of Marilyn Monroe's movie, *Some Like It Hot*. One eve-ning Jack Lemmon, one of Marilyn's co-stars, threw a party at Romanoff's for the Chicago delegation of newspaper people. And who but Mrs. Horace Dodge II sat down at our table. As I mentioned earlier, former showgirl Gregg Sherwood Dodge's path and mine crossed time and again. I was the first to interview her when she came to Chicago from the boon-docks for a career. I bumped into her in England after she gave that up to marry one of the richest men in the world, the heir to the Dodge auto for-tune. Hollywood columnist Mike Connolly, it turned out, had invited Gregg to be his "date" for the night.

After awhile, we left Romanoff's and it was on to the Slate Brothers nightclub—in other words, a typical, somewhat boring, Hollywood night on the town. Mike had gotten loaded along the way and had to be carried out. But first he requested that I take his date home. When we got to the car, she insisted on driving, though she was in no condition to take the wheel, to the swank Beverly Hills mansion she and Horace had recently rented. The previous occupant had been multimillionaire Dominican Republic playboy Rafael Trujillo, Jr.

As we drove down La Cienega Boulevard, I discovered that Gregg was not an ardent fan of Jack Webb's "Dragnet." This became evident after she waved to a passing squad car and, when it pulled alongside of us, greeted Officers Lawrence Brown and Kenneth Bonnard with, "Hello, you motherfuckers! You sons of bitches!"

They pulled us over and she couldn't pass the drunk test. I'd had a few drinks, but I wasn't drunk. They asked me to walk a straight line, which I did. They asked me to stretch out my hands and touch the tip of my nose, which I did. In desperation, they requested that I submit to a drunkometer test. I refused—I'd already passed all their testing. So they charged me with being drunk anyway and took us both down to the station. There we were fingerprinted and photographed. Mrs. Dodge was led away to the Women's Department, and I was tossed into a cell with 59 men—by actual count—being charged with drunkenness. Most were Skid Row habitues. The cell was designed to accommodate 25.

I was allowed to make one local call. But the catch was that I didn't know any phone numbers. I knew some lawyers in Los Angeles, but didn't know their phone numbers offhand. I knew Danny Thomas and Bob Hope and many other stars. But their private home phone numbers were back in my hotel room. The authorities refused to let me use the phone book or dial Directory Assistance, not that the phone numbers would be listed anyway.

So, for the next six hours I sat in a cell surrounded by 59 new-found friends. Actually, I didn't sit. I stood by the bars all night, occasionally yelling for the guards to *get me out of here* and put me in another cell. They didn't. I learned later that Mrs. Dodge also rebelled against being incarcerated—by engaging in a slugging match with two jail matrons. Gregg's story was that the matrons roughed her up and she struck back in self-defense.

Shortly after dawn, bondsmen finally showed up and I was released. Mrs. Dodge's husband hadn't been notified by the jail matron until four hours after Gregg made her request, so I made bond for her, too. Horace E. Dodge II arrived on the scene just afterward and drove us both home.

At least my arrest was good material for a few opportunists. When he heard about it, Jack Benny inquired, "Is that a sun tan—or did you get that under the third degree lamp?" Red Skelton, then starring at the Riviera in Las Vegas, long-distanced us in the wee hours at the Beverly Hills

Hotel, our home away from home, to exclaim, "I just read the newspapers. Some guy in trouble is impersonating you. Get yourself a lawyer and stop him from using your name." Jack Webb, whose "Dragnet" was produced in cooperation with the L.A. police department, was most solicitous: "Now that you're an expert on the workings of the Los Angeles force, how about a role in my series?"

The three-day trial, which took place a couple of weeks later, was even more bizarre than the initial arrest. The City Prosecutor, the Judge, and of course, the two police officers had their fangs bared for the reporter from that mecca of Al Capone who'd made a few waves in their fair city. The implication time and again was that I wrote my column from behind bars—cocktail bars. I don't want to give the impression that it was another Scopes trial. . . but they did their best to try to make a monkey out of me. And I won't say I left Chicago for the trial with trepidation, but it did disturb me when I was told that L.A. viewed drunk driving more seriously than any big city in the nation. In a word, they made a federal case out of it—only 5 percent of the cases resulted in acquittal.

Friends tenderly bade me farewell, promising to bring cigarettes and food. A prominent L.A. police official--an old friend who had served as technical adviser on "Dragnet"—strongly recommended that I plead guilty "because nobody beats a drunk driving charge out here." I was tempted, but decided against it. I *wasn't* guilty. I did try to hire Perry Mason as my attorney, but Raymond Burr refused to come out from behind his TV screen for what he was sure would be his first defeat. So I hired someone with almost as good a record—former Chicagoan Maynard Davis, who was recommended by one of my closest friends, attorney Sid Korhsak. Korhsak, who settled million dollar cases without ever stepping into court, broke his own record. He sat through my entire case as a spectator, one of the rare times he made an appearance in court.

The trial began with the L.A. City Attorney, sensing his case was weak, offering to reduce the charges. Instead, Judge Kepple asked to see the police report on the arrest, and suddenly said that in his opinion it was stronger than he had seen in many other drunk driving cases and the motion was denied.

After three days, justice was finally done and the jury acquitted me. But that wasn't good enough for Judge Kepple. His anger and disappointment were obvious after the jury returned its verdict. He dismissed them and requested me to remain seated. "I want to say to the defendant that there's been an attempt to fix this case, because the City Attorney offered to reduce the charge from drunk driving to reckless driving. Cases cannot be fixed in L.A. Being from Chicago, the defendant may not be aware of this. But this is not Chicago!"

I couldn't believe what I was hearing. I asked His Honor for the right to reply. "Request denied!" he shouted.

With my lawyer tugging at my sleeves so hard that I'd soon be sans jacket, I shouted back: "Your Honor, that's the most prejudicial comment I've ever heard in any court. You've slurred the entire judicial system of the City of Chicago!" I could see he was thinking about charging me with contempt, but instead stormed off the bench and slammed the door to his chambers.

After I returned to Chicago, I found out that I was still on trial. With Essee. She said, by her count, I had told her nine different versions of the story. She is still deciding which one to believe.

When it was all over, I tried to get some satisfaction from Mike Connolly by giving him hell. After all, the rambunctious Mrs. Dodge had been *his* date. And if he hadn't gotten so loaded, I wouldn't have had to chaperone her to jail.

He just shrugged his shoulders, winked at me and said, "*Oooops!....*"

8

The Funny Men

As you may have gathered, I love a good joke...even if it's on me. But the humor I've enjoyed most has come from the "funny men" (and women) who have mastered probably the greatest challenge in art or entertainment: Making people laugh. I've known—and *enjoyed*—all of them, for more than five decades.

Bob Hope and Danny Thomas were the first of the great comedians I came to know. Danny made a name for himself in Chicago, where we started our careers at approximately the same time—in the early 1940s. He was booked for a week at the 5100 Club and stayed for almost four years until New York and then Hollywood grabbed him. I caught one of Danny's first shows and sensed instantly—the way you do maybe half a dozen moments in a lifetime—that a star was born. I immediately began mentioning him in the column (which I'd just begun)—and it was a pleasure.

Even though Danny was breaking up the place with his humor, that night I saw as complete an entertainer as showbiz has ever known. He could sing, as he later did so movingly with tunes like "It Had To Be You" and "What'll I Do?" (to Doris Day in the movie of songwriter Gus Kahn's life, *I'll See You In My Dreams*). He could act, as proved by his hit television series, "Make Room For Daddy." His multi-talents also led him to produce many of TV's most successful series and discover many of today's stars. It's no accident that his daughter Margaret, later changed to "Marlo," became one.

In those early days, Danny was a just-married, practically broke, undiscovered talent playing in a converted auto sales showroom at 5100 North Broadway Avenue in Chicago. The $75 a week barely covered the expense of his apartment on Surf and a new baby. We became fast friends, as did our wives. Essee had just had Cookie, and she and Rose Marie would stroll down the street, walking the babies in their buggies.

At times darkly complex, the former Amos Jacobs was anchored by his strong religious beliefs. Danny never missed Sunday mass or confession—he would be the first to say that he had things to confess. And in those early days he vowed, through the poverty and the struggle, that if he ever made it to the top he'd return much more than he was given. To many, the statue of St. Jude on his Hollywood estate may be ostentatious. But the St. Jude's Children's Research Hospital in Memphis that he built almost single-handedly is no pretense to the thousands of parents with children who have been saved from formerly fatal leukemia.

Rose Marie never lost her roots, either. After they moved to Hollywood, she insisted on being known only as Mrs. Jacobs. When I asked her why, with typical Thomas humor she said: "Out here they charge according to your name. When we first arrived, I purchased a gown as Mrs. Danny Thomas and they really soaked me. I went back to the same store to buy pretty much the same dress a few months later. I told them my name was Mrs. Amos Jacobs, and they charged me half."

After Danny hit it big, he returned to Chicago's Chez Paree to honor commitments made long before. Whether it be at Pullman car cleanings, Baryshnikov's dancing or Bernstein's conducting, I have a habit of catching 40 winks on the job. Essee will tell you that I've awakened near the end of the last act of many a play and asked, "Dear, did we enjoy this one?"

Danny's show was no exception. Yet on his triumphant return, I made the supreme effort and stayed awake. In the middle of his act, he rushed over to my table. "Kup!" he exclaimed. "You're *awake*—aren't you enjoying my show?"

The routine for which Danny was best known in those early days was the "jack story." It became a legend in show business. Danny wasn't a comedian with a string of one-liners. He told stories, hilarious stories, often incorporating the many dialects he had mastered. And the "jack story" was his masterpiece. Many of you probably know it. But I have to repeat it, as best possible, for those who don't. It's the story of a salesman working a rural territory. On this day, he strikes out. He doesn't make a sale. As he's driving home late at night, he gets a flat tire. Pitch dark and 10 miles from nowhere. He goes to the trunk of the car to get his jack. But no jack. Somebody had borrowed it. So he locks the car and starts walking to the nearest gas station, 10 miles away. As he starts trudging, there comes a downpour and he's soaking wet. To add to his troubles, he has a nail in his shoe. As he trudges painfully, he begins to think the worst. It's possible they don't have a jack at the gas station. Maybe they won't let me use their jack. Or maybe they'll charge me $50. Fifty dollars just to use a jack. Those goniffs. He's still trudging and building up animosity. If they do have a jack, I'll have to walk all the way back to my car. His imaginary anger is building up to a boiling point. Finally, he reaches the gas station, ready to explode. He spots the innocent proprietor and bursts out, "You know what you can do with your God damn jack!"

Danny officially retired the "jack" story when he performed at the Diplomat Hotel in Miami Beach in 1969. Two of his long-time Chicago friends in the audience, Jack Arvey and Sam Ruby, called for the story, whereupon Thomas explained that he no longer tells it, "I've retired the 'jack' after using it 10,000 times." Thomas then pointed to this reporter in the audience and continued, "and there's the man responsible. He presented me with a real jack, gold-plated. . . after the 10,000th telling." Actually, Danny gave me more credit than I deserved. It was Aleck Gingiss, a tuxedo tycoon, who thought up the idea of presenting Danny with a jazzy jack.

Danny has received hundreds of awards, but a special honor came from a young priest. One New Year's Day in Chicago Danny was attending early mass at a nearby church. The priest had delivered a sermon that sounded familiar to Danny, whose act often includes little sermons. After the service, the young priest came over to Danny, took him aside, and confessed: "I think you ought to know that most of what I said today was inspired by one of your performances. You played a benefit which I attended, and I was so impressed with what you said that I jotted down most of it, and have used it ever since." Then with a twinkle in his eye, he said, "I suppose you could refer to me as the Reverend Milton Berle. . . ."

"Unca Miltie," the first television star, has become synonymous with comedic pilferage. One thing that's certain is that Berle didn't win any early popularity contests with his fellow comics. I saw Berle's movie, *Always Leave 'Em Laughing*, with Jack Benny. Benny broke up throughout, but then turned to me and said, "I'm laughing, but I'm *not* enjoying myself." And when Berle, Red Skelton and I had dinner in Chicago, the conversation went like this:

BERLE: What did you see in New York?

RED: Among other things, the Mayflower.

BERLE: Any of my old material on board?

RED: No, I saw that at the Smithsonian Institution in Washington.

BERLE: Very funny fellow, this Skelton, Kup. Be sure to give me the punch line when you write it.

Berle wasn't always good-natured about the charge that he stole material. Once, after knocking them dead on Broadway, Berle and fellow comedian Jackie Miles bumped into each other at Toots Shor's. It was one thing for Jack Benny or Red Skelton to harass Milton, but it was another thing for the upstart Miles to do it, and Berle let him have it. Afterward, Jackie apologized. "I'm sorry, Milton, I guess I just lost my head." "You know," said Berle, "you look better that way."

If nothing else, it proved that Berle could come up with a keen ad lib right off the top of his own head.

I know he did it many times when I was with him. When the name of Lucille Ball, then recently divorced from Desi Arnaz, came up: "She's one of America's great patriots. She broke off relations with Cuba at the same time the U.S. did." And: "The reason I'm so crazy about Chicago is that I was born in one of the outlying suburbs—New York. The stork that brought me only flew with one wing—he was holding the other over his nose at a joke I told. I didn't start kindergarten until I was six. For the first year I was teacher's pet—she couldn't afford a dog. Some comedians may not like me now, but I was the most popular kid in school—I was the only one with the *Racing Form*. I don't bet to win, place or show anymore—I just bet my horse to live. Anyway, later on I started out as a singer. I sang 'Swanee River' so movingly in Iowa that four people dove off the balcony. Then I got my big break in movies. They were retiring Rin Tin Tin."

The truth is that if Berle did "borrow" material from other comics, it wasn't as much as they, or Berle, led the public to believe. And, as Joe Laurie, Jr., a leading wit of the 1940s and 1950s, explained: "Sure, he steals other comics' material—but Milton improves on their jokes with his delivery. It's the *way* he does the material that matters—his delivery is absolutely the best." Certainly the public didn't mind where Milton's material came from. His many years of being Number One in the early days of television, and his durability afterwards, are unsurpassed.

I recall one dinner with Jack Benny, who was discussing his Sunday night TV show with Groucho Marx as guest. It sounded more than familiar to Essee, who told Jack that Milton had used almost the same script.

Benny was stunned. He hadn't seen that Berle show, although his writers may have. His first impulse was to scrap the entire program, but there wasn't time. Instead, he got Berle on long-distance phone in New York. Milton was totally gracious about Jack's dilemma, and gave Benny his blessing—though he couldn't resist adding, "What a funny world this is, Jack. Imagine, *you* stealing from *me!*"

Another time, Danny Thomas was booked at the La Martinique for his New York debut. He was terrified about the critics and wisecracking New Yorkers and he confided the problem to the more experienced Berle. "Don't worry about it, Danny. I'll be at your opening. The first one that throws a crack at you, just bring the mike over to me and say, *I've got a fellow here who takes on all my small fights.*" Berle made good on his promise, and the debut went beautifully. Danny has been grateful to Milton ever since.

I once asked Milton's mother who was her favorite comic. "Bob Hope," she quipped. Then she added, "I stole that one from Milton's daughter. See—I'm a real Berle!" When Mrs. Berle died suddenly in her seventies, it broke Milton's heart. He couldn't stop crying throughout the funeral, nor for a long time afterward. A New York paper paid her this tribute: "Nobody loved Berle except his mother and the public. Now Milton has lost half his audience."

It's interesting that almost all the giants of comedy had unusually close relationships with their mothers. Freud probably had the answer. It could just be that they always laughed at their sons' jokes. Fortunately, the world is still laughing at Milton Berle's jokes, even though some of them belong to Bob Hope, Johnny Carson. . . .

Here are a couple of paragraphs I once wrote on one of my favorite comics. You'll know who it is.

> I'll never forget when he invited me into his lavish Beverly Hills home. I had the most wonderful meal I'd eaten in years—and very reasonable, too. A steak was only $4.50 (for old friends, that is).
>
> After the meal, he personally collected our paper plates. He mentioned that they'd only been used a few times. We adjourned to the living room, and spent the next half-hour listening to probably the most wonderful collection of records in all of Hollywood. I would have listened longer, but I ran out of nickels.

Jack Benny, of course. Through an unsurpassed sense of timing (which Johnny Carson has so successfully used as a model) and an unrelenting portrayal of himself as the tightest of tightwads, this gentle, beloved man was at the top of his craft for half a century. One of Jack's other trademarks was a long-running feud with his friend, satirist Fred Allen, who delighted in ribbing Benny about being humorless without the aid of his writers. "Without his writers," Allen quipped, "Jack couldn't ad lib a burp after a Hungarian meal."

I recall when a rumor went around Chicago that Benny had died of a heart attack in New York. I immediately put in a long-distance call to Jack's home. Fred was visiting Benny at the time, and picked up the phone. "Is it true?" I asked. "Jack isn't dead, is he?"

"I don't know," replied Allen. "I've been sitting here talking to him for about an hour, and I really can't tell."

The fact is that Jack could be very funny without writers. Once after we'd had lunch and went out to his car, he stared disgustedly at the parking meter. "What's the matter, Jack?" I asked. "I still have three minutes to go on my nickel," he answered.

When I inquired what he felt about people not recognizing him for being a pretty fair violinist, he answered: "It's enough that I know I play the violin just like Jascha Heifetz. . .under my chin." During a concert at Ravinia in 1962, his violin playing was interrupted by a jet plane passing overhead. With a typically perfect pause, Benny looked up at the sky and said, "W-e-e-e-ll, I hate to think they're hearing this up there for *nothing.*"

But those occasions *were* exceptions. When not before an audience, Benny was the audience. George Burns played pranks on him and ribbed Jack unmercifully, and Benny loved it. It was no accident that when Fred Allen died, Jack Benny received hundreds of letters of condolence.

Jack made himself the butt of the humor on his shows, too. His wife, Mary Livingstone, was continually poking fun at him. An interesting sidelight is that Jack met Mary when he was a vaudeville performer playing in Vancouver. Someone set up a blind date for the two of them, but it turned out that Mary was barely out of her teens. "What am I doing here with this kid?" Jack exploded in a rare display of temper. "I became so enraged myself," Mary told me, "that I decided to get revenge someday, and I did. I *married* him."

It was the role of Benny's valet Rochester, though, which was truly revealing. In an era when blacks were portrayed as shiftless and unintelligent, Jack and his writers created a relationship where Rochester got the laughs by having the smarts.

Because of his public persona, people in all walks of life thought they could kid around with Jack. When he was invited to perform at the White House, Benny arrived with his violin case. The guard at the entrance asked him what was in the case. Said Benny, looking for a laugh, "It's a machine gun." But the guard was equal to the situation. "Thank goodness," he deadpanned, "I was afraid it might be your violin."

Jack could let himself be one-upped and enjoy it because, unlike so many of the current comedians, he wasn't insecure. Jerry Lewis once said, "I open the refrigerator door, the light goes on, and I do 20 minutes." Jack was the opposite. He enjoyed laughing, often at himself, as much as he liked making others laugh.

And he was so generous. Jack gave more than $100,000 a year—a huge sum in those days—to worthy charities, even in the days when it wasn't as fashionable or as tax-deductible. He tipped more than $10,000 a year, largely to offset his reputation as a tightwad. Wherever he went, waiters, barbers and porters made a beeline for Benny. Ironically, it was Jack's generosity that once saved his life. In 1962, he was scheduled to fly back from New York on the American Airlines plane that crashed, killing 95 people. Hours before the flight was to leave, Jack was asked to do a benefit in Hartford, Connecticut, for a new university music building. As always, he couldn't say no and wound up helping to raise close to a million dollars. Because of it, he had to take a later plane.

When at last he did leave us, another Bennyism—that no matter how many birthdays he celebrated, he was always 39—comes to mind. His hometown paper, the *Waukegan News-Sun*, put it this way in their lead paragraph: "Waukegan's favorite son, who for more than 72 years of his life entertained people, died early today. Jack Benny was 39."

Joe E. Lewis, a contemporary of Benny's, was the childlike master of laughter because he never aged in another sense. He drank, smoked cigarettes, played the horses and loved human beings to a fault. More than probably any performer I know, he had the rare strength, on-stage or off, to display his weaknesses. Essee and I spent more wee hours of the morning than was good for us trying to keep up with Joe, but Essee adored him. To know him was to love him.

The proof is that Hollywood made a movie of Joe E.'s life, a rarity in showbiz, especially for comedians. Joe E. downplayed it, of course, saying: "*The Joker Is Wild* is a different kind of picture. Children will not be admitted—unless accompanied by a drunk." Frank Sinatra starred in the 1957 film and did a good job, but the film failed to capture Joe. The two romantic interests in Joe E.'s life were played by two of Tinseltown's then most tempting dishes, Jeanne Crain and Mitzi Gaynor. After watching Sinatra make love to them, Lewis cracked, "Frank had more fun playing my life than I had living it." The truth is that the Hollywood formula circa 1950s simply couldn't deal with this pixie-ish giant whose close friendships ranged from occupants of 1600 Pennsylvania Avenue to members of the mob.

The Joker told how Lewis got his croaking voice when hoodlums slashed his throat and left him for dead in a Chicago hotel room (the Commonwealth on Diversey) in the Roaring '20s. It didn't tell how he got his voice back. Father J. A. Heitzer, an English instructor at Notre Dame University, heard of Joe E.'s case while visiting his ailing sister in the next room at Columbus Memorial Hospital. The priest introduced himself, and vowed that he would teach Lewis to speak again. Every Sunday thereafter, Father Heitzer came up from South Bend for the painstaking task of trying to give an adult his voice back. He began with the letter "A." It was six weeks before Joe E. could master the first letter of the alphabet. About a year later Joe was singing before packed audiences—in a voice he described as "an all-clear signal for a floating crap game."

Joe was constantly being told by doctors to quit drinking. One time, I itemed in my column: "Is it true, Joe, that you were ordered to stop drinking by six doctors?"

"Yes."

"And you gave up those doctors for one who gave you permission to drink?"

"Yes."

"Why, Joe?"

"Because," Joe E. replied, "I like a doctor who isn't afraid to take chances."

Now and then, he did climb on the wagon, referring to himself as a CPA—Certified Public Alcoholic. When he went on Ed Murrow's "Person To Person" in 1956, Murrow laughed louder and longer than in any other interview. Afterward, Joe E. told me: "I was ready for the one question he didn't ask: *Joe, how many drinks do you consume in one day?* I would have told him: *One for every cigarette you smoke, Ed, and what I consume tastes better.*"

He tried to give up gambling, too. He made the supreme effort on his honeymoon with starlet Martha Stewart, promising to give up gambling for reading. After a few arduous hours, Joe made the sensible compromise: He took out a subscription to the *Daily Racing Form.* Joe E.'s best-known quip on his gambling was, "Betting the ponies is actually my work. Showbiz is my hobby. I'm constantly taking money from my hobby to invest in my work." And once when he arrived in Vegas to play a club, he greeted reporters with, "I'm really here for a legal separation—from my money." It was his close friend and "guardian," Chicago's Judge Abraham Lincoln Marovitz, who arranged to put aside and invest some of Lewis' money, or Joe would have wound up a pauper. Instead, he left a sizable estate.

He gave away as much as he gambled away. Johnny Black, the song-writer who tragically died broke before his "Paper Doll" became the nation's rage, once was Joe E.'s partner, accompanying the comedian at the piano. One afternoon Black came to Lewis and said, "There's a gent out here who wants to buy our song." They were both broke, of course, so Lewis told him to go ahead and sell. Black said he would, but he wanted both their names on the sheet. "To hell with my name," replied Joe, "just get some money for yourself. It's all yours." And years later, starring at the El Rancho in Vegas, he was stopped by a supposed former bigshot who pleaded not for a $20 handout, but for $200. As usual, Joe E. immediately obliged. Abe Marovitz was with him, and berated Joe for "giving that phony any money. He *never* was a *bigshot*."

"He's a *phony?*" repeated Lewis. "Well, why destroy a legend for only two hundred bucks!"

He risked more than his money on his fellow man. Finishing a show at the Mounds Club in Cleveland, he and his pianist, Austin Mack, were walking to their hotel when they saw smoke sifting from a low-rent apartment building. They dashed into the building and began ringing bells to warn the occupants. Only one person answered. Frenetically, she explained that hers was the only bell that worked. Lewis rushed up the stairs, knocked on all the doors and got all the people out before the fire truck arrived—and just in time to save his own life.

He got himself into some other tight spots, too. Once Joe was inveigled into attending a political dinner in honor of Senator Joseph McCarthy, the last person in the world he would have admired. Hand-picked speaker after speaker walked up to the podium, and called McCarthy the greatest living American. Finally, the toastmaster spotted Lewis in the audience and asked him to say a few words. In the several seconds he had to walk to the dais, Joe's quick thinking saved him. "I agree with what the previous speakers have said about Joe McCarthy," Lewis exclaimed, "but I haven't seen too much of him since he quit managing the Yankees." Then he stepped down. Sports fans will remember that another Joe McCarthy managed the Yankees to six pennants.

By the same token, anyone who was as openly vulnerable on-stage as Joe invited hecklers. "I want you to know, young man," he once said to a persistent heckler, "*you* are not obliged to entertain *me*—nor are you equipped." But his classic heckler line was: "You know, I thought *I* was drunk—until I saw *you*."

Inevitably, time caught up with him. When he celebrated his 50th birthday in 1952, he said to me that the party was held over his objections. "I told my friends that I didn't care to advertise the fact that I'm now 50. In showbiz, that's not too smart." I asked him why he'd agreed to the celebration. "Because they told me that everyone thinks I'm 60!" When he was 65, there was a huge party hosted in Las Vegas by Frank Sinatra. Lewis made this brief speech: "There are three signs of old age. The first is loss of memory. I forget the other two."

He was 20 pounds lighter then, recovering from a stroke that had partly paralyzed him, but he returned to work Feb. 19, 1967, on the "Ed Sullivan Show." Still, it was dusk for this man who had spread so much sun in the lives of others. For example, he had trod the most remote beaches of the South Pacific to entertain World War II GI's. One site was so dangerous and out-of-the-way that the Commanding Officer, trying to pay tribute to Joe, could find nothing better to bestow on the comic than naming the camp's newest structure for him.

As a result, Joe always announced, somewhere in the Pacfic there is a Joe E. Lewis Latrine.

The only other award he would acknowledge came when the liquor industry presented him with a gold shot glass for downing his one millionth drink. Or so he said.

No, Joe E. wasn't the type who won awards.

Only your heart.

On the other hand, Groucho Marx, one of the indisputable kings of comedy, was not known for being bighearted. He was hugely successful on the stage, radio and TV. But it was his movies with his brothers Harpo and Chico that make his unique acerbic humor live on for each new generation.

Groucho didn't need writers. When the *New York Times* asked him to write a review of an important book pertaining to comedy, he sent in a minor masterpiece with this note attached: "I spent so much time on this review that I never got around to reading the book."

My very first mini-interview with him, in a restaurant before he was about to attend a St. Louis Browns baseball game, was a good example of tart, off-the-cuff wit that knew no equal:

GROUCHO: Interview? *Interview?* Why pick on me? I haven't married some other man's wife lately. I can't make it today anyway.

I'm going out to see the St. Louis Browns. I'm dying for the smell of big league baseball, and there's no team that smells like the Browns.

KUP: The Radio Academy voted you the No. 1 comedian. Do you agree?

GROUCHO: Yes, I was No. 1 comedian. Jack Benny was No. 2, Amos 'n Andy were No. 3, and the St. Louis Browns were No. 4. Personally, I think the Browns are much better comedians than Benny, Amos 'n Andy and myself. How funny do you think *we* would be with a bat in our hands? Anyway, I never heard of the Radio Academy. Well, that's not true. It consists of myself and two relatives in New Jersey.

KUP: I also see that—

GROUCHO: Listen, I've never met you before. How do you spell your name?

KUP: K-U-P-C-I-N-E-T.

GROUCHO: Sounds like a disease to me.

Al Jolson, celebrating a wedding anniversary at the same restaurant, spotted Groucho and came over to introduce his latest young wife. Before Jolson could say anything, Groucho greeted: "You have a beautiful granddaughter, Al." After a few more Marx jibes, the introductions were finally made, and the Jolsons returned to their table.

KUP: When you have the time, I'd like to have you on my TV show, Groucho.

GROUCHO: I don't blame you. What kind of a show is it? Don't tell me— I know. A bad one.

A friend waved to Groucho from another table and he rose to go over. Suddenly, he stopped and picked up his cup of coffee to take with him. "Can't trust you newspapermen." When he got back, it was time to leave for the ball game.

GROUCHO: Don't worry about the check. I'll sign your name. If only I could spell it. Can anyone spell a name like that? Why don't you change it to something people will remember? Like Hopper, or Parsons. Well, goodbye, Mr. Fidler! (Hedda Hopper, Louella Parsons and Jimmy Fidler were the leading gossip columnists of the day.)

Groucho always had a not-so-kind word at the drop of any hat which smacked of pompousness. When he finally went on television, I asked him what he thought of the medium. "I find it very educational,"

Groucho said with a straight face. "Every time somebody turns on the set, I go in another room and read." When another leading TV comic asked Groucho for a critique, Groucho replied, "I never miss your show." The comic beamed. Then, Groucho added: "I never see it, and so I never miss it."

Nothing was sacred to Groucho except for the truth spoken in jest. In the 1952 Presidential campaign, he was asked to comment on Dwight Eisenhower and Adlai Stevenson. "America is a remarkable country," Groucho countered. "It's the only country in the world where the people can go on the radio and kid the politicians—and where every four years the politicians go on the radio and kid the people." Always one with an eye for a pretty girl, Groucho was once imposed upon for advice by an actor with a goody-goody image. "I can't find the right girl," the actor complained. "You see, I'm looking for a girl who doesn't drink, smoke, swear or is promiscuous." Groucho just stared at the actor. "What for?"

He first gained national recognition in movies as one-third of the Marx Brothers. A big part of their success was the contrast in the three personalities. No small part was their Chicago roots. They were reared on the South Side of the city, and got their show business start in Chicago. When I came to know Groucho better, he would talk seriously (for as long as a minute) about those early days, recalling how the then four Marx Brothers were earning a standard $100 a week in vaudeville. "We learned that a six-person group automatically got $150 a week, so we pressed our mother and aunt into the routine. Later on, when we were making enough money, we went back to a foursome and then to a threesome." Groucho confided, "We had a key word that always stopped us from being complacent. *Greenebaum*. We owned our own home, and the mortgage was held by the Greenebaum banking firm. Whenever we began to break up on stage and stray too far from our routine and laugh among ourselves and become sloppy, our mother, always in the wings, would shout, *Greenebaum!* And we would immediately get serious again, thinking of the small fortune we owed.

"Chicago is a beautiful city today, but I'll never forget the slum area we lived in. Of course, it wasn't a slum until we moved in. Seriously, there were my mother, father, grandfather, four brothers, an aunt and uncle and their child, and there was only one bathroom. It was the most crowded bathroom in the city."

Harpo Marx (the one who never talked) was not only a sensitive musician, but a cultured speaker off stage. The moment with him that stands out most in my mind was when he did a pantomime interview with Chicago's "curbstone cut-up," Ernie Simon. Suddenly, Harpo felt a jab in his you-know-where. He whirled around and there was a smiling woman holding a huge hatpin. She had decided to find out for herself if Harpo could indeed talk, and stuck him in the behind to see if he'd let out a screech. He didn't—only because the hatpin didn't quite make it all the way through his topcoat.

Chico Marx was the truly zany one in real life. An avid gambler, he lost several fortunes on the ponies, cards, dice and just about anything else he could place a bet on. One time, I asked him how much money he'd lost in his lifetime. "I can tell you right to the penny," he replied, surprisingly. "It's $1,850,456.91." I asked him how he could possibly know the figure to the penny. "Because," answered Chico quickly, "that's exactly how much money Groucho has in the bank."

The two brothers made perfect foils for Groucho—but then, anything did. He insisted, though, that his humor was not insulting. "I don't *insult* people," he told me. "I *lampoon* them. There's a difference. Like being a *writer*—or a *newspaperman.*"

If Groucho would pass through Chicago and we didn't get a chance to talk, he'd drop me a note like this one: "Sorry I didn't see more of you while in your toddlin' town—but one can take only so much of Kup. By pony express, I'm sending you a lighter emblazoned with my mug. For a small fee, this can be erased by one of the cheaper jewelers in your town. Hoping this finds you, I remain—and I intend to as long as possible—Groucho."

With the exception of Bob Hope—who is a chapter in himself—no funny man appeared in my column more than Henny Youngman. You don't segue into writing about Henny because *he* never segues. Breaking just about every rule for comedic performance, he simply walks out, stands there with a non-sequitur fiddle under one arm (on which he occasionally strikes a single note) and rattles off dozens of rapid-fire one-liners which have broken up audiences for more than 50 years. His only segue from one subject to another is his deadpan expression.

Like Danny Kaye and Jackie Gleason, you can't describe Henny. You have to be there. All I can do is give you the opening of a typical Youngman routine:

—We sent another astronaut into orbit three weeks ago. He's still waiting for his luggage.

—I just bought a new sports car with four speeds—fast, faster, fastest—and dearly beloved.

—I've been married for 46 years—where have I failed?

Hardly anyone heckles Henny. Who could get a word in edgewise? I remember one time when someone tried. Before the heckler could utter three syllables, Youngman turned on him, "You know *before* and *after*? You remind me of *during*."

Once in a blue moon, Henny also does a joke which is a two- or three-liner. Like the one about Rip Van Winkle being awakened from his long sleep by his wife. "Get up, you've been sleeping for 20 years," Mrs. Van Winkle says. "Give me five more minutes," says Rip.

Now you take my wife. . .please—

That line, of course, is in every Youngman monologue. Once you've seen Henny, you wait for it, knowing that a string of jokes about his wife Sadie will follow. But Sadie had the last laugh. She handled the money in the family.

As popular and enduring as Henny has been, I don't think the public has ever seen him at his best—at the "roasts" of other stars. Whenever the top dozen or so comics and entertainers perform at a roast, each gets up and pans the guest of honor in every way possible. Henny is in demand for roasts because he commits the ultimate insult—he *ignores* the guest-of-honor *completely*! Henny walks up to the dais and for his entire 10 minutes does the same act as he does on TV or clubs. It gets funnier and funnier as it goes along and, by the time he sits down, without even looking at the guest of honor, everyone is in convulsions. At the Johnny Carson roast, Johnny was totally in stitches after just 10 seconds of Henny:

—My wife thinks she's a lawyer—she makes a federal case out of everything.

—If she loses, she takes it to a higher court—her mother.

—My wife is always lecturing me. She lectures me so much, in fact, I carry around my own slides.

—My wife does bird imitations—she watches me like a hawk.

—My wife's mouth works faster than her brain—she says things she hasn't thought of yet.

—If I ever left my wife, I'd die—she'd kill me!

Though not a performer, any chapter in any book on those who have made America laugh would be incomplete without Art Buchwald. He has no writers—he is a writer. I know how difficult it is to find a humorous quip to close a column six days a week, a custom I adapted from the show biz injunction, "always leave 'em laughing." But Art comes up with a whole column of *original* humor thrice weekly. Because of America's commercial fabric, most top comedic writers end up working for performers. My favorite comedians usually use several writers. Yet Art "performs" his own material. . . in print. I recall sitting with him and his ever-present cigar in the Pump Room early in his career.

"The telephone company is taking over the world," extemporized Art. "Did you ever stop to think how helpless we would all be without telephones? Women would go mad, teenagers would be speechless, and business would come to a standstill.

"The telephone company knows what each and every one of us is saying. They listen to all our conversations. They know the innermost international secrets by listening in on what President Kennedy says to Nikita Khrushchev on the phone. They know all domestic secrets, too, by listening in when a wife calls her husband to make sure he is at the office and then picks up the phone to call her lover."

"How do we put an end to this tyranny?" I asked.

"We can't," answered Art. "We're trapped. If we phone for help, the phone company just cuts us off. We can't communicate. Did you ever stop to think how difficult it would be for you to write your column without a telephone?"

I shuddered. "You mean I couldn't pick up the phone and call Rome and ask Liz Taylor how *Cleopatra* is going?"

"You couldn't even get Eddie Fisher. What we gotta do is take over the phone company ourselves, so we can control the world. By the way, I'm glad I'm in Chicago during Brotherhood Week, because I have been inspired by the good that Brotherhood Week can do. I just read where the Black Muslims met at the International Amphitheatre and invited George Lincoln Rockwell and his American Nazis to attend. This, to me, is a brotherhood lesson for all of us. And I should like to pass on this Brotherhood Week slogan: *Take a Nazi to lunch.*"

"What about Communists, Art?"

"There just aren't enough to go around," he explained. "I have been making speeches all around the country and almost everywhere I've gone, there are people who want to fight Communists."

"What's wrong with that?" I asked.

"What's wrong with it is that you can't find a single Communist to fight. There aren't enough in the country to go around. I attended one of these meetings in Waco, Texas, and saw people fully armed for battle. And there wasn't a Communist closer to them than New Orleans. What we should do for these people is insist on a more equal distribution of the

Communists in the United States. Instead of having them concentrated wherever they are concentrated, they should be forced to circulate around the country and let people see at least one. What good are all those guns and bombs if there are no Communists in the area?"

"Talking about Communism," I said, "do you foresee a world war?"

"Not at all," said Art. "The phone company won't permit it."

Recently, Art was "roasted" by the Society of Professional Journalists. When at last it came his turn to answer the shots everyone had taken at him, Art simply walked to the dais and said: "It looks like I'll have to save the evening."

And he did—with one-liners like, "The definition of a moderate Iranian is one who has run out of ammunition" and "The trouble with George Bush is that he looks like every woman's first husband."

There are others who belong among the greats.

Jackie Gleason, particularly through his characterization of Ralph Kramden in "The Honeymooners," will live on in our laughter. I never thought Jackie would die in a hospital as he did, because this bizarre bon vivant used to check into hospitals for relaxation. Once I called him when he'd put himself in a Miami hospital for a few days. He wasn't there. The nurse told me, "Mr. Gleason checked out this morning. He wasn't feeling well."

Red Skelton has to be one of the top 10. They say that all comedy is born of tragedy, and Red never got over the great tragedy of losing his beloved son to leukemia. Yet he kept making us laugh through his tears.

And George Burns, the most durable of them all, who made a career for decades by playing second banana to his wife Gracie (though George got off many good ones himself: "Isn't it funny that she can see a blonde hair on my coat at ten feet—but can't see a garage door at five?").

And Danny Kaye, the master of visual humor (and so many other things, including gourmet cooking).

I remember at Hollywood's Hillcrest Country Club how the "Knights of the Round Table"—the top comedians of the day—would try and top each other. As George Burns said to me, "We never listened to anyone else's gags. As soon as you started telling them, the rest of the Knights began thinking up their own stories to top yours. They wouldn't hear a word you'd say, but when you finished, they'd give you this business of *Very funny, very funny, here's a much funnier one.* One time," Burns went on, "Groucho was telling a story and saw no one was listening. So he threw in the line, *And that's the story of my father's funeral.* When he got through, either Danny Kaye or Red Skelton or somebody said, *Very funny, very funny, Groucho, but let me tell you one that's positively hilarious. . . ."*

Though a handful of these still reign, through the years a new group of greats has grown to prominence. Buddy Hackett can break up anyone. Shecky Greene at his best is hilarious. The multi-faceted Steve Allen is brilliant and, if he devoted himself completely to humor, would probably be unsurpassable. Bill Cosby, the current king, undoubtedly will go down as one of the all-time greats.

And then there were those who could have been kings of comedy, but for one reason or another, fell from grace. Lenny Bruce comes to mind. One of his funniest routines was a takeoff on this reporter. (Laugh? I thought I'd never start!) He began brilliantly on the cutting edge: "Did you hear about the beat poet who wanted to commit suicide? All his poetry rhymed." Lenny was among the first of the four-letter comedians. No foul word was beyond him. But he brought an intelligence to his comedic remarks that made his audience think. For better or worse, he broke out of the language limitations. I once brought Bob Hope to see Bruce in a small Chicago club. I wasn't sure how Hope, the All-American boy, would take Bruce. But Hope recognized talent. "This guy's a genius," was Bob's review. But then he went over the edge. When in a hospital for a drug problem, he answered his phone: "This is a recorded message. I died at 7:01 this morning. . . ." It was more than sick humor. It was prophetic.

Shelley Berman had a wonderful wit, but his temperament too often got the better of him—as when he once ripped a telephone off the wall on national TV. Dick Gregory got off winging, a black comedian breaking new ground by telling black-white jokes. The list of the best goes on and on—Red Buttons, Jackie Leonard, Jan Murray, Jay Leno, Alan King, Jerry Lewis, Mort Sahl, Sid Caesar and, as night club comedians, Woody Allen and Dick Cavett (before they moved upward and onward in other fields), Phil Foster, David Steinberg, and Joey Bishop.

And one could write a whole book on the "funny women," from Lucille Ball to Phyllis Diller.

To me, the greatest comedians are like the finest wines. We've had many comets who blazed brightly for a brief period. But if you stand the test of time, you're a *real* star.

9

Ike and the '50s

The 1950s—coming after what we hoped would be the *last* world war, and preceding a decade of new frontiers and revolts—were epitomized by our President during those years.

Dwight Eisenhower, like all American leaders, was not the uncomplicated hero we wanted him to be. Still, probably more than any American President, he came across that way. I don't know if Ike made the 1950s what they were or if they made him, but he and the times were certainly right for each other. Eisenhower personified the "if it ain't broke, don't fix it" theme of American character.

My first real Ike memory took place in Harry Truman's Oval Office some six months after World War II had ended. I was talking to some governmental heavyweight whose name I don't even recall when President Truman came over with General Eisenhower and introduced them.

"I met you a few years back, General Eisenhower," the man greeted. "And I'll never forget you." Both Ike and Truman took deep breaths, expecting the customary string of compliments about Ike's great war record, place in history, saving of the world and so forth. But the General was surprised and delighted when instead, his fan said: "No, I shall *never* forget you—the day we met you gave me four winners at the racetrack!"

When Ike arrived at the Blackstone Hotel in Chicago for the Republican National Convention, in 1948, he put an immediate and absolute stop to a draft-Eisenhower movement.

One magnificent moment at the convention was when Big Jim Thorpe, America's greatest all-around athlete, walked up to Ike. The General had made some highly complimentary remarks about Thorpe in a recent speech and the Indian wanted to thank him personally. Like Truman—and unlike L.B.J. and Nixon—Ike had the ability to relax and enjoy the *little* things.

Ike and Thorpe reminisced about the last time they had met. It was 36 years before, when the Carlisle Indians defeated West Point, 27–6. Thorpe, the greatest football player of his day, had run wild against the Cadets and scored every touchdown but one.

Ike's famous smile flashed. "And on one of those touchdowns," he said, "I tried to tackle *you*, didn't I?" Thorpe nodded, smiling. "And," Ike continued, about to break into laughter, "I got a stiff arm in the face that knocked me out and I had to be carried from the field."

Eisenhower won the presidency in 1952 and again in 1956, of course, and his presidency for those eight years was inextricably attached to the story of another political giant whom I knew intimately. . .Jack Arvey.

I first came to know Arvey when I was a child. We lived in the 24th Ward, and he bossed it with a benevolence that made him second only to God. He was a one-man forerunner of the welfare state, making sure his "subjects" had food, coal to heat their flats and, in many cases, jobs on the city payroll. This brought forth such loyalty that in one election I can recall the Democrats got a whopping 29,000 votes to the Republicans' 700.

As a student at John Marshall Law School, Arvey showed the quality that made him the ruler of his ward for 28 years and then Cook County Democratic Chairman. Stumped by a difficult question on an exam, he deliberately ignored it and instead handed in a 20-page essay on something he knew quite well. The professor responded as follows: "You don't know a damn thing about the case referred to in this examination. For that you get an F. But your ingenuity shows an amazing instinct and feel for the law and its ultimate purpose. For that you get an A. The two grades average out as a C. You pass."

In Washington in 1948, when he testified before the House subcommittee investigating the paroles of the four former Capone-ites, Jack Arvey was subjected to considerable grilling by Congressmen Hoffman and Busbey, both Republicans. Congressman Hoffman particularly wanted to know about Jake's Place. Where was it located and who ran it? His face turned crimson when Arvey explained it was the figment of a cartoonist's imagination and was merely political propaganda used during the last mayoralty election. The congressman also asked Arvey if he knew a "Joe Kostner." "Very well indeed," replied Arvey in his most polite manner.

"But I'm sure Mr. Kostner had nothing to do with the paroling of the four men in question. He died, you see, in 1925."

As the 1948 elections approached, Arvey shrewdly realized that new faces were needed in the Democratic Party. So first, Jack convinced no less than the mayor of Chicago not to run again. Ed Kelly had served as mayor longer than anyone in Chicago's history (a record which would stand until Richard J. Daley ruled for more than 20 years) and had been a helluva boss himself. But his popularity had dipped and Arvey figured if Kelly ran again, he could bring down the whole Democratic ticket with him. Jack was able to convince Kelly to step aside in favor of Martin H. Kennelly, a well-known civic and business leader who had *not* been active in politics, and thus had no chinks in his armor for the Republicans to attack. By the same token, Arvey was able to put forth Paul Douglas, the former University of Chicago economics professor, for U.S. senator and, above all, Adlai Stevenson for governor. Their victories laid the groundwork for the surprising victory of Harry Truman in 1948.

Jack had overcome obstacle after obstacle to achieve these across-the-board triumphs. For example, Stevenson was originally slated to run for U.S. senator, an office he far preferred to that of governor. But the Republican incumbent, Senator C. Whelan "Curly" Brooks, owed much of his popularity to his military record in World War I. Arvey knew that Paul Douglas' unblemished reputation, not only as U of C prof but also Marine combat veteran, would make the difference.

About the only thing Arvey couldn't manage was. . .Ike.

Though Arvey in the end worked night and day for Harry Truman's nomination at the 1948 convention, Jack a short time earlier had been a key member of a small group of party leaders who maneuvered behind the scenes to sponsor Dwight D. Eisenhower for president on the Democratic ticket. This began when a group of U of C scientists, headed by Harold Urey, which produced the atomic bomb that ended World War II, called on Arvey in late 1947. They brought ominous tidings—they described in detail the destructive potential of nuclear weapons and predicted intercontinental ballistic missiles, military bases on the moon and, unless there was leadership in the White House *beyond* partisan politics, a world-threatening situation between the United States and Russia.

Arvey was moved by their impassioned plea. He changed his game plan. But who—*who* was above politics *and* could win a presidential election? The answer came to him in an instant.

General Dwight David Eisenhower, of course, then president of Columbia University.

Arvey also, like every other expert, had to consider the polls that predicted *any* Republican could defeat Harry Truman in '48. When Arvey
tried to relate this to Truman, he became *persona non grata* at the White
House. Truman no longer would take his phone calls. So Arvey made his
decision, flew to Washington, contacted key national Democrats, including Jimmy Roosevelt, the son of F.D.R., and William O'Dwyer, mayor of
New York, and Eisenhower was sounded out.

And Ike was "favorable"!

Jack, with the help of Roosevelt and O'Dwyer, then put into action a
battle plan of operation which the general himself would have admired.
First, it was agreed that Ike would have to be *drafted*—under no circumstances would he *campaign* for the nomination. Second, they had to agree
on how the story should be "leaked" to the public. One key Democrat
said he could arrange for Arthur Krock of *The New York Times* to interview Eisenhower and establish Ike's "reluctant" willingness to accept a
draft.

But the rub was that the Democratic Party seemed to be coming apart
at the seams. There were the "Wallace-ites" and the "Dixiecrats" who
had abandoned Truman completely. At the other end, "ultra liberals"
wanted Supreme Court Justice William O. Douglas as their nominee. Add
to that a litany of problems, such as the fact that Truman had more vetoes
overridden by the Congress than any president in U.S. history. Then at
8:15 one morning late in 1947, Arvey received a phone call. "It's all off,"
the caller said. "He won't accept under *any* conditions."

Did Ike pull out because he thought he couldn't win as a Democrat,
or because he didn't finally want to become any part of a move that would
be disloyal to his World War II Commander in Chief? (At the time, the
mutual admiration between Truman and Eisenhower was great, though
some years later it would dissipate and develop into a feud.) What happened is that a number of top Republican business giants, for whom Ike
had great respect, got wind of the Arvey plan and dashed to Ike's side.
They urged him not to pull the Democrats' chestnuts out of the fire.
Compounding their argument was the fact that Ike at one time had indicated to Truman that he would not be a candidate while he, Truman, was
in office. When word reached Truman that Ike had decided not to run, he
instantly exclaimed, "He's a man of his word." Ike, after some stop and go,
apparently was keeping that word.

Jack Arvey was equally as loyal. . . to the Democratic Party. As soon
as he received the news, he rushed to New York, met with O'Dwyer and

Roosevelt, and a public statement was issued pledging support to Truman. Roosevelt, interestingly, declined to sign the statement because he believed it was impossible for Truman to win. Jack returned to Chicago, incognito, wanting to avoid the press completely because "we" were clamoring for information on the Eisenhower story. He secluded himself in the Lake Shore Drive hotel apartment of an old friend, Col. Charles Baron. No one but Baron, myself, and one or two others who never would violate Arvey's confidence knew where he was. Yet, as Jack lay down that night to really sleep for the first time in days, the phone rang. He picked it up.

"The White House calling," announced the operator.

Arvey suspected a Kup prank. He was thinking of hanging up. But, a moment later, President Truman came on the phone.

"I just read the statement you issued on my behalf, Jack," said Harry, "and I want you to know that you will never have any cause to regret your support." From that moment on, the Truman–Arvey relationship, which had been on dry ice, thawed into a friendship that blossomed throughout the remainder of their lives.

In 1952, Arvey also stage-managed the nomination of Adlai Stevenson for President. Adlai was truly reluctant, but Arvey, with an assist from Truman, overcame that.

I loved Stevenson for his eloquence, his sensitivity, his vision and because he was a Democrat, albeit a reluctant presidential candidate. Once Truman tried to buoy the Illinois governor's spirits, saying, "You have no idea how popular you are, Adlai. Last time we were together, I even heard one person say, *Why, there's that Governor Stevenson of Illinois and who's that little son of a bitch riding with him?*"

On another occasion, the president told me, "I had to speak to Adlai like a dutch uncle to get him to run." What was apparent at the time, to Truman as well as others, was that Stevenson was trying desperately to disassociate himself from the Truman adminstration, which was in disrepute at the time and carried so much baggage. The last thing he wanted to happen was to be known as Truman's choice. Adlai wavered for a long time before deciding to bite the bullet and become a candidate.

In one significant way, Ike and Harry were alike. Both had terrible tempers—and big hearts. Just after Eisenhower's nomination at the 1952 Republican convention, when the last volley had been fired in the bitter struggle between Ike and Senator Robert A. Taft, Ike received news of his victory in his suite at the Blackstone Hotel. Contrary to all protocol, Ike didn't wait for Taft to make the traditional call on him. He picked up a phone and called Taft at the adjacent Conrad Hilton. "I want to come over and see you, Bob," he said. Ike and his bodyguard, Chicago policeman Lou Swee, pushed their way laboriously through the crowd in the lobbies and on the street outside so that the general could publicly pay his respects to a gallant campaigner who was heartbroken at having lost his last chance to follow in the footsteps of his father, President William Howard Taft.

I voted against Eisenhower because of my affection for Stevenson. But I, too, *liked* Ike.

At the other end of the spectrum from Ike, Arvey and Adlai, was Governor Jimmy Davis of Louisiana. Jimmy had been a very popular vocalist and singer of western songs—he was the composer of "You Are My Sunshine," one of the big hits of the day—and he had been elected on a campaign which consisted largely of singing, rather than issues. When Essee and I visited his capital in Baton Rouge (which was modeled after the White House), Jimmy immediately said, "I want you to meet my cabinet." He then introduced us, saying, "This is my secretary of state—he was the drummer in my band. This is my secretary of the treasury—he was the trumpet player in my band. . . " and so on. Virtually all his cabinet members were. . . his band!

Preachers, as much as politicians, typified the 1950s. Billy Graham was probably most representative of a country which uniquely had found a way of separating church and state. He has come in for a lot of criticism through the years, but I've always admired Billy. He is definitely not a religious hawk. He is always calm beneath the impassioned rhetoric and, possibly most important, did something from the beginning that would have saved TV preachers today a lot of grief: He gave a public accounting of his funds.

It was a prosperous, somewhat ingenuous time—possibly the last years in which we as a country—and this reporter personally—unquestionably accepted the dreams of our nation's childhood. Debbie Reynolds and Eddie Fisher found each other. Notre Dame kept winning. Christian Dior's new flat-chested look quickly went flat. There was a war in Central America, but we knew it wouldn't really affect us and couldn't last long—the news commentators couldn't pronouce Tegucigalpa. And 1952's Miss America was the tallest in our history. Colleen Kay Hutchins was six foot, two inches in high heels. When I shook her hand, it was reminiscent of Heavyweight Champ Joe Louis' grip.

Tommy Manville was also somehow typical of the 1950s. He inher-

ited so much money that his main pleasure in life became marriage—
something he did almost a dozen times. Bandleader Artie Shaw was
ahead of Tommy for a while, but when Manville married No. 8, it looked
like he was champ once and for all. Then, lo and behold, I had to call
Tommy at his palatial New York residence and relate tragic news: A Texas
oilman, Jack White, had just married wife No. 9 and dethroned Tommy.

I found out about it when the wealthy Texan stopped in Chicago to
visit an acquaintance, lumber tycoon Danny Ellman. During a lull in the
conversation, Ellman introduced Jack to a pretty lass, Joy Lansing. Forty-
eight hours later, Joy became the ninth Mrs. White. Though Tommy was
almost in shock when I told him, he recovered enough to be critical of
White, saying: "Well, Jack always did believe in long engagements."

It's true that Tommy, who married more because he enjoyed the publicity than the women, seldom took 48 hours to tie the knot. The moment with Tommy that stands out most, though, is when he was dining at
the Pump Room with wife No. 6 or 7 after knowing—and courting—her
for all of four hours. He saw me, waved, and I went over. "Kup," he
greeted, "I want you to meet the next ex-Mrs. Manville."

The humor of the decade reflected both Ike and Manville. We were
enjoying ourselves, but underneath it we were beginning to be troubled.
As a result, psychiatrist jokes proliferated—such as the one where a patient sent her therapist a postcard from a vacation spot. It read: "Having
wonderful time, wish I knew why."

Mrs. Oscar Hammerstein told me a story that best combined Ike's "if
it ain't broke, don't fix it" philosophy with the cracks which were beginning to show in our armor. It was about the child who was absolutely perfect in every way—except for one thing—he didn't talk.

At the age of two, his parents began to worry. When he was three,
they hustled him to specialists and child psychologists. Every effort was
fruitless. At four, five, six, the boy, though obviously highly intelligent
and fine in every other respect, still was mute. The parents had just about
given up hope that he would ever talk.

Then one morning at breakfast, the boy turned to his parents and
said, "This cocoa stinks."

The mother and father leaped with joy. "Son," his mother exclaimed,
"you can talk! And a complete sentence!"

"Of course I can talk," the boy said.

"Then why," the father asked, "haven't you said anything up until
now?"

"Because," replied the boy, "up to now everything has been all right!"

Yes, the 1950s were the Eisenhower years—outwardly, nothing was really broken. But deep within our country, our cities, ourselves, we could detect some very dangerous cracks in the cornerstones.

10

Competition, Critics and Kudos

When I first began the column in 1943, the only competition was from Nate Gross of the now defunct *Chicago American*. It was just a week between the time my editor asked me if I wanted to do the column and the day it first appeared. But in that week there must have been a hundred people who told me I was making a mistake and to stick to sportswriting. Nate, they said, had the town locked up. He was a lot older and more experienced, had all the contacts, and so forth.

But I had my assignment and I was going ahead with it. Nate was a good reporter, but he had little flair for writing a column. He gathered a lot of his information over the phone from his hotel room. I was going to cover this beat *no* differently than I covered a football or baseball game. I'd be *there*. I'd be *visible*. If someone had something worth printing, they'd know where to find me—if I wasn't already within earshot.

That meant being almost *everywhere*, because my beat turned out to be many beats. I kind of liked the way the paper put it with an ad on the cover of our trade publication, *Editor and Publisher*, in 1968:

A celebrity columnist.

And society writer.

And book reviewer.

And financial writer.

And sportswriter.

And feature writer.

And music critic.

And art critic.

And film critic.

And drama critic.

And public relations man.

Irv Kupcinet is a very busy man. Six days a week he writes a column for the *Sun-Times* which covers so much ground we can't say exactly what kind of column it is.

The jump to general columning was eased somewhat because of my sports columning. In the early days, I depended a lot on my friends like George Halas, Phil Wrigley, Arthur Wirtz and Charlie Bidwill, who had contacts in the political and social world as well as in sports. Yet, covering all these beats had some drawbacks, above and beyond being thrown in the jug for alleged drunk driving or unwittingly pre-empting the Pope.

There were the inevitable lawsuits. Mine were kept to a minimum. When they did occur, I'd simply pass them on to the legal department— and never hear of them again. In the interests of honest reporting, I mentioned a few in the column, like the one about:

A gent whose name I can't recall at the moment is suing me for $100,000. The old flatterer! This can be very embarrassing. No sooner did the news leak out than my creditors, who had been waiting long and patiently, sprang to life. "One hundred thousand dollars, eh?" I could just picture them saying to themselves. "And all this time he's been giving us that brother-can-you-spare-a-dime business."

There also was the inevitable hate mail. One beat which wasn't mentioned in *Editor and Publisher,* was...*causes.* I had no power—but the column did, and part and parcel of that power was to fight for the underdog, the minority, the needy. That wasn't always welcomed by those in the drivers' seats.

A sample "fan" letter:

You must have a lot of money invested in Negro speculations where the almighty dollar is your only god, and not the self-preservation of the white race which our forefathers fought and died for. I am very proud to be a member of the White Circle League and I think Mr. Joseph Beauharnais is a very fine upstanding man. If anybody is scum to the white race, it's you.

It was signed by someone who wrote 90 percent of my hate mail—
anonymous. In a lighter vein came this fang letter from a University of Illinois student:

> I thought it might interest you to know that I used one of your articles—
> word for word—as a rhetoric theme. To my complete astonishment, I received a grade of "C." Never again shall I plagiarize your column.

In spite of such criticism, I kept writing the column and, in September of 1948, *Time* astonished me by devoting one of its own columns to mine. I told them I would have been a bigger stinker than I already was if I didn't bow low from the waist and say thank you, since they were unduly laudatory and devoted a ludicrously large amount of space, considering the subject. However, I felt forced to picayunishly point out a couple of things to them. One was that the accompanying photo looked like me. . . the face only a mother (and a very understanding one at that) could love. Essee also was upset with the picture. Poor girl, she thinks I'm a look-alike for Cary Grant.

On a slightly more serious note, I took *Time* to task when it said: "Every night, sportily-dressed in a shirt with long Sinatra-style points (and with KUP loudly emblazoned on his handerchief, tie clasp, cuff links and gold ring) he patrols. . . ." *Time* must have been peeking in my boudoir. Though I did have exactly such a set of handkerchiefs, tie clasp and cuff links with KUP loudly emblazoned on them, I'd never yet worn them. I suppose the only thing that really bothered me was when they called it a "sometimes ungrammatical column." With Winston Churchill, that was the kind of pedantic nonsense up with which I would not put.

With TV now in full swing, I decided to make the leap on the theory that the two mediums went together and one would complement the other. In 1952, I began a late night news/interview show on the CBS station in Chicago. I left that in 1957 to become the Chicago anchor for a new NBC show, "America After the Dark," the successor to Jack Paar. The show was brilliantly conceived but poorly executed as it traveled from New York to Chicago to Los Angeles and, on occasion, San Francisco each night to cover worthy events. It was short lived and made way for Johnny Carson.

Still, after a decade or so, the column was visible enough so that you might say even Hollywood beckoned. Not exactly Hollywood per se, but my good friend Otto Preminger, the only producer with the vision to see me as an actor. He used me in two of his movies, *Anatomy of a Murder* and *Advise and Consent*. No other producer, since, has had the same appreciation of my acting.

The movies were fun, but I always made it a hard and fast rule never to have my name associated with any business enterprise because of the obvious conflict of interest. Once the column was pretty well established, there were offers from every conceivable kind of commercial enterprise from Kup's Koffee Kup to Kup's Klothing. On the other hand, something that genuinely pleased me was when a copy of *Swiat* arrived on my desk one summer. One of my closing laugh lines had been published in the far-off Warsaw monthly, giving credit to "Kommentator Ivo Kupcinet w dzienniku Chicagowskim Sun-Times."

All this didn't make Nate Gross, or even my other competitors, very happy. Nate in particular found that the friends he had counted on for so many years as sources of information had now become my sources. He became very bitter about me and his "friends." But when you cover the same beat, you run into most of the same people. As soon as it became evident that I had cut into his readership and emerged with a reputation of my own, he stopped talking to me. He'd simply ignore me when we ran into each other. I've always adopted the old philosophy of "kill them with kindness" and was even gracious to him, always offering a handshake. That burned him up even more.

On a similar note, though I've never told this until now, I was frankly flattered when in the early 1960s the King Syndicate was having trouble with Walter Winchell and asked me to come to New York. Not that I thought they preferred me to Winchell. I knew what the plot was: Fly in this hotshot from Chicago to make Winchell sign his newest contract. I played along with the game, because it was an experience being wined and dined by the top New York newspaper brass. They never would have let Winchell go, and even though a part of everyone in this business wants to make it in New York, a bigger part of me wanted to stay in Chicago.

A couple of years later, in 1966, when Hedda Hopper died, Don Maxwell, editor of the *Tribune*, called and asked if we could meet. I said sure. Wilfrid Smith, sports editor of the *Tribune*, was also at the meeting. He was six foot, four inches and 250 pounds and had been a professional football and basketball player as well as a teacher and sportswriter. More than that, he had been my football coach and civics teacher at Harrison High School and was, to put it simply, my boyhood idol. I was touched and flattered that Wilfrid was there...but I knew that there had to be a reason for it.

The reason for the meeting soon became apparent. The *Tribune*, which syndicated the Hedda Hopper column, wanted me to replace her. The offer included Hedda's home, her office and the right to travel the world. The salary: a mind boggling (in those days) $75,000. But it meant being based in Hollywood. Essee and I gave serious thought to the generous offer, but we both came to the same conclusion. Cookie's tragic death left us as desolate as we were bitter about Hollywood at the time. The memory was too fresh and to live and work in that atmosphere would be impossible. It was a heart-breaking decision professionally, but not personally. I regretfully informed Maxwell of the decision Essee and I had reached. "The timing is wrong," I told him and thanked him for the offer. Neither Essee nor I had any misgiving. We would have a little more piece of mind away from the Hollywood that had sucked our daughter into its maelstrom.

Between writing the column and appearing on radio and TV, plus the tremendous amount of reading I had to do to keep abreast of developments—in a word, working 16-hour days—it was inevitable that I'd get a reputation for catching 40 winks at private screenings and public appearances. It *was* a little embarrassing now and then—Joe E. Lewis once broke into Brahms' "Lullaby" when I nodded off during his act—but it may have saved me, too. Bob Hope has the same ability to fall asleep anywhere instantly (we've often had contests over who can leap into unconsciousness faster), and it's no doubt been one key to his durability.

My annual vacation helped, too. In the early years, I wanted to keep the continuity of the column going even if I was at Nippersink, a resort in Wisconsin, with Essee and the kids or deep-sea fishing in the Bahamas. So I had celebrities in all walks of life do guest columns. Parts of some are worth rereading. Jack Benny, for example, wrote an entire column about being sorry that he was not able to do the column. One highlight of the itinerary that prevented him from writing the column that he wrote was:

We left Colorado Springs on a Wednesday night and arrived home Friday. Mary was really glad to see me. In fact, she gave a party the night I got in. . . . I'm not sure she expected me early, though, because there was one extra man.

Equally as funny was Bing Crosby. He wrote a column from the shadow of the Canadian Rockies where he was filming *The Emperor Waltz*, telling all the wonders of that beautiful spot. He then ended with this line:

There is one other advantage to this location that I've thus far refrained from mentioning. There are 2,000 miles between us and Bob Hope.

And Mae West:

In answer to the question, "Is love an art or a science?", let me answer by saying: *Love is what you make it . . . or who you make it with.*

Betty Grable, one of the leading glamour girls of the 1940s, played it straight:

I owe Chicago the best part of my happiness. In 1939, Harry [James] was playing at the College Inn at the Sherman Hotel, while I was appearing at the Chicago Theatre. Dick Haymes, who sang for Harry then, introduced us.

And, of course, they were married, albeit a sometimes stormy marriage. And speaking of stormy marriages, a sparkling guest column came from one of Elizabeth Taylor's husbands, Mike Todd:

There's a shaft of golden California sunlight slanting through a window of my office as I sit writing, but in my mind's eye the yellow beam fades slowly as it filters through Chicago's smog and I am again deposited in a room in the Drake. Spike, that genius among bellhops, having stowed away my bags, has just departed, leaving me clutching a stack of neatly typed telephone messages. Right on top: "Listen, lizard, you're late." And I am. Riffle the slips. Henry Crown, your mother, Ashton Stevens, Dave Goldbogen (Todd's original name), and some guy named Kupcinet. Chicago, I love you.

It was a mistake to have said what time I thought I'd arrive. A lot of fine folks think Todd is a bum—again. Well, I won't phone any of 'em yet. Instead, I'll bounce over to the Shubert for a show called *Up In Central Park*—holding forth at $45,000 each and every week. Chicago, I love you.

Some day I ought to ask Kup to run a line presenting my apologies to this fair city for foisting on it that stinky company of "Star and Garter." Well, like the feller says, that's show business.

Now for a leisurely walk back to the hotel. I should walk more, if only for the waistline. State Street is still very imposing. I once had an office 50 feet from here (Randolph and State) the size of a phone booth, only it didn't have a phone. Those were nice, quiet days, and I didn't know how well off I was. Chicago, I love you.

More profound was that of Bishop Bernard J. Sheil:

We have failed youth miserably in the past, rather than youth failing us. We dare not fail them now when the world of tomorrow for which so many of them fought and died hangs in the balance.

But the best of all (seriously, it was damned good) was the one Essee wrote for me:

When Irv switched from sports to this column, he gently hinted that a wife's place was over a hot stove in the kitchen instead of traipsing around night clubs with her husband. However, I put my foot down, only to find his size 13 brogans on top of mine, which is our normal dancing position.

Everyone says, "Oh, you're so lucky! Your husband's job is so glamourous and exciting. You must meet the most interesting people." And they're right.

While Irv is table-hopping (the only exercise he really gets these days), I usually remain at our table, talking or dancing (depending on the sex) with our visitors. In that way, I've picked up a number of interesting little tidbits on their personal likes and dislikes which you may appreciate. Frank Sinatra always requests "Laura" when he gets up on the dance floor. And, bobby soxers, he really is a swell dancer. George Burns, Gracie's husband, tells the most fabulous stories in the world. And when you ask, aghast, "Really?" he replies, "No. I just made it up!"

Most of all, there's Irv Kupcinet, my favorite character, who sleeps, eats and writes this column. People invariably ask me how we had time to have two children. Our stock reply is that Bobbe Lynn ("Cookie"), 5 years old, was born during one of Joe E. Lewis' songs at the Chez. And 21-month-old Jerry was born somewhere between the Singapore and the Chez Paree.

Pretty good, eh? So good I didn't let *her* write one again.

A lot of other famous men and women from politics to science, show business to sports, did give me some entertaining and at times insightful guest columns. Yet after a few years, it became apparent that the celebrities' press agents, not the stars, were writing the guest columns. So, instead, we just substituted the words: KUP IS ON VACATION.

On Oct. 28, 1957, I wrote the last piece at what had been my home-away-from-home for 22 years. Ever since 1935, first as a sportswriter and then as a columnist in '43, I had wended my way, day and night, to and from 211 W. Wacker. In those final days of October in '57, the hulking figures of the steely-eyed movers stood over my shoulder ready to seize my typewriter, and everything else, for the big move to the new 15 million dollar home of the *Sun-Times*. There were farewells to Mike the barber, who shaved me every day at five o'clock shadow time...Max, the genial spirit behind the cigar counter...Joe, the building engineer and sports authority ("every game's fixed")...Nick, the schnapps dispenser next door where the clan gathered after working hours...the elevator boys Gene, Tom, Eddie, Ivan and Irish with their cheerful good mornings... and then into a cab to the new diggings at Wabash and Wacker. My office was on the Wabash side of the building—in fact, it was the only office that went up and down with the bridge, or so it seemed. The view was breathtaking.

I always took cabs to get around. I've probably ridden in more cabs than anybody in Chicago, maybe anybody anywhere. I never had to waste much time waiting because doormen always had a way of getting them for me. You can learn a lot from cab drivers and sometimes it translated into items for the column. As Checker cabbie Eddie Hamilton used to say: "It's too bad that people who know how to run the country best are so busy driving taxicabs."

Frequently, of course, I had to fly. Almost anyone who travels in his work has a close shave airplane story. I've had several, but the first is the one I remember best. The famous broadcaster Johnny Neblett had asked me to fly in his private plane on one of his assignments, and I welcomed the experience and whatever might come from it for the column. We made a date, and at the last minute a major Chicago story broke and I had to cancel. Months later, we made another appointment to duo in the sky on some major story he was following. Again, something came up, and I couldn't go up.

Finally, we cast it in bronze. But one more time, fate came up with a story I couldn't refuse to cover. Several feverish hours after what would have been take-off time, I completed the story and switched on the radio. So help me, the very first words I heard were: "Johnny Neblett late today died in the crash of his own plane...."

And death took no holiday on the newspaper itself. There are times when you pound away at your typewriter not with your fingers, but with your heart. One of those times was in 1955 when Richard J. Finnegan, the legendary editor, died. If he'd asked me once, he'd must have asked me a hundred times, "How's the family, Kup? Are you spending enough time at home with them?" It was paradoxical that Finnegan's heart gave out— he had such a great one. The following year, on Nov. 9, 1956, the stillness and shock encompassed us once again as Marshall Field III died.

The *Chicago Sun* was founded by Field at the urging of President Roosevelt to give Chicago an opposing view to the ultra-conservative, anti-F.D.R. *Tribune*. The *Sun* made its debut on Dec. 4, 1941, with this page one headline: "Oh, What a Beautiful Morning" from the hit musical of the day, *Oklahoma!* Four days later, however, came Pearl Harbor and the purpose for which the Sun was founded disappeared. Both newspapers were now on the same team, supporting the war effort. Field's proposal to take on the *Tribune* evaporated in the overwhelming spirit of patriotism. The *Sun*, which was having financial difficulties, and the *Times*, a vibrant, lively tabloid but with a small circulation, merged in 1948 to give birth to the present *Chicago Sun-Times*.

Consequently, the publishers under whom I've worked were Emory Thomason, founder of the *Chicago Times*, his successor Richard Finnegan, Marshall Field III, Marshall Field IV, Marshall Field V, Jim Hoge, Rupert Murdoch and, now, Bob Page. Most were mint. One had extreme mental aberrations. I frequently implore Page to stay on the job because I'm tired of breaking in new publishers.

But no matter what, the column seemed to take a couple of steps forward for every time it stumbled. And, so help me, every single competitor strangely seemed to go into eclipse for one reason or another. Nate Gross died but, long before that, the *Chicago American* ran another column of exactly the same type by Roy Topper. Roy died suddenly, and Maggie Daly took over. She had physical problems, had to retire and lost a leg afterward. There were so many others—from Jimmy Savage of the *Trib*, Jon and Abra Anderson in the *Daily News*, Bob Wiedrich in the *Tribune*, to Michael Sneed and O'Malley and Gold. Sneed, of course, has survived by coming over to the *Sun-Times*. Maybe it was on the theory that if you can't beat 'em, join 'em.

The *Trib* in the early days had no similar columnist. After they saw that more could be done with the column, they hired a guy named Jimmy Savage. Jimmy had been a press agent for the Balaban and Katz theater chain. He was bright, a clever writer, and would have been real competition, but he went out to California to cover the Oscar awards with me and died suddenly while there. The *Trib* then hired another B&K press agent, Herb Lyon. He was strong competition. He even went so far as to get my first edition (his first edition went to press later) and steal items out of it. Naturally, I had to put a stop to that, so one day I printed the birth of a child to a famous couple—but deliberately gave the child the wrong sex in the first edition. I made the boy a girl. Then I quickly corrected it in the more important next edition.

Meanwhile, Herb printed that "it's a girl!" about the same time our second edition came out with "it's a boy!" He looked *bad*. After that, he was *very* careful about lifting my items. As fate would have it, Herb was a three-pack-a-day smoker and died of pancreatic cancer in his early forties just as his column was really getting established.

I'm not superstitious. For many years I belonged to the Anti-Superstition Club that met annually to demonstrate the *un*truths of all those beliefs. But it seemed that whenever some columnists would start to make a real run at me, they'd become incapacitated or quit or die. I certainly didn't wish anything ill on any of them. Frankly (my ego speaking), I felt confident I could, and did, top them fair and square.

11

"Home" Life

One year in the late 1950s I received this note from high school buddy, Erwin "Red" Weiner: "I saw you at the Harvest Moon Festival at the Stadium Saturday night, turned on the TV at home and there you were into the wee hours on your 'At Random' and after I got up late on Sunday, I turned on WGN for the Bears–Detroit game, and there you were with Jack Brickhouse on the radio doing the play-by-play from Detroit. To get away from you, I went to the movies that night—and there you were in *Anatomy of a Murder*. Seriously, Kup, *when do you sleep?*"

As you know by now, the question isn't *when*, but *where*, and the answer is that I sleep almost everywhere. From my job cleaning Pullman cars to the recent opening of *I'm Not Rappaport*, several times every 24 hours I manage a short nap. When I was dating Essee and had to ride the streetcar to her house, I frequently caught "20 winks"...that frequently turned into a sound sleep till the end of the line. So what if I arrived two hours late?

Shortly after I started the column, I adopted the habit of putting on my pajamas as soon as I arrived home for dinner, assuming we were having dinner at home. That habit was born of a suggestion from Lou Lurie, the former "Mr. San Francisco" and before that a prominent Chicagoan. "Getting into your pajamas forces you to relax," he explained. "Then, when you dress again to go out, you'll feel refreshed." He was right. And I've been doing the pajama bit ever since.

So, one way or another, I did manage to get enough sleep—but not in the right places. The tougher challenge was to find enough time during my waking hours to be with Cookie and Jerry, and with Essee at home—to have a real home life.

I was so busy columning, for example, that I missed the birth of Jerry. I was at Toots Shor's in New York on Nov. 1, 1944, when a long distance call came through that Essee was being rushed to the hospital. A couple of hours later—I was then in the Zanzibar—our obstetrician, Dr. Ralph Reis, phoned to tell me that I was the father of a boy. Dale Harrison, a competing columnist, took great delight in announcing the birth of Jerry before I did—calling it one of his biggest scoops. But I *was* present for the birth of my daughter Cookie three years before on Mar. 6, 1941. However, I left the next day for Florida to cover baseball spring training.

On normal nights, I'd start making rounds around 10 o'clock. First the Pump Room, to case the spa for some visiting celeb or local newsmaker, then on to the Chez Paree and the Latin Quarter where some top entertainer was appearing, ending in the wee hours on Rush Street at either the Singapore or the Trade Winds.

Essee was always with me. We were a team—we *are* a team. . . . I remember a night that we came home and the kids were getting dressed—but not in their school clothes. We'd been out with Joe E. Lewis at one of the late, *late* spots. I said to Essee, "What time *is* it?" And she answered, "It must be about 8 a.m.—and it must be Sunday—because the kids are going to *Sunday* School."

We had our arguments, of course. Once in a while they even got bitter, but they always ended with kisses. I maintain that the right philosophy for a couple is to never go to bed angry—stay up and fight! Seriously, people usually argue over little things, so my method of arguing is to try and ignore it completely. Naturally, at times that made Essee even angrier and, when Essee is angry, she has a sarcastic wit second to none. Considering how much time we've spent together, though, I think we've gotten along remarkably well.

We were lucky to go into marriage knowing that neither of us was going to have it all our own way. Today, too many kids get married, have one big argument and phone the divorce attorney because they're in shock that the marriage didn't work out like some B movie. There's *some* truth to "marriage is a 50–50 proposition." But the real truth is that a successful marriage is more like 75–25—for *both*.

Essee loved the life we led. But when I first got the column, she was dubious. She thought—as did her mother—that I'd be surrounded by glamour girls at all times. It was true that a lot of other columnists through the years, beginning with Walter Winchell, had at the very least strange marriages or, soon, no marriages at all. Walter never took his wife anywhere, and he was hardly ever at home, so you can draw your own conclusions. Earl Wilson of the *New York Post* had started his column about the same time as mine, and Essee and Rosemary Wilson decided they weren't going to end up like Walter's wife, that they'd accompany their husbands as often as possible. It was fine with me. I'll be the first to admit that I like looking at, talking to and, sure, even being admired by a beautiful gal. Who doesn't? So we had the perfect ménage à trois: The column, Essee and me. The Wilsons weren't quite as fortunate. Rosemary went everywhere with Earl. But she fell victim to demon rum.

Because I was married to the column, I wasn't with my two children as much as I would have liked. I definitely was not the ideal father, which I realized later in life. Cookie and I adored each other, as some lucky fathers do with their only daughters, but I never spent the time with her that I should have. Jerry was more rebellious, which made sense for a son of a father who was so visible, but we came to a marvelous rapport and love which is one of the deep joys of my life. Still, I wish I had spent more time with them. Fortunately, there were wonderful people helping us out at home—mainly, Johnetta Clark, our cook, who has been with us for more than 40 years and helped rear two generations of Kups. We also had a young Japanese girl, June Yamaguchi, who was with us for 13 years. Her parents had been interned in a concentration camp with thousands of Japanese-Americans in a sad chapter in American history.

Like so many fathers just starting out, I devoted too much time to the business instead of to the home in an effort to make life better for my children. In so doing, I deprived myself of the pleasure of being with my kids enough as they grew up.

Yet being a columnist also gave me experiences with my family that I could *never* have known with an ordinary nine to five job.

There was the time they allowed me to be the engineer on the Super Chief and I actually drove the train between Raton, New Mexico, and Las Vegas. Before going up front to realize my childhood dream, I informed my wife and daughter (Jerry was an infant and too young to make the trip) that, until we reached Las Vegas, I was captain of their ship. I must admit I expected more of a reaction. Well, I knew I'd receive the proper appreciation and acclaim from them upon my triumphant return.

Some six hundred miles later (and not as many minutes as usual, because the speed of our run had strangely exceeded the usual 85 m.p.h. with me at the throttle), I strode rather haughtily back to our compartment where Essee, Cookie and I then repaired to the dining car to eat a marvelous meal of mountain trout actually picked up as the train went through Colorado.

And I waited patiently for one of them to acknowledge my accomplishment.

Finally, Cookie said: "Were you the jerk who was jerking the train?"

As I said, Jerry was just an infant then. But about ten years later, on a holiday trip, it was *all* father and son.

How does a non-gambling father-son team from Chicago spend several days in Las Vegas? Easy. We swam, he accompanied me at golf at Wilbur Clark's Desert Inn, where we marveled at the horticultural achievement of a beautiful 18-hole course in the middle of the desert, visited Hoover (nee Boulder) Dam, went fishing and yachting on the nation's largest man-made body of water, Lake Mead, and took in some dazzling floor shows at night. No, you really don't need to have your hot little hands around dice, chips or blackjack cards to have a great time in Vegas. I know my 12-year-old son didn't even take a second look at the slot machines. As for me, I'll admit it *was* tempting now and then because I do enjoy action of any kind, but. . . there was a lot more action to be had with Jerry.

And, of course, I bumped into many people I knew. Joe E. Lewis, for one. Joe E. anywhere was twice as much fun as beating the house at blackjack, and in Las Vegas he was incomparable. Jerry and I caught up with him at Beldon Katleman's El Rancho Vegas. The movie of Joe's life had just been made. Jerry asked how much it cost to make a movie like that. "Two million five hundred thousand dollars," said Joe. Jerry's eyes opened wide. Then Joe added, "But they could've done it for two million dollars—it's just that they insisted on using real scotch." Then, as an afterthought, Joe said to Jerry, "I don't want you to think your dad has drunks for friends. I do drink, son, but I've never been drunk. I figure I'm sober as long as I can lie on the floor—without holding on."

As planes began to replace trains, Essee and I—as often as we could, with our children—flew to the West Coast. Frank Casey, the Midwest PR chief for Warner Bros., frequently was on the same flights. He was like a third child to Essee and me, and a real practical joker. One night we were scheduled to fly to California when Essee got a phone call, supposedly from an official at United Airlines. They said that our plane couldn't leave until the morning. So, Essee unpacked our bags to get out the stuff we'd need for another night at home, and got undressed.

"What are you doing in your nightgown?" I asked when I walked in the front door.

"United called and said the flight wasn't leaving until tomorrow morning. I don't know why—the weather's fine."

Without blinking, I said: "Get dressed quick. *I* know why. It wasn't United—it was *Frank Casey.*"

And it was. Essee repacked the bags, got dressed, and we made the plane with about 30 seconds to spare.

Another time, we were on a plane going to Montreal with the Marshall Korshaks. They served Essee the usual meal, but not Marshall and me. "You have a special diet," they told us. It turned out that Frank had called ahead and told the airline that Marshall and I could eat nothing but kosher food. Actually, the joke backfired because it was much tastier than the usual airline fare.

In a way, vacations actually became the cement of our "home" life. Every summer we'd go to Nippersink, a resort in Wisconsin, and take a couple of bungalows. June would be in one with the kids, and Essee and I in the other. Days we'd play golf, while June took the kids to the swimming area. Nights? Our nights were delightful because dear friends, Judge Henry Burman and his wife Florence, had a home on the grounds, where they entertained the Kups and two special friends, drug tycoon Louis Zahn and his wife Frieda. Actually, when I think about it, my golf game was more powerful than my football game. I could outdrive almost anybody. The only problem is that the drive generally ended up on the wrong fairway. I drive a car the same way, too. Essee says that when I get behind the wheel of an automobile, much as I love my hometown, Chicago beware! There is nothing in front of me or in back of me and, no matter how heavy the traffic, all lanes are open.

Essee also covered the coronation and all the Oscars with me, but at times she simply couldn't accompany me. She would have gone anywhere, but Bob Hope's junkets in particular were completely restricted because of their military nature. And there was my annual all-male chauvinist deep sea fishing trip in the Bahamas aboard Arthur Wirtz's 123-foot yacht, The Blackhawk, named after the hockey team he owned. Once a year I would take a week off with a few close friends, which in recent years includes Red Weiner, Jack Musick, the retired president of Hiram Walker, former *Sun-Times* executive Chuck Fegert and Howard Mendelsohn, and go looking for Hemingway's "big one."

On my most recent fishing expedition, we were joined by my son Jerry and his son, 10-year-old David. Three generations of Kupcinets failed to catch a big one, the first time in 25 years that our fishing group came back empty handed after seven days at sea. But it wasn't a total loss. David enjoyed himself so much that at trip's end he whispered to his father, "This was the greatest week of my entire life."

On the wall of my office is a 120-pound sailfish. But that wasn't the big one. The big one was a 435-pound marlin, eleven and a half feet long. It's on the wall of Shaw's Crab House in Chicago.

The only time I missed a column on my fishing trips was because of that damned elusive marlin I finally landed.

It happened this way. I wrote the column, and in order to get it to Chicago in time, I gave it to an airline hostess leaving the Bahamas for Miami. In Miami, she was instructed to turn it over to Western Union, which then would file it to Chicago. But the column never showed up. It turned out that the airline hostess forgot all about it. The paper, with all that blank space, covered it humorously:

GONE FISHING...

The above notice—and the following communications—will explain why Irv Kupcinet's column on this page today is conspicuous by its absence. It's not that he didn't write one.

It's just that nobody can find it.

It's possible that an airline stewardess has it. Or it may be in Miami. Or it may be lost somewhere on the Spanish Main.

Kup is on a fishing trip in the Caribbean, and his column was supposed to have been filed from Miami in time for this edition. The following messages between THE SUN-TIMES in Chicago and a Miami telegraph office show that no effort has been spared to locate the missing document:

NEED KUP FROM MIAMI—CHICAGO.

WILL CHECK—MIAMI.

WHAT'S THE WORD ON KUP FROM MIAMI? SUPPOSE TO HAVE BEEN FILED HERE LAST NIGHT. IF U HAVE RESEND. UNFIND HERE—CHICAGO.

MR. KUPCINET IS AT SEA ON THE YACHT BLACKHAWK. NO COLUMN FILED AS YET. WILL EXPEDITE WHEN FILED—MIAMI.

OK. THANK YOU VERY MUCH—CHICAGO.

WHAT'S THE WORD ON KUP? NEED URGENTLY HERE— CHICAGO.

KUPCINET GAVE INSTRUCTIONS TO AIRLINES STEWARDESS TO FILE UPON PLANE LANDING AT WEST PALM BEACH— MIAMI.

OK. THANX—CHICAGO.

Thanx for nothing.

Europe long has been our favorite vacationland—London, Paris, Rome. One August we decided it was time to take Cookie, then in her teens, and Jerry with us to let them see what the rest of the world looked like. In Rome, two Italian boys fell in love with Cookie and sang half the night under our balcony at the Excelsior Hotel. In Israel an Egyptian boy fell in love with her. He was really head over heels for her. She fell right back in love with him, so much so that she wanted to move to Israel. But boys were falling in love with Cookie wherever she went, so she got over it.

It was a vacation just to be with Cookie and Jerry.

12

The "Show Biz" Beat

Though I'd broadened the column so that it encompassed everything from professional gamblers to professional hoboes, Presidents to Popes, most days a majority of my items orbited essentially about
two beats. One was Chicago. The other was show biz.

Often, in the 1940s and 1950s, I covered the show biz beat in our own
apartment. At the very least, 442 Wellington was another Pump Room.
Literally. Essee and I spent so much time in the Pump Room that we decided to have an exact replica of it in the apartment.

We had a booth that looked just like the white leather Pump Room
booth, a glass table eleven and a half feet long, all the trimmings. When
Ernie Byfield, the legendary hotelman who operated the Ambassador
East heard about it, he was so thrilled that he sent over an entire set of
cutlery, glassware, plates, ashtrays and you-name-it, even including a
Pump Room cart to wheel the food in and out. But the pièce de résistance
was the time he also sent over Phil Boddy, his maître d', wearing impeccable white tie formal attire, to greet and handle our guests for our first big
party at home. I got a rise out of Essee that night when I walked over to
her and kiddingly whispered in her ear that I had seen several of the
guests slip Boddy money to get a good seat.

The apartment was so large that we almost had as much space as the
Pump Room. There was a slot machine, for example, that everyone loved
to play. We set it at 90–10, and gave the winnings to charity. And there

were other show biz touches. Harry Belafonte wanted to have a room named after him, so Essee put a plaque with HARRY'S HIDEAWAY on the door of one of the bathrooms. He loved it.

Those were great times. Stars could do whatever they wanted at our Wellington apartment. And they did.

Famed songwriter Hoagy Carmichael brought his 5-iron one night and practiced his golf swing for hours. Essee was terrified that he'd take a divot out of our brand new carpeting. He didn't.

David Niven was also a visitor. He was as charming and sensitive off-screen as on. The very first time he visited us was not long after his wife had died as a result of a freak fall during a party at Tyrone Power's Hollywood home. Yet David kept his irreplaceable loss hidden. Unless you knew him extremely well, only the most subtle signs of Niven's heartbreak filtered through.

John Wayne also shocked his fellow stars. He was at our home for dinner in 1964 right after his surgery for lung cancer. There must have been 30 or 40 people there that night, from members of the press to other celebs and, simply because he physically towered over everyone else (plus the fact that he'd only been out of the hospital a couple of weeks), all eyes were on him when we sat down to eat. Before taking a bite, Wayne reached inside his jacket, pulled out a cigarette, lit it and...puffed deeply. Everybody was aghast.

I guess I wasn't really shocked, because it figured. And the fact is that Wayne lived a long time after that cancer surgery. He was as stubborn about giving in to death as he was about everything else. We didn't see eye to eye on politics, but I admired the fact that his strong stance really came from loving America. We became close through the years, and he was as loyal to his friends as he was to his country.

But Duke also had a surprise for me that night. He stood up in one corner of the room, rapped for attention and then, in a manner that would rival an Oscar presentation, announced that I had been made a member of his *Old Shoe* club and presented me with a pair of gold cuff links, shaped like well-worn boots.

"As comfortable as a pair of old shoes" was Wayne's favorite way to describe a friend. Hence the name of his club. I thus joined a select group of the Duke's best friends.

I have a number of pieces of jewelry that tell a story. Circa 1950 readers, and probably most others also since a book about it was recently published, may recall when movie queen Lana Turner's daughter stabbed and killed playboy-hoodlum Johnny Stompanato. At the time, Lana was estranged from husband Steve Crane, himself a big gambler. One night, at the Kon-Tiki in Hollywood, Crane got into a dice game with a good friend of mine, Broadway producer Harry Bloomfield. Harry not only won Steve's money, but his ring—on which was inscribed TO STEVE FROM LANA. Harry immediately sent the ring out to an engraver, who took off the inscription and substituted KUP. I wear the ring to this day.

Clark Gable turned the women's heads at our parties more than anyone, though. After the tragic death of Carole Lombard, everyone wondered if Gable was going to marry again. When he was at the house, I asked him. "Tell you what, Kup," he replied. "Five bucks says I'll still be single when I come back from Europe." We shook. Five minutes later, he gave me back my hand. It was probably the only one that hadn't been offered to him in marriage.

Six-foot, four-inch, 240-pound Paul Robeson also stood out. Paul had one of the finest singing voices ever, and was really the first black in his profession to speak out against racial injustice in America. Unfortunately, he visited Russia, where they put on a good show for him and Robeson decided Communism was the answer to America's race problems, turning his voice in that direction. Still, I liked him and didn't feel he was any threat to our country.

No visitor to our home had more class than Archie Leach. He was the quintessential movie star—strikingly handsome, articulate and witty. And never petty. Though many of his 72 movies are considered American classics as well as being box office bonanzas, Cary Grant—his Hollywood name—never won an Oscar for performances that no one could have matched. The reason he was never given an Academy Award may have been, as with so many other overpowering stars such as Paul Newman and, until the end of his career, John Wayne, that Grant was seen to be "playing himself" and not acting. On one occasion, I asked him if it bothered him. "Not in the least," Cary replied. "I think I can speak for Archie Leach as well."

Cary delighted in keeping his real name alive—and poking fun at it. In one movie (*His Girl Friday*) he improvised this line: "The last person to say that to me was Archie Leach, just a week before he cut his throat." And in *Arsenic and Old Lace*, the name Archie Leach appeared on a tombstone. Though his clipped British accent made it evident he was from England, Cary was one of the most "American" of movie idols: Dashing, defiant, resourceful and. . .a winner.

A one-of-a-kind character was Errol Flynn. It has often been said of the many bisexuals in show business that they are usually only homosexuals trying at times to be straight. In a lot of cases, that's true. But with Errol Flynn, he was the closest thing to a genuine bisexual I've ever known.

He played a reckless Romeo and adventurer on the screen, and played it even more indefatigably off screen. His marriages were as stormy as his affairs. I recall his telling me with a twinkle in his eyes that the battling Flynns in '48 had reached an agreement about an upcoming trip they were taking together. "Any trouble and I ship Nora home right away," he said. "Before we started, I told her I was arranging for friends to stand by in Pasadena, Albuquerque, Kansas City and Chicago just in case we started fighting. If we did, off she'd go—and I wanted someone to make sure she got back to Hollywood." At a white-tie-and-tail party a few months later at Errol's palatial Hollywood home, the highlight came when Flynn nabbed a snooper rifling through drawers in the back of the house. Though the robber was carrying a pistol, Flynn decked him and disarmed him—as he'd decked the huge and formidable director John Huston a few years before. Another highlight of the night was the race between Flynn's trained white mice. They were named for the celebrities present. And Jack Benny took a huge risk by betting a nickel on the mouse "Jaybenny". When Jaybenny lost, Jack shouted: "I smell a rat!"

Errol phoned me long distance on occasion, trying to shock me with what he had to say. Once in a while he did. In '45 he phoned me and said, "Have you read today's papers yet?" I told him of course I had. "Well, I have too," Flynn said, "and I just learned I'm a daddy again!" Shortly after Rory Flynn was born, Hollywood's most on-again off-again marriage was off and running again in Flynn fashion. One time when it was "on," the two stopped at my table for lunch in the Pump Room:

ERROL: I don't know why the press insists we're reconciled. We were never separated.

NORA: If we weren't separated, why are we living in separate homes, Errol?

ERROL: Let's see, now. Let's just say that's our mode of living—or something. Get me out of this, Kup.

NORA: I think I'll just put some adhesive tape over your fat mouth.

It began to look like the marriage might blow up then and there. Nora said that Chicago had always been their danger point, that every time they traveled through Chicago together, they ended up battling. "How much time do we have before the train?" she asked. "I don't know if we'll make it—and I don't mean the train."

One of the best Errol Flynn stories was when he was conked with an egg in a Hollywood nightspot. A playgirl known from coast to coast was arguing with another gal at the table next to Errol's. As the battle waxed violent, Flynn remarked aloud, "Well, here's *one* fight in which I'm *not* involved."

Whereupon the playgirl screeched, "Oh, *yeah?*" And pitched a perfect strike at Flynn's face with a raw egg.

One of the most interesting pairs who passed through was Humphrey Bogart and Lauren Bacall. Bogie and "Baby" had one of Hollywood's better marriages, and really were made for each other because both had a "tough," sardonic persona that protected not only their bighearted vulnerability, but also their ardently liberal beliefs and championing of the underdog. I first talked to Lauren at length in the Pump Room before they were married. Bogie had given her a huge diamond ring set in gold. When I asked her if a wedding was in the offing, she leaned over and, feigning seriousness, whispered in the most confidential tone, "I'm already married. . .to Errol Flynn."

It was next to impossible to one-up Bacall or Bogie. Another time when we lunched, Bacall was constantly being bombarded by whistles from men because of her famous line in *To Have and Have Not* in 1944 when she told Bogie that if he wanted anything, "Just whistle. . . ." How did she handle the whistlers? Lauren whirled around langorously, gave the wilting whistler as knowing and sexy a look as I've ever seen, and then assaulted him in that sultry voice with, "And *what*. . .can I do for. . . *you?*"

The best example of what was beneath the Bogie/Bacall bravado was their wedding itself. It took place on May 21, 1945, at the home of Bogart's best friend, author Louis Bromfield—and Bogie's one dictum was that even with all the newspaper, newsreel and magazine photographers on hand, *no* pictures were to be taken *during* the ceremony. After the wedding, everyone knew why. Bogie, the movies' toughest tough guy, wept openly throughout the entire ceremony.

But there were no tears the next day when the newlyweds paused in Chicago en route to Hollywood. Naturally, they visited the Pump Room, where they were the bruncheon guests of famous hotelier Ernie Byfield, who was responsible for creating and populating the Pump Room. Ernie invited Essee and me to join the Bogarts at table No. 1. What I remember best was the lovelight in the eyes of both Bogie and Baby and the feeling that here was a marriage of two strong people who would make a go of it.

An interesting sidelight to the wedding was that Bromfield was an arch-conservative and Bogie an ardent New Dealer who played an active role in the re-election of President Roosevelt (and alongside whom I would fight against blacklisting in Hollywood a couple of years later). Bogie and Bromfield had an agreement: Never talk politics. That's how they stayed best friends. On the other hand, Bogie's previous wife, rabid Republican Mayo Methot, argued politics with Bogart at the drop of an issue—and ended up not only an ex-wife but, frequently, black-eyed.

Later, I attended a party which Bogie gave in honor of Betty, where he surprised her with a $12,000 mink coat. Though it was the first mink she'd ever owned, the coat caused considerably more excitement among the guests than for Betty. And considerably more excitement for their pet boxer dog, Harvey. Thinking the coat was a rival for Bogie's affections, the dog, as soon as Betty took the coat off, attacked it viciously and ripped it to shreds.

For the longest time, Betty only took parts in pictures with Bogie, partly so that they could work together, partly because it was thought she was limited as an actress. She later proved this wasn't true. However, it was true that her marriage was more important to Bacall than any movie part. When Bogie died, a part of her died. She tried unsuccessfully to make it come alive again through a number of men, from Frank Sinatra to the brilliant but downbeat Jason Robards, Jr. But no one could replace Bogie. No doubt he could have lived longer and not fallen prey to cancer of the esophagus if he hadn't smoked and drunk to excess. But Bogie was Bogie, and you had to take the bitter with the sweet. *He* did.

Director Alfred Hitchcock and actor Paul Newman were two of so many whom I first came to know when they came to my town. Hitch, famous for his tongue-in-cheek slaps at women, once had made a trip to Marrakesh and compared it to a beautiful spa in Palm Springs, California, "except that in Marrakesh the women have the decency to keep their faces covered." When Newman arrived in Chicago for the opening of the picture that sprung him to stardom, *Somebody Up There Likes Me*, he made many people angry. The movie was a hit, and so was Newman's driving. As he left the scene of an accident in Chicago, he assaulted a police officer and made some *very* tasteless jokes about a recent kidnapping. Paul obviously wanted to be a race car driver even then. In fairness, Newman's energy was later channeled into more admirable avenues,as he developed into a major star.

One of the moments I recall best was when I *had* to go backstage. . . or the performers wouldn't have gone *on* stage.

Martin and Lewis were opening at the Chez Paree, and Essee and I were at ringside waiting for the show to start. Dean and Jerry had become the hottest thing in the country through their movies and were doing the same thing in clubs. But. . .the show didn't start.

The club was packed and the natives were becoming restless. So were the chiefs. Finally, one of the owners came up to me. "Kup—could you go backstage for a minute?" he asked. I told him sure, asking him why on the way.

"They've got stage fright—or they're fighting over something. I don't think they're going on!"

I went backstage and just kind of shot the breeze with Dean and Jerry for a couple of minutes. Then I said, "Listen, you guys, please get out there. I need my sleep."

They laughed and loosened up. They knew what I meant. I went back to my table, 20 seconds later they were on stage, and about 20 minutes after that, I was happily asleep.

Yul Brynner was another fascinating character I met during the column's first 15 years. Yul was always ambiguous about his background. Every time I interviewed him, he would tell a different story about the line of his birth. When we talked in Chicago one spring, he stressed that he had sprung from European gypsies. That summer when I saw him in Hollywood, he was from Mongolia. I figured he may have been from Brooklyn.

Yul and Joan Crawford have one characteristic in common. Both were demanding stars who insisted on all the comforts of home when traveling. Joan was famous for the 20-page list of demands she sent to hotels in which she was planning to stay. Brynner's list was almost as large, for both his hotel accommodation and his dressing room in the theater. I recall one of Joan's demand was an ironing board in her suite. She did her own ironing. Yul's most unusual demand was the fresh paint job he ordered for his dressing room. It had to be done in brown. And not any shade of brown, but the one he specified. If the shade was off, the paint job had to be done over. These perks were part of stardom and really, a small price to pay to keep them happy. For who shall ever forget Yul's performance in *The King and I*? It brought happiness a thousand fold greater than his own "make me happy" demands. *The King and I* and Yul Brynner were forever entwined and he loved the role so much that he played it, on and off, for 25 years.

And there were stars who stopped off in Chicago because Chicago was their home town. The list is long. Robert Ryan, one of Hollywood's early and most impressive angry young men, learned boxing at the Illinois Athletic Club. He went on to become Intercollegiate Heavyweight

Champion, which stood him in good stead for the many boxing movies in which he starred. His first break, as a matter of fact, came in the fight flick *The Set-Up*. Ryan, who wanted to be an actor almost from the time he could talk—and earned two dollars a day as an extra at the old Essanay Studios a mile away from his North Side home when he was only eight— got the part because he was a student of poetry as well as uppercuts. As a sophomore at Dartmouth, Ryan discovered a poem by Joseph Moncure March, "The Set-Up." He became enamored of it, and with the help of his English professor, popularized it on the campus. From there, the po- em's fame spread to other Eastern colleges. Eventually, "The Set-Up" was bought for a movie by RKO's Howard Hughes. March had written the script for Hughes' first movie, *Hell's Angels*. When Ryan found out RKO owned the rights to "The Set-Up," he wrote Hughes, asked to make a movie based on it, and Hughes agreed.

Another movie tough guy I liked who had a Chicago connection was Burt Lancaster. He wasn't from our area, but his vaudeville partner Nick Cravat was. Before Burt ever became an actor, he and Nick were an acro- batic team. If you or a relative went to vaudeville shows in the Midwest in the 1930s, you might have seen why Lancaster (then going under the name of Lang) would later be able to do his own amazing stunts with Tony Curtis and Gina Lollobrigida in the movie *Trapeze*. Lancaster, after he made it in Hollywood, financed a vaudeville tour of theaters starring Cra- vat and himself. Nick was overjoyed with the idea, but insisted that Burt pay him only $100 a week. "After all," Nick said, "I don't mean anything to the public. They'll come to see *you* and you deserve 90 percent of the money."

Lancaster laughed. "Remember the days when we got $5 a night— and we each took $2.50?" Cravat nodded. "Well," Burt exclaimed, "that's the way we'll operate now." And they did.

On the West Coast, I sometimes stayed at the home of some performer/friend. No matter how many Hollywood palaces I'd seen, the huge winding staircase inside the entrance of Jack Benny's Beverly Hills mansion was something special. Their Palm Springs mansion, in which Essee and I stayed when Jack and Mary were in New York, was almost its equal. Essee often shared a room with Joan, the Benny's adopted daugh- ter, when I returned to my typewriter in Chicago. One of Mary Benny's closest friends was Jane Wyman, who happened to be in Palm Springs at the time. She had recently divorced Ronald Reagan, and in the course of the conversation, we asked Jane what caused the divorce. Jane's explana- tion may have been a tip on Reagan's political future. "How would you like to go to bed with your husband and every night get a half hour lecture on politics instead of what you expected?"

Joan Crawford's home was sumptuously spotless and Danny Thomas' Beverly Hills manse is a story in itself. When the Thomases first moved in, it was a fairly expensive but not really impressive Spanish-style house. With each new success, Danny added a wing. Eventually, they couldn't add any more without putting the master bedroom across the Mexican border. Danny then more than made up for that with what he did *inside* the house, from the lighted statue of St. Jude to an immense wood carving of *The Last Supper* covering the entire wall of the dining room. Danny also added a unique U-shaped dining room table so that no one would have his back to *The Last Supper*. Danny and Rose Marie now occupy a much larger home atop a mountain. The home is so large that it is often described by ribbing friends as a hotel. With all its religious artifacts, including the previously mentioned art works, the home is known as "Vatican West."

Bandleader Artie Shaw was getting married again (wasn't he always?), and I took him to task when he said that all of his half-dozen ex-mates would return to him. That included some pretty heavy names, such as Lana Turner, Ava Gardner and Kathleen Winsor (author of the bestseller, *Forever Amber*). I talked to some of the gals in question, and not one said she'd even dream—make that *nightmare*—of returning to Artie. At the time, I didn't reveal *why* in the column. But now, let's put it this way: As Chicago comedian Jackie Leonard said, "I don't have to tell jokes for a living. I've got the band-aid concession for Artie Shaw's ex-wives."

Ava Gardner did accompany ex-husband Artie to Jazz Limited once when we also were there. After a few minutes a quarrel registering 8.7 on the Richter scale ensued. Finally, Ava threw up her hands and shouted, "Let's stop fighting, Artie. People will think we're still married!"

I ran into the irrepressible Mickey Rooney on almost every West Coast jaunt. The time which stands out most was with Rooney's dad, Joe Yule. Joe confided how Mickey made his debut at the age of three: "My wife and I were doing an act together in vaudeville at the time. After one of our performances, I heard little Mick singing a song we used in our routine. I was amazed that he could carry the tune and knew all the words. So I said, *Mick, I'll bet you can't do that on stage*. And he came right back with, *I'll bet I can*. And he did." He's been on stage ever since.

Though Abbott and Costello became famous with their "Who's on first?" baseball bit, Yule actually invented the routine. Yule did it with a cleaning-and-dyeing scene, as follows:

"Where you going?"

"I'm going down to dye."

"What's the matter, you sick?"

"No, I'm not sick. If I were sick, I couldn't dye. In fact, I'm dyeing in my father's place so we can keep the money in the family."

"You mean you get paid to die?"

"Sure, you don't think I dye for nothing?"

"Can I die with you?"

"No, you gotta belong to the union."

"You mean you gotta belong to a union to die?"

"That's right."

"What's right?"

"Not always. Watt's the salesman."

"Who's the salesman?"

"No, Hoos the boss."

And speaking again of ex-husbands, which you do often in Hollywood, I once bumped into Maxine Andrews of the famous movie and recording singing sisters and asked how things were going with her ex-husband, Lou Levy, who ruled one of the biggest music publishing companies at the time. "Well," she answered, "the last time he visited the kids, he brought them an elephant."

Levy had been driving along Ventura Boulevard and wondering what would be an appropriate gift to bring his children that day. Lo and behold, traffic slowed and a few cars ahead he spotted a circus truck transporting an elephant. Levy hit the accelerator, pulled alongside the driver and offered him $10 for an hour of his time. The driver then followed Levy to the former Mrs. Levy's home, where they unloaded the elephant and led the beast into the backyard as a surprise for the children.

Many stars in those days, though, were not movie stars. Radio ruled the country in the 1940s and for much of the 1950s. Names that you now hear on "When Radio Was Radio" type shows were household names. Possibly the most popular show was Ralph Edwards' "Truth or Consequences." Later, he began an even more popular program, "This Is Your Life." Your reporter played an off-stage part in many shows. One in particular I'll tell you about in a chapter or three.

By the middle 1950s, though, TV had taken over. Milton Berle and "I Love Lucy," still so popular in reruns, were the leading shows. A sobering statistic was that the average TV audience at 9 p.m. on any given night was larger than the electorate which would choose the President of the United States. We were also spending as much time on that single leisure activity as we did on our jobs.

And there was a world of celebrities outside of movies and TV.

Ernest Hemingway and Mickey Spillane, two of the more popular writers of the day, were feuding and, as usual, I wound up in the middle. I had a couple of drinks with Spillane when he was in town to promote the first movie made from one of his books, *I, The Jury*, which opened at the Chicago Theatre on July 24, 1953. I asked him about Hemingway's caustic comment that Mickey had started out as a comic book writer and was still one. "There are lots of scared little bank clerks and office boys who read Spillane," Hemingway said. "They couldn't read *The Old Man and the Sea*. People who read him don't read me."

"Hemingway's a real %!*%!'" Mickey replied, "I've sold 60 million books, and is he saying 60 million Americans are scared little bank clerks and office boys? To be honest, I can write dogs. I'll match my *Kiss Me Deadly* with his *Over the River and into the Trees*. We both loused up the writing business with those two."

And when Victor Borge, an accomplished pianist turned piano humorist, was playing the Civic Opera House in 1958, he related that Arturo Toscanini once told him: "I tried to contact you as a guest soloist, Victor, but when I heard your price, I nearly fainted." Borge, who one-upped *everyone*, instantly replied: "And when I heard your orchestra, Arturo, I thought you *had*."

13

Marilyn, Grace, Judy and Joan

Marilyn Monroe.

Joan Crawford.

Judy Garland.

Grace Kelly.

To me, these were the four actresses who created the biggest headlines of their era. There were others, of course, but Judy and Joan, Marilyn and Grace, were the ones I knew best—and the ones the public seemed to want to know best. Let me count some of the ways.

My first meeting with Marilyn Monroe gave little indication of what the future was to hold. She came to Chicago to promote a movie starring Groucho Marx and in which she had a small role. While in town, she agreed to appear at a benefit in which Essee and I were involved. When she arrived at the Hilton Hotel, Marilyn looked so bedraggled, her clothes unkempt, her hair (then brown) in a tizzy, that Essee whispered to her, "Let me take you to the ladies' room to fix your makeup." Twenty minutes later they emerged and Marilyn was more presentable, for which she thanked Essee. My introduction for Marilyn's benefit apprearance was the standard one, in which guests are extolled extravagantly: "Ladies and gentlemen, may I present a brilliant newcomer to the screen . . . a young lady who just completed a movie with Groucho Marx, and one for whom

I predict stardom." Little did I know how prophetic my pro forma intro would prove.

So much has been written about Marilyn—whole books by people who never spent 10 minutes with her. Almost always it comes down to descriptions of her as a dumb, "easy" blonde or...a portrayal of her as a stifled genius. Because Marilyn's looks personified American maledom's fantasy of a sex symbol, both the public and the critics wanted to put the finishing touches on the Hollywood image and view her either as a consummately bad actress or another Julie Harris. She was neither.

She *was* an excellent extemporaneous comedienne. I recall my very first interview with her in 1952. Mere months before, she had been an unknown. Upon seeing her—and interviewing her—there was no doubt in my mind that within a short time, she'd be *un*known to hardly anyone in the United States. My introduction of her really was coming true. Here's an excerpt of that conversation with her:

KUP: Marilyn, there is controversy over the fact that you supposedly sleep in the nude at night. What *do* you have on when you go to bed?

MM: Only the radio, my dear boy, only the radio.

KUP: They make you out to be a dumb blonde, but I hear you've read Freud. True?

MM: No—I'm waiting for the movie.

KUP: I know you're rushed now—would you hold still for a longer interview next week?

MM: How long would I have to hold still for?

KUP: Half an hour?

MM: I don't know you that well, Kup.

When newly-elected President Eisenhower went to Korea just before Christmas of that same year, he was greeted with a sign that said

OFF LIMITS TO EVERYONE
(EXCEPT MARILYN MONROE!)

It has been more than well established that Marilyn was a classic example of someone who couldn't bridge the gap between the fantasy of the public's perception and the reality of her life. The more worshipped by millions as a love goddess she became, the more she felt starved for one-to-one love. There are ludicrous stories of her walking up to strangers on the street and blatantly offering to go to bed with them. Those stories fit in only with the sexual fantasy of American males toward their love god-desses (later termed "the zipless fuck" by Erica Jong).

The *fact*, not the fantasy, is that Marilyn didn't need to strike up con-versations with strangers, nor did she have the time. I know of several in-stances where she refused brief, secret one-night stands which not only would have given her a temporary "love fix," but would have enhanced her career as well. For example, Harry Cohn, head of Columbia Pictures and one of the most powerful and ruthless Hollywood moguls at the time, had the hots for Marilyn (as did most heterosexual men in Hollywood) and invited her to spend a weekend on his yacht on the premise that he wanted to discuss "the kind of role you've always wanted to play." Marilyn did want to prove herself as a dramatic actress and was always looking for such a role. But she was smart enough to ask: "Will Mrs. Cohn be along?" Cohn replied that his wife wouldn't be on the boat—she was out of town. To which Marilyn immediately replied: "Then *I* won't be on the boat, ei-ther."

On the other hand, she *always* needed to be involved with a man—and no one man could fill her needs. That she had much more than looks was shown by winning two of the most accomplished and admired men of the day. Baseball immortal Joe DiMaggio, a class act, carried a torch till the day of her death, long after their marriage had ended. In fact, it wouldn't be inaccurate to say that he's still carrying it.

Marilyn Monroe and Joe DiMaggio, two of the most glamorous figures of the day, united in marriage. It was fairy tale time and the press loved it. But reality set in too soon. Marilyn's career was booming. Joe's was behind him. The demands of movie-making are tremendous. DiMag had few de-mands on his time. She was the one sought after for interviews, picture-taking, public appearances. Joe virtually became a tag-a-long. He spent most of his time at home, watching television. The odds were stacked against a successful marriage and the divorce followed shortly.

But Joe's love for Marilyn continued until her death, and thereafter. His remembrance of a single rose graced her mausoleum for years. He be-came estranged from Frank Sinatra over an incident involving Marilyn. To this day, DiMag is clutching her memory as dearly as he once clutched a bat.

When Marilyn married playwright Arthur Miller, she went from star light to star bright. Miller was recognized as one of the greatest artists in his field (Studs Terkel once called him an American eponym). Being No. 1 was about the only thing DiMag and Miller had in common. Joe was re-ligious and held a simplistic view of life. Miller, once idealistic, was supremely sophisticated and cynical. And Marilyn, now on a self-education kick, hoped Miller would write the adult vehicle by which she could bring together the ever-widening rifts within herself.

The Misfits—which sadly turned out to be the last film for Marilyn as well as Clark Gable—was that vehicle. Yet the ingenuous part of her that had loved Joe felt more and more a misfit in Miller's world. Her career became a bumpy landslide of pills and booze.

Who but Marilyn Monroe could have such men in her life as President John F. Kennedy and his brother, Robert, as well as Joe DiMaggio and Arthur Miller? In the language of the old New York Yankees and their batting power, that was "Murderers' Row."

Her affair with J.F.K. was brief and not serious, more of the "wham, bam, thank you ma'am" genre. But that it did happen, none on the inside would deny. L'affaire Robert, on the other hand, was far more serious, so serious that it may have pushed Marilyn over the edge. Marilyn, in her fantasy world, envisioned the day Robert would divorce Ethel and marry her. She put pressure on Bobby in their trysts and he decided the time had come to break it off. That was the night he secretly visited her at her Los Angeles home and told her, in effect, that they had to make a clean break—that it was over forever. The next day Marilyn was found dead. Whether she overdosed on pills by accident or design remains moot to this day.

Not moot was the role played by Peter Lawford, a member of the Kennedy clan by virtue of his marriage to Patricia Kennedy, in that final and dramatic scene. He enlisted the aid of local and federal law enforcement authorities to cloud the fact that Bobby was in Marilyn's home the night before she was found dead. He was the one who maneuvered to spirit Bobby out of L.A. and back to D.C., hoping thereby to erase Bobby's fingerprints, so to speak, from the death scene.

It was well known that Jack was a ladies' man, both as a bachelor and as president. But with Bobby it was an aberration that defied reason and added another dimension to a man known as a devoted husband and father, devout Roman Catholic and dedicated public servant with presidential aspirations.

The Kennedy Camelot was not a shining hour for the media. Many members of the press, including this one, were aware of Jack's and Bobby's liaisons, yet remained silent in keeping with the code of the day. It was a far different era than today, when investigative reporting sheds light on so many infidelities, as witness the Gary Hart-Donna Rice headlines. Perhaps a discreet note of warning in the press at that time would have served as a warning to J.F.K. to keep his sexual affairs out of the White House and would have derailed Bobby's mad crush on Marilyn.

Unlike Marilyn, Joan Crawford was about the least likely candidate for suicide. She lived by a different set of rules and reveled in it. Those around her were not always so enthusiastic.

The book *Mommie Dearest* by Joan's daughter Christina revealed, among many other shocking things, how Miss Crawford the disciplinarian tied her children in bed at night so they could not go to the bathroom until morning. Essee and I were at her home enough to know this was true. The first time she visited our home, in fact, Joan gave a similar display.

Always seeming quite tall, though she was only of average height, Joan arrived in a long white ermine coat, looking every inch the star. The elevator konked out that night, and our guests had to take the freight elevator up. Seeing Joan Crawford, who had a fetish for cleanliness, alight from that freight elevator in her white ermine coat and other regalia was a scene in itself.

However, no freight elevator—nor oncoming freight train—could make Joan Crawford miss a beat or lose control. Upon entering our apartment, she immediately requested a tour. Essee led her around the apartment and, when they reached the children's rooms, Joan actually ordered Cookie out of bed, threw her white ermine onto Cookie's chair and did calisthenics with our daughter on the bedroom floor!

As fascinating a guest as Joan was, she wasn't the kind of person you'd want to stay for a visit. "Traveling light" for Miss Crawford was nine suitcases and a trunk. Moreover, whenever she was going to a hotel for a few days' stay, she sent ahead 25 pages of directions and demands a la Yul Brynner. She was bizarre, extreme and dictatorial, yet not out of caprice or cruelty. When we lunched with her at the Pump Room, where they serve telephones with meals, the first thing Joan would do was open her briefcase, take out a perfectly ordered looseleaf notebook, turn to a neatly typed list of telephone numbers, and put in long distance calls to Hollywood producers, agents, daughter Christina at school, and so forth. She *was* a loving mother—albeit one who thought it best for her children to be strapped into bed at night.

If she made the rules for everyone else around her, Joan followed them to a T herself. During one period in her career, she got along on $15 a week! She told her business manager, Mort Blum (Jack Benny's brother-in-law), to allow only that much. What occasioned the "allowance" was Joan's salary temporarily being cut off because she was suspended for refusing a role that she didn't feel measured up. Of course, if she needed a pair of shoes or an ermine coat, she merely signed for it. Nevertheless, not many actresses were willing to walk around with only three fivers in their purse. Maybe that's why Miss Crawford's rating with Dun and Bradstreet was excellent long before she married Pepsi president Al Steele.

Her marriage to Steele was stormy but it lasted largely because Al was so complacent. . .and so in love. Essee and I joined them for their wedding breakfast in the Pump Room and Al soon learned about Joan's discipline. He put out his cigaret in a butter dish, which brought Mr. Steele a steely look from his bride. "Never, but never," she scolded him, "use a butter dish for an ash tray," whereupon she summoned a waiter to remove the cigaret butt and butter dish.

They repaired to their suite shortly thereafter and Essee, remembering she had something to tell Joan, followed them and walked into a veritable fist fight, with each slapping the other with resounding blows. Remember, this was still their honeymoon. But, as I said, Steele was the compliant type and the marriage lasted until his untimely death.

Joan was as demanding of herself as of others. For instance, guests at her Brentwood home were told to take off their shoes on entry, lest they darken her all-white carpeting. And when she checked into a hotel, guess what this paragon of cleanliness did? She would get down on her hands and knees to scrub the bathroom floor and anywhere else she spotted a speck of dirt. That probably was the most unusual role for a reigning queen of Hollywood. Her addiction to discipline is one reason she stayed on top through three generations of moviemaking.

Sometimes, though, her male co-stars weren't too happy about taking orders from Joan. I remember her confiding to me about a movie she made with Van Heflin. In one scene, she was to slap him, and hard. It took four slaps until the director was satisfied. But this wasn't to say that La Crawford hadn't put everything she had into each of those slaps.

Strangely, the easily irascible Heflin merely grinned after each blow. "Are you *enjoying* this?" Joan finally asked him.

Heflin grinned. "Yes, as a matter of fact I am," he said, rubbing his hands gleefully. "You evidently haven't read the entire script. On page 120, I . . .slap. . .*you!*"

Joan was on my TV show a number of times and something seemingly small which took place somehow sums her up best for me. Each of my guests always had a cup of coffee in front of them. Because Joan was married to Al Steele, a bottle of Pepsi was placed in front of *her*. But behind it was a Kup's cup—our show's trademark—filled with pure vodka.

Grace Kelly and Judy Garland were the center of controversy and the eventual stars of the most exciting Academy Awards I've covered (and I saw them all but one from '45 to '88—I missed '87, when surgery laid me low for a month). It was 1954, and Best Actress had come down to a bitter battle between Grace for *The Country Girl* and Judy for *A Star Is Born*. Everyone had taken sides. Hollywood itself was divided sharply into two camps. Behind Grace was the Bing Crosby/Bob Hope delegation (including such luminaries as Jimmy Stewart and Ginger Rogers). Behind Judy was Frank Sinatra (with Bogart, Bacall, et al.). It seemed that the backers for Garland and Kelly were almost evenly divided and the suspense reached an incredible crescendo as Oscar night drew near.

But the suspense went much further than *who* would win.

Judy and Grace were protagonist and antagonist, depending upon where you stood, in a real life battle that was more dramatic than any movie. Each represented, probably better than any other actress before or since, opposing values in the Hollywood community and, to an extent, in our society at large. And many insiders, as well as millions of fans, felt that a victory for Grace or Judy would be an affirmation for *their* way of life. Judy and Grace...in a way, the *names* told you *everything*.

Judy...saucy, middle class, a typically American creation. And even the name itself was a show business creation. It was Frances originally. And her last name was not Garland, but Gumm, a name Georgie Jessel gave her when she was appearing in vaudeville with him.

I had many memorable times with Judy, including lunches in the Pump Room whenever she passed through town. I witnessed her frequent battles with husband Sid Luft and even flew to London with her for the premiere of one of her movies. Flying with Judy could be nerve wracking. She was a white knuckle flier all the way and Essee and I were almost as tortured as was she in just watching her agony.

But the incident I recall best occurred when she was scheduled to be on my TV show. As show time approached, no Judy. So Essee got on the phone to her hotel and obviously awakened her. "Oh, Essee, I'm in bed with my boyfriend and I don't want to get up." But Essee's pleading worked, and Judy arrived in the nick of time. And what she said on the show was even more memorable. She revealed during the course of our interview that she never liked her mother, who, she said, abused and resented her. "We never got along," she confided.

Grace Kelly was...Grace Kelly, stately and, oh, so proper.

Whereas Judy took some wild chances with material (sometimes with great success, sometimes flopping), Grace carefully hand-picked each movie role she played. Always, those roles fit her public persona: Cool, aloof, finely-bred, often pristine and always principled. This was epitomized by *The Swan*, in which she woos and wins a prince. From that picture, she went on to co-star with Bing Crosby and Frank Sinatra—two previous arch-rival candidates for that crucial Academy Award—in *High Society* (a remake of *The Philadelphia Story* and, of course, Grace was the biggest Philadelphia story in years).

In a fundamental way, Grace Kelly's background was not unlike that of John F. Kennedy's. Her background was not really to-the-manor-born, but to-the-palace-made. Grace's father, John B. Kelly, like Joe Kennedy, Sr., was a fun-loving self-made millionaire who was more impressed with money than with titles. When Prince Rainier later went to the Kelly home to ask for Grace's hand in marriage, the robust father gave his blessing but said, "There's just one thing. I can't address my future son-in-law as *Your Highness*. So I'll just call you. . .Laddie Boy." Which he did.

Interestingly, the seemingly distant persona which Grace played on the screen was the opposite of Grace in real life. She would spontaneously seize upon a situation, act boldly and never look back. There was no better example than her romance with Rainier. And before that, Grace was promiscuous as hell. Few actresses to hit Hollywood had the reputation of going to bed with virtually every one of her male co-stars, from Gary Cooper to Bill Holden. On the other hand, the warm and affectionate Judy, while her marriages didn't always work out, was a one-man-at-a-time woman. An item in my Aug. 1, 1976, column shed new light on the Judy vs. Grace Oscar competition 22 years before:

Princess Grace of Monaco, as ravishing today as when she was actress Grace Kelly, engaged in some reminiscing with this reporter at the 20th Century Fox gala at Zorine's the other eve. We took her back to 1954, when Grace won an Oscar for best actress for her role in *Country Girl*, in an especially heated race with the late Judy Garland, who had been nominated for *A Star Is Born*. Grace recalled receiving letters from Judy's fans demanding that she withdraw from the Oscars and let Judy win.

After Grace won that crucial Oscar from Judy, her career ascended to a pinnacle. Grace had the grace to become a princess in real life, to make the screen fantasy a reality. . .until her untimely death in an auto accident a few years ago. Judy, on the other hand, though she would hit some high notes, went downhill. Between a weight problem for which she took uppers, deep insecurities for which she took downers, and washing them all down with booze, she died long before her time.

Marilyn Monroe in her thirties, Judy in her forties, Grace in her fifties, Joan in her sixties. It seems more difficult for women than men to survive as superstars.

Yet, even though these four were given to us for a shorter time than so many of their contemporaries, they dominated—and still do to some extent—the American psyche in a special way. Though they are as different from one another as gold from silver, rubies from emeralds, each is an American touchstone.

14

Diana

B ut to Essee and me, the leading lady who made the most indelible impression was...Diana Barrymore.

For openers, Diana fell head-over-heels in love for the only time in her life with a man who would never marry or could never make love to her, the most brilliant playwright of the day, Tennessee Williams—a confirmed homosexual.

Diana, of course, was the daughter of an early American matinee idol, the incredibly handsome, talented, charismatic and alcoholic John Barrymore. To understand how she came to fall futilely in love with Tennessee, you have to understand the father for whom she first had total adoration. A few little-known stories about the Great Profile reveal a larger-than-life figure who, either drunk or about to drink, was in command of every situation. When he appeared on Broadway in *Hamlet*, for example, a London critic who covered the opening had the temerity to include two lines of minor criticism. Immediately, Barrymore summoned the producer. "I want to move the show to London," he said. The producer had no choice but to give in to Barrymore, who further said, "I want you to find out the greatest consecutive number of performances any actor has ever given of *Hamlet* in London." The producer did some homework and told John it was 160. "Then I shall play 161," exclaimed Barrymore, "after which we shall triumphantly return to America."

And so he did—all to make a single critic eat about 20 words.

Barrymore could not abide hecklers any more than critics. During one performance, a drunk in the balcony wouldn't shut up. John called a halt to the play, turned and pointed to the man. "Have a heart, fellow," the Great Profile hissed. "I only have two hours to make a fool of myself. You've had your entire life."

On another occasion in New York, Barrymore visited a haberdashery to purchase a shirt. He selected the most expensive, and asked that it be sent to his home, fully expecting instant recognition of his face. But this clerk was a rare exception. "Your name?" he asked.

John stared at him. "*Barrymore*," he seethed.

"And the first name?"

The Great Profile looked down on the clerk coldly for another few seconds. Then he snapped, "*Ethel!*"

He was as imperious with royalty as he was with clerks. When a Balkan princess was visiting Hollywood, she requested the autographs of a number of celebrities, wanting Barrymore's the most. The Great Profile was totally unimpressed by a princess' request. His studio, sensing super promotional possibilities in a meeting between the two, at last coaxed Barrymore into personally giving the princess an autograph. As a battery of cameramen filmed away, John took pen in hand and in letters a foot high, autographed the white coat of the Balkan princess with the letters P-E-S-T.

Another time, Barrymore attended the funeral of a dear friend at Forest Lawn and was nipping at his ever-present bottle throughout the services. Walking unsteadily out of the cemetery afterward, Barrymore was stopped by an old man. "I once appeared on the stage with you," he said to John. Barrymore studied the fellow for a minute. "Tell me, my good man," he said. "How old are you?" "Eighty-nine," the old codger said proudly. "Hmmm," said Barrymore, turning to go. "It hardly pays for you to leave here."

But the Great Profile had a softer side. When John appeared in *My Dear Children* in Chicago, I introduced him to artist-restaurateur Riccardo, who also had a classic profile and was somewhat of a look-alike for Barrymore. The two hit it off and Barrymore made a habit of imbibing brandy heavily at Riccardo's restaurant after each show. Yet "Ric" did better than anyone ever had to keep Barrymore within safe limits. The show moved on to New York and, on closing night, there was a gala party for John and the cast. When Barrymore rose, he devoted his entire speech to Riccardo. "The most fun I had in this play was in Chicago where I met a fellow named Riccardo, a snake-charmer...no, a hypnotist," said Barrymore. "That's what he must be, a master hypnotist, because he put me in a trance and made me eat solid food for the first time in 25 years."

No normal man could compare to a father who, onstage or off, was never second-best. So Diana searched futilely for a man she could somehow look up to. All she had to show for it was a string of failed marriages and romances—until she met Tennessee Williams. "Tennessee is the one man for whom I'd give up the Barrymore name," Diana confided to Essee.

"But how could it work?" Essee asked Diana. "He's been homosexual all his life." Diana's answer was a fantasy: "I'll *make* it work. It's *got* to work. He's the Shakespeare of the 20th Century! We'll have a ménage à trois. His boyfriend will always be in bed with us. It will work. I haven't had a drink since I met Tennessee!" That was saying a lot for a girl who followed in her father's footsteps where alcohol was concerned, too.

Impossible dream though it was, if it were Diana's dream, Essee wanted it for her. The two had become close almost from the first moment they'd met, when Diana was appearing for six weeks at the Civic Theatre in 1959. Diana had always wanted a sister; Essee had always wanted a sister. A typical telegram to Essee from Diana was this Nov. 16, 1959, wire:

In all this world to have found a sister who understands me is a miracle. Love, love, love, Diana...

One corner of Diana's apartment in New York was a shrine to John Barrymore—walls covered with pictures and memorabilia of him. But now the Barrymore corner played second fiddle to the shrine to Tennessee which was in her heart.

I got to know the playwright some years before when he'd written *The Glass Menagerie*, now considered an American classic. It was written about his sister, Rose. He was very fond of her—though not so fond of his brother, Dakin, and with good reason. Tennessee's brother wanted to be a writer, too, but didn't have the ability. So he became a lawyer. But his real career was living off Tennessee's fame. The first time Essee saw Dakin before she knew who he was, she exclaimed: "What's a hobo doing here?" He did look like someone you'd see living out in a park somewhere. "That's Tennessee Williams' brother," I told Essee. She found it hard to believe. And Tennessee found it hard to believe how far his brother would go to tread on his fame. Yet the worst episode was after Tennessee died in 1983. He'd long expressed a wish to be cremated, his ashes put to sea. His brother countermanded the request, and had him buried in St. Louis—a city T.W. hated even more than W. C. Fields hated Philadelphia.

When Tennessee's *The Glass Menagerie* opened in Chicago, he was an unknown and the play was in danger of failing. But *Tribune* critic Claudia Cassidy and Hearst critic Ashton Stevens recognized his genius and got behind the play. I did, too, but my column was relatively new and wasn't as much of an influence. Soon, others boarded the bandwagon. This was great theater and Williams was going to be our greatest playwright, they kept telling the public. As a result, the theater-goers responded and the play, once so close to closing, became a success and went to New York. There it was hailed as a masterpiece and Tennessee Williams was recognized as the genius he was. If *The Glass Menagerie* had failed in Chicago, Tennessee might never have been heard from again.

Yet if I was certain that Tennessee was a great playwright, I was equally certain that he was unalterably homosexual. Essee knew it, too. Tennessee took her and Diana to a drag ball in New York where everybody called him by his drag name—Mona. Diana dressed in a very masculine outfit, walking with a cane. She didn't have a lesbian bone in her body, but would have changed anything for him. But he *couldn't* change. Several years after his relationship with Diana ended, for instance, he was a guest on my TV show with Gore Vidal who refused to acknowledge his presence and wouldn't talk to him, wouldn't look at him. Their relationship was that bitter—a case of a homosexual and a bisexual who'd had a falling out. I got a little upset with Gore and, during the break, asked him what was going on. He told me he was simply so bored with the show and with Tennessee Williams that he'd fallen asleep. After the break, nothing changed. "Why don't you talk up, Gore?" I kept interjecting. "You're never quiet like this." And he'd continually reply, "I have nothing to say at this particular moment." It was about the only time I've ever known Gore Vidal having nothing to say.

Essee still has a scrapbook at home which is a poignant elegy to Diana's impossible dream. Paraphrasing Diana's autobiography, *Too Much Too Soon*, she titled the scrapbook. . .*Much Too Soon*. A couple of entries:

"Sis Darling—
The boy. . . tonight.
Business is practically a sellout (Miami). They pulled the panic button too soon.
He's going to stay in the Coconut Grove. *Stay here, Tennessee, I miss you, miss you, miss you.* The laughs we had. Whatever he wants. Love to all, but especially to my sister."

A photo of Diana with Tennessee, sent to Essee. Tennessee's inscription: "The roof is hot, but the cats are cool. Love—10." (for Tennessee)

Essee was pregnant then, but lost the baby. And Diana then lost the most crucial part in a play in her life—the lead in *Sweet Bird of Youth*. . . by Tennessee Williams. Tennessee chose Geraldine Page. It was the one play Diana wanted to do on Broadway and every time the curtain would go up, every night at 8:30, Diana would stop wherever she was, shudder and say, "*I* should be there. *I* should be on his stage."

Essee may have been the last to see Diana alive. We knew she'd fallen off the wagon some months before. The career setback when Williams chose Geraldine and the gnawing truth—deny it though she did—that Tennessee could never be her lover, were too much to bear. In an earlier intimate moment with Diana, Essee had questioned the sexual side of her relationship with Tennessee, sensing that nothing had really taken place despite Diana's fantasy of a menage. "We lock our little fingers together," Diana had revealed euphorically, "and it's more sensuous than anything I've ever known."

Shortly after, in 1960, our daughter Cookie went to New Jersey to star in *Father of the Bride* with Pat O'Brien. Essee stayed there for six weeks with Cookie, so she had time to see Diana. It was at Diana's worst time. After one performance, Essee phoned Diana in New York, became terribly worried after the conversation, and went to see her. There were several people in the apartment, but they seemed unaware of Diana's dangerous state of mind. A month before, doctors had told her that her liver was in terrible shape. If she took one more drink, they warned, she would die. So, instead of "liquor," she was alternating tall glasses of vermouth with pot. "She's in terrible shape, Irv," Essee told me when we talked long distance late that night, "and there doesn't seem to be anything I can do to help." In the middle of the night, Essee's phone rang. It was Diana. "Essee," she said, "I'm off the wagon for good."

Essee rushed over, in time to see her, but not to save her. No one could do that. She was found dead the next day, Jan. 25, 1960, lying naked in the bedroom of her converted brownstone apartment at 33 E. 61st Street, by a maid. Essee knew where Diana kept her marijuana and she hid it, hoping in some small way to protect Diana in death as she could not in life. To this day, the police don't know that the pot was a contributing factor in Diana's dying.

Yet the pot wasn't the real cause. Nor even the liquor, though her death certificate was almost identical to that of her father's:

Cause of Death—Heart and kidney failure, due to chronic alcoholism.

It should have read:

Cause of Death:
The Barrymore Name.

The story in the *New York Journal American* read as follows:

The *New York Journal American* learned of Diana's premonition of death from Mrs. Essee Kupcinet, who visited Diana the night before her death.

"Diana was almost psychic at the time," Mrs. Kupcinet said. "She had a morbid foreboding all last week, saying 'I'm running out of time' and 'I will soon die.' In fact, she said to me, 'Go out and buy a black hat and dress.' I kept telling her to snap out of it—and she would for a while."

Tennessee sent a gorgeous blanket of flowers for the casket, and was of course at the funeral. But he refused to talk about her. When he was at our home for dinner some months later, Essee said to him, "I want to show you a picture." It was the photo of Diana with him...two "cats" on a hot tin roof.

"Don't even talk about that to me," was all he could say, turning away from the photo.

You couldn't blame him any more than you could blame Diana. His homosexuality and his genius were inextricably bonded in a way that was sometimes dark, sometimes shining.

As for Diana, her need for a man who was feminine may have been a desperate, unknowing attempt to find something she'd never known. That last night in her apartment, she whispered to Essee: "You're here to spend six weeks with your daughter. Do you know that in all my entire life put together, I never spent that much time with my mother?"

Saddening as was Diana's death, it was no surprise. We feared it had to happen and, when it did, at least it happened after many laughs, many highs and, if not in old age, at least in middle age, after the sweet bird of youth, if not her youthful dream, was spent.

After Diana's funeral, Essee stayed on with Cookie. My wife is very strong, but when we talked about it her first night home, she was still visibly shaken and tearful over Diana's death. Then, though, we soon had the joy of talking about Cookie. I know it occurred to us both that even though Essee in particular had suffered a terrible loss, it was not a supreme loss. I thought of my 19-year-old daughter, fresh from her new triumph, so full of life, the promise of so many years in her unlined face.

Not in my blackest nightmare did it ever cross my mind that three years later...*she* would be taken from us.

15

Meanwhile, Back at the Ranch . . .

C hicago was always my number one beat.
Kup's Column may have been widened to include the Oval Office of the White House, the private study of the Pope or Joan Crawford's swimming pool, but I never stayed away long. Something was always happening in Chicago. Because there is something special about Chicago.

Where, but in Chicago, could you have a coroner's report that read: "The victim was five foot, six inches in length"? Coroner Al Brodie was reading that to the press about a man found murdered in a sewer in the late 1940s.

"You mean in *height*, not length, don't you, Coroner?" a reporter interrupted.

"No, in *length*," said Coroner Brodie. "We measure them *lying down*."

Where but in Chicago could a jockey be put in the hospital by . . . an angry bettor? It happened to Steve Brooks who was riding the heavily favored champ Spy Song at Washington Park. But the horse ran out of the money, and a patron who had lost $15,000 broke through security and broke Brooks' nose.

Where but in Chicago could you have someone like Fred Snite, Jr., known as the "Iron Lung Kid"? Snite, his respiratory system crippled by bulbar polio as a child, spent the rest of his life in an iron lung and still became a champion at bridge as well as marrying and then fathering several children.

Only in Chicago could this have happened: Municipal Judge Charles E. Dougherty reluctantly dismissed the indecency charges brought against Val de Val for her performance at the now-closed 606 Club, whereupon

Attorney Bailey Stanton requested that the court return Miss de Val's costume, since it had been confiscated as evidence. She was opening at the Rialto Theater, another strip joint, and couldn't work without it, Stanton explained. The clerk thumbed through a sheaf of papers on his desk and finally located an ordinary letter-size envelope...containing Miss de Val's complete costume.

Only in Chicago could this have happened: Jazz star Dave Brubeck opened at the Blue Note to a standing ovation and recalled to us the time four years before when he played the same club and only a handful of patrons turned out. Brubeck, one of the all-time jazz greats but then just beginning, was so discouraged that he asked owner Frank Holzfiend if there was a way to get out of the contract. Frank put his hand on Dave's shoulder and said, "You just worry about the *music. I'll* worry about the crowds. Some day they'll pack this place to hear you." They did, of course.

Only in Chicago: Dr. Percy Julian, a leading research scientist, was named Chicagoan of the Year (sponsored by Kup's Column) in 1952. Julian attributed much of his success to the day he came home from grammar school proudly waving an arithmetic examination paper marked "80." His father, ordinarily a kind man, sternly told Percy: "Never be satisfied with mediocrity—that's what 80 is. Only be satisfied with 100." After that, Percy Julian achieved many 100's and was never satisfied with anything less. The day he left home in Montgomery, Alabama, to go to DePauw University in Greencastle, Indiana, his family was bidding him godspeed. Waving most wildly was Julian's 99-year-old grandmother, who once had picked a record 350 pounds of cotton in a single day, and her husband (from whose hand two fingers were cut off after his master had discovered he had secretly learned to write). The grandson of a slave, Percy Julian was a credit to his race...the *human* race.

Other typical Chicago happenings in the 1940s and 1950s included the cancer-fighting radioactive cobalt unit (then one of two in the world, and a hundred times more effective than X rays) being installed in Cook County Hospital...Burr Tillstrom, creator of "Kukla, Fran and Ollie," signing a $10,600 per week contract to make him the highest paid puppeteer in the world...and the death on Jan. 1, 1951, of the one Chicagoan *everyone* loved, six-foot, two-inch, 550 pound Bushman, the most celebrated gorilla in the world. One report had him dying of a broken heart because he was the only gorilla not subpoenaed by the Kefauver Senate Investigating Committee.

In the 1940s and 1950s, like New York and L.A., Chicago had a booming nightclub and theater business where all the greats performed. Many more stars started in Chicago and wound up on one coast or the other. In 1954, for example, three Chicagoans were the talk of Hollywood: "He-man" actor Rock Hudson, sexational actress Kim Novak and deadpan comedian George Gobel. Hundreds of radio and, later, TV shows emanated from Our Town. One of the most memorable, characteristic of the side of Chicago that Carl Sandburg called "hog butcher to the world," was the National Barn Dance. Bursting with old-fashioned corn and tied together with homey philosophy, it was as enduring as any show radio has ever known.

Another top show of the day was Ralph Edwards' "This Is Your Life." Ralph went anywhere and everywhere to find worthy guests to surprise. When the show came to Chicago, which it did on occasion, I usually helped Ralph to line up those who would surprise the guest of honor. It wasn't always someone famous—I'll never forget when Checker cabbie No. 5000, Eddie Hamilton, was the subject.

The show took place in January of 1955 and spread a warm glow in our sub-zero town. But it almost didn't come off. Ralph wanted someone who typified the spirit of Chicago, and bypassed the big shots in favor of a man who proved that no matter what your station in life, you can always bring the job up to the man. Eddie was popular because he provided all the "comforts of home" in his cab—newspapers, magazines, cigars, cigarettes, orange juice, coffee, even needle and thread...everything free to his passengers. Also at no charge were Eddie's wonderful mini-lectures on the many wonders of Chicago.

For those few of us who sat in on the original decision several weeks before Hamilton's "life," keeping the secret was probably as difficult as it had ever been for any of Edwards' shows. For one thing, cabbie No. 5000 knew just about everybody in town. For another, Eddie's wife had never lied to him. She was notified a day after the decision was made and confessed, "I've never told Eddie a lie since we've been married. I'm going to have to tell him a little white lie almost every day now to keep him in the dark."

It was always a huge challenge to get the subject *to* the show completely unaware that his life is about to unfold. In Hamilton's case, I knew that his cab was frequently parked in front of the *Sun-Times* building at the noon hour, giving me the opportunity often to ride with him. I made more of a point of it in the coming weeks and in the course of one of the rides, I mentioned in my most off-hand manner that Edwards was bringing his show to Chicago and needed a driver to spend all Wednesday afternoon going around town on errands. Eddie was interested. So I added that it was also possible that Edwards might open the show by driving up to the Studebaker Theater, site of the show, in his cab. Finally, the whole thing was set up perfectly...until a rival newspaper learned at the last moment that Eddie was to be the surprise guest and printed the story that afternoon! Only once before had a surprise ever been tipped in advance (in the case of actress Ann Sheridan, whereupon Edwards immediately cancelled). In this case, Chicago ingenuity came to the fore. I suggested that Edwards send Hamilton on a "mission" to Skokie, a suburb, that would keep him busy and away from anybody who might have read the story. It was worth a shot—and it worked, though not without more perils of Pauline.

Because of the icy roads, the drive to Skokie and back took *much* longer than expected. Came 7:30 p.m. and no Checker cab No. 5000. Come eight o'clock...ditto. Edwards, anxiously pacing the floor at his Conrad Hilton Hotel suite, was faced with doing "This Is Your Life—Eddie Hamilton!"...without Eddie Hamilton.

At the last minute Eddie arrived, explaining that...Chicago was his beat. He'd never driven to Skokie before—and he got lost!

One thing was for sure: He didn't have time to read a paper.

That night, Ralph Edwards said, "Eddie Hamilton...this is your life." And cabbie No. 5000 almost fainted. An interesting sidelight, though, was that though Eddie of course knew about the show, he didn't remember Ralph Edwards' name—because the cabbie always watched the competing TV fights on Wednesday night.

Inevitably, there were those stories where no one could grin. I remember being in a ground-floor apartment at 3634 S. Damen for a short while during Christmas of 1958. But there could have been no Christmas spirit in the small flat of Mrs. Loretta Grimes and her daughter Theresa, 19, and sons Joey, 15, and Jimmy, 13. A few day after Christmas two years before, her two younger daughters, Barbara and Patricia, disappeared.

Loretta Grimes hadn't had the heart to put up a Christmas tree since then. But she didn't make that decision herself. She left it up to her three surviving children. They didn't have the heart to put up a tree, either. There were a modest pile of gifts piled neatly in one corner of the bleak living room. However, most of them were marked for survivors of the Dec.

1, 1958, Our Lady of the Angels school fire where 92 children and three nuns perished, and with whom Mrs. Grimes felt a bond.

Loretta Grimes wasn't at home when I got there. She was at work selling stockings at Goldblatts' 47th Street store, getting off work at nine and reaching the apartment at 10:30. "Working late gives me something else to think about," she told me.

We talked for a while. "Here, let me show you my three angels," she said, and returned clutching a folder from which she took photographs of Barbara, Patricia and another daughter, Leona, who had died of uremic poisoning in her twenties. Every day for the two years since the girls had disappeared, detectives from the Chicago Police Department had come over to Loretta Grimes' home to tell her of their progress. Yet there really was no progress. An oddity in this respect was that, though a number of psychologically disturbed and guilt-ridden people confess to all highly publicized murders, more came forth to admit to killing the Grimes girls than almost any other. Of course, none could shed any light on the true nature of the girls' disappearance, though each new confession was a new heartbreak to the Grimes family.

"There's only one thing I'm praying for this Christmas," Mrs. Loretta Grimes told me. "I'm praying that somebody will come forward with some information about my Barbara and Petie [Patricia's nickname]. The *not knowing*...week after week...month after month...." The case has never been solved.

There were the visiting greats who inexorably came to my town. One of those I remember best was Sir Alexander Fleming, the Scottish scientist who discovered penicillin. He wanted to see the penicillin exhibition at the Museum of Science and Industry. Fleming was so moved by the museum's exhibit that he presented it with the glass-sealed locket in which he carried the culture of the original mold from which he made his apocalyptic discovery.

Sir Alexander seemed like a man with a good sense of humor, so I asked him if his "wonder drug" could cure a hangover?

"Oh, my goodness," replied Fleming, "penicillin isn't *that...wonderful!*"

There were the titans of Chicago industry—none more unforgettable than the single-minded Henry C. Lytton, last of the State Street pioneers. He vowed to live to be one hundred and he made it—his birthday cake for the occasion a six-foot-long replica of State Street with each of the big department stores, including his own, prominently displayed. Henry raised the knife to cut the cake, studied the situation for a second, and then slashed into the building of his rival, Maurice L. Rothschild.

There were our two baseball teams, the Chicago Cubs and White Sox, who between the Cubs' pennant in 1945 and the Sox' in '59, had a long, bleak period. Chicago sports fans are ever loyal, though, and so the Cubs instituted a policy of giving carfare home to any kids separated from their elders at the ballpark. Gradually, the number of lost kids from Evanston, Glencoe, Winnetka and other distant suburbs showed a dramatic increase. The Cubs front office checked it out and found that hundreds of wily youngsters who lived in the vicinity of Wrigley Field had not only been sneaking into the ballpark, but sneaking out with carfare to a distant 'burb which more than covered the price of a ticket. It was a lot different than when I was a kid sneaking into Comiskey Park at age 10, or hiring on to pick up papers in the outfield prior to the game to get a free ticket.

But the story of Chicago goes far past and far deeper than the always-visible sports franchises, ever more powerful titans or Nobel Prize winners.

More to the point of posterity was Carl Sandburg. He epitomized the Chicago/Midwest writer (along with Ernest Hemingway, James T. Farrell, Nelson Algren and Saul Bellow) who said what they had to say without pomp or pretense.

An unusual Sandburg item came to me via Red Skelton. Red was having lunch at the MGM studio with Les Weinrott, a Chicago radio producer, Louis B. Mayer of MGM, and the redoubtable Sandburg, most popularly known to the public as *the* authority on Abraham Lincoln. During the very serious luncheon, Bunny Waters, a tall and beautiful model, and later the wife of maestro Johnny Green, strolled past. Skelton, ever in the market for a laugh, nudged Sandburg and whispered, "That's Bunny Waters. She's six-foot, two-inches."

Sandburg took a look, turned back to Skelton, and harrumphed: "Lincoln was six-foot, four."

Partly as a result of that meeting, Sandburg turned over to MGM the script of his *Remembrance Rock*. The contract required him to finish the writing in 10 months, but Carl became so engrossed in the story that he asked for repeated extensions—and got them—finally finishing five years later. More than once during the long (for MGM) half-decade, the studio wanted Carl to remove or alter some portion of his writing. The immovable Sandburg gave Hollywood writers a lesson on how to win points in the inevitable debates with producers when he simply went off into a corner, strummed his familiar guitar, hummed his familiar ballads, and did *nothing else*...until the producers finally acceded.

Yet Carl was as hard on himself as on any producers. In 1955, when he was about to celebrate birthday No. 77, we asked him how he felt about his longevity. "It's a crapshooter's delight," he replied. A tribute on NBC put the question to him as to how he felt about not getting the 1954 Nobel Prize for literature, which went to Chicago suburbanite, Ernest Hemingway (who thought Sandburg should have won it). "Shucks, it makes no difference," replied Carl. "Twenty years from now some fellows will be sitting around and one of them will ask, *Say, did Sandburg ever get the Nobel?* And another will answer, *Sure, he got it in '54 and Hemingway presented it to him.*"

A place that has long made Chicago *Chicago*...is the most progressive educational institution in the world: The University *of* Chicago. The one man who epitomized the U of C was President Robert Hutchins. When Harold Swift of the meat packing family and Chairman of the Board of the U of C was looking for a chancellor who would make Chicago the envy of Harvard, Oxford, et al., many stories about Hutchins reached his ears—so many that he thought they must be apocryphal. The one in particular which most caught his interest was that Hutchins was such an early riser that he had half a day's work completed before most men reported to their offices (rising at 4:30 a.m. and being in the office at five o'clock). Swift decided to check the report personally and one morning at six o'clock Eastern time placed a long distance call to the Yale Law School where Hutchins, then barely 30 years old, was dean. "Is Mr. Hutchins in his office?" Swift asked the operator.

"There's never *anybody* here at this hour *but* Mr. Hutchins," she replied.

Swift did not talk to Hutchins that day, but he was so impressed that he made sure Hutchins ended up running the U of C.

And run it he did, emphasizing academics and de-emphasizing athletics. One of his favorite quotations, appropriately, was from an Oxford professor who, when asked his opinion of a colleague, replied: "The time he can spare from the adornment of his person, he devotes to the neglect of his duties." And when the *Chicago Maroon* (the student publication at the U of C) celebrated its 55th anniversary, Hutchins sent a congratulatory note which read: "I was amazed to learn that this is the 55th year of the *Maroon's* existence. Congratulations!"

When Hutchins celebrated his 50th birthday, the editors of the *Chi-*

cago Maroon sent him back this greeting: "We were amazed to learn this is the 50th year of the Chancellor's existence. Congratulations!"

But Hutchins had the last word: "Dear *Maroon*—I am, too. I should have thought that somebody would have killed both of us off long ago!"

Maybe the best capsule of the U of C came a year later when the college basketball and West Point football scandals made our nation heartsick. One U of C student noted that "for better or worse" there were more *Bibles* being sold in America than ever before. And another, when asked if there was any examination cheating on the Midway, answered: "Why should we cheat? We don't play football."

Speaking of the U of C brings me to New York. So much of what Chicago *is*...New York *isn't*. The friendly (and once in a while not-so-friendly) feud between my town and the Big Apple was there before I started the column, but I must admit I frequently fueled the fire. Not that I don't have a huge amount of respect for New York. It's a great place....

To *visit*.

16

Chicago Criminals

I saw my first gunfight when I was 12.

I was leaving the Central Park Theater on the West Side with a bunch of boys, when we heard a series of gunshots coming from the alley behind the theater. I raced to the scene and saw a gunman lying dead, blood spewing out from a hole in his head. It was horrendous, especially for a 12 year old.

Those were the days when Al Capone—and Paul "The Waiter" Ricca, Johnny Torio, and Bugs Moran, among others—ruled the roost. By the time I had put 10 years of the column under my belt, Capone (let's not forget that he was originally a New Yorker) occupied a cemetery plot instead of 50 rooms of Chicago's Metropole Hotel. His brother "Bottles" was busy with a quarter of a million dollar back tax case. His widow Mae and son Albert spent most of their time filing law suits connected with movies and TV shows. The days of the syndicate's nine-passenger compact car—two in the front, two in the back, five in the trunk—were gone.

In an earlier chapter, I related how during my trip to Israel in the late 1940s I learned a word coined over there for the rat-a-tat of machine guns: *Tsk-caw-go*. No book by a Chicago reporter could be complete without a chapter on crime in our city. In the late 1940s and early 1950s, Chicago was just beginning to pull itself out of the blackest era in our history—an era that earned us nicknames which were synonomous with crime and violence. When Chicago does something, good *or* bad, it goes all-out.

Al Capone came to epitomize all of this. Al died in 1947. That same year, *Look* magazine did a story on Mayor Kennelly, titled: "Chicago Gets An Honest Mayor." The obvious inference was that he was our *first* honest mayor. Certainly we'd had some politicians with questionable connections. Probably the most flamboyant I recall was Mathias ("Paddy") Bauler, the Near North Sider who was known as "the last of the saloon-keeper aldermen." One of 13 children, Paddy began his career as a singing waiter and master of ceremonies in a saloon owned by his older brother, Herman, who preceded Paddy as alderman. As an entertainer, Paddy always wound up his act by holding a half gallon of beer at arm's length, then slinging it over his shoulder and draining it in one long, unbroken swallow. As alderman of the 43rd Ward he used to hold court in a back room of his saloon (now closed), which he had registered in the name of his lawyer because municipal employees were prohibited from selling alcoholic beverages. Paddy, wearing a tall silk hat, would hoist a beer stein, and bellow, "Awright, everybody, come on and have a drink!" He was responsible for such bon mots as, "Sit down, you slobs, you look like a federal grand jury!" But his most memorable quote was: "Chicago ain't ready for reform!"

Judge John Gutknecht once urged Bauler, an inveterate traveler, to keep a journal of his journeys: "Paddy, I've been to Europe twenty-five times and around the world three times, and I've always had a diary."

"Judge," replied Paddy with the utmost seriousness, "you can get rid of that with Pepto-Bismol."

However, that was the *past*. Still, an obviously honest mayor—to say nothing of an array of accomplishments in industry and the arts and education—didn't stop the naive and headline-hungry from characterizing Chicago as a gangster town. Hollywood was the greatest contributor to this image, with its flood of movies depicting the Capone era. Upon Big Al's death, hundreds of stories immediately spewed forth about the late and unlamented Capone, most of them apocryphal. A true story, known to only a few intimates, was that Capone once took a liking to a florist on the West Side of Chicago near the scene of his Cicero headquarters. Al decided to make the florist wealthy by giving him all of his business. This meant that the florist had to prepare those fancy and expensive wreaths sent out by Capone to those he himself had ordered rubbed out. But Al had one demand: That his floral offering not only be the most lavish, but also the first to arrive. It was a mild form of camouflage to show that the dear departed was a friend, not a victim. Once, in his aim to please, the florist slipped up.

The wreath arrived before the police had identified the body.

Crime, corruption and criminals have become less and less a factor in the fabric of my town since I began the column. Still, to the degree that they existed, I covered bookies, gamblers and even syndicate figures as part of my beat. Frankly, I worried a lot less about the items they gave me than those coming from many prominent citizens or politicians. Though outside the law, the criminal element at least had its own code of honor. If they told you something, you invariably could count on its being true.

Because I hobnobbed with this element of society as well as with corporation presidents and movie stars, I had to make it clear to them where I, as a newspaperman, was coming from. Some of them insisted on trying to use me or buy me off. After I had written the column for a few years, for instance, I mentioned a major Chicago nightclub's show favorably, as it deserved to be. One night later as Essee and I were on our way out, the owner—who was "connected"—shook my hand. It wasn't an ordinary handshake—he had 10 crisp one hundred dollar bills in his. I simply stuck them back in his lapel pocket and said thanks but no thanks.

Others found it harder to take no for an answer. One day I printed an item that syndicate hoodlum Sam DeStefano had threatened some reporters. The next day I received a call. "I don't threaten nobody, Kup. I'm not that type," Sam told me in a Little Lord Fauntleroy voice. I mentioned the name of the reporter on a competing paper who had been threatened. "Oh, him!" exclaimed Sam. "That was some time ago. I mean I haven't threatened any reporters *lately*. I wish you could make that clear to your readers, of whom I am one." I asked Sam about one Alvin Shultz, who came to DeStefano's home to complain about exorbitant interest rates on a loan from Sam, and had been threatened—then slugged—by DeStefano. "I do not engage in fisticuffs at any time," Sam replied. "It is not the gentlemanly thing to do."

I decided to take another tack, and simply asked Sam what he did for a living. "I do not work any longer," he replied. "I am retired." I asked him how he accumulated enough money to retire at a comparatively early age. "My finances are an open book. I worked hard all my life with never a day off. I own a 21-apartment building on LaSalle Street, which is a model for cleanliness. And you may remember from reading your own newspaper, Kup, that I worked for the city and received a remuneration that ranged from three thousand dollars a year to six thousand dollars a year—until I was fired for telling a little fib. With that kind of income and by living economically—no nightlife and wild spending—you can save enough to retire." I asked Sam if the little fib wasn't that he had lied to the Civil Service Commission about not having a criminal record.

"I have no secrets from you, but if I'd told the truth, I never could have gotten the job. So I told this little white lie, as you yourself might call it. I think everybody knew it was a fib."

I asked Sam if the little fib didn't involve bank robbery. He quickly changed the subject.

"Kup, I have to be going now," DeStefano answered. "I'm having my portrait painted. I only really called you to say hello and to say don't write anything nasty about me. *Or else.*"

I wrote about our conversation the next day.

Another time, the police were looking for some hoods in connection with a murder. I happened to know that the suspects played cards every Saturday afternoon in a downtown hotel. So I told the police—in the column. The next morning, one of the hoods rang me up and asked not to be given any more publicity. "What size suit you wear, Kup?"

"Why?"

"I thought I'd send a dozen of them over to your house." It was a better offer than cement shoes, I'll admit, but I turned it down.

I also turned down a request from the boss man of the syndicate, Tony Accardo. And nobody ever said no to Accardo. One year when I was on my annual trip to the Bahamas for that big marlin that got away from Hemingway, I noticed a roster on the pier listing the largest fish that were caught. Tony Accardo was at the top of the list. He had caught the biggest tuna. I knew it would be interesting to my readers, so when I got back, I ran the item. Catching that fish was how Tony got his nickname: "Big Tuna" Accardo.

The following day this terse, unsigned note was on my desk: MR. AC-CARDO WOULD LIKE YOU NOT TO MENTION HIM IN THE COLUMN AGAIN.

Accardo was hardly ever seen in public. But Essee and I would often bump into a couple of his henchmen, the Fischetti brothers, at the Chez Paree. The Chez had a key club, with secret gambling. One time I had to go back to the paper late at night on a story, while Essee sat in the key club with a couple of celebs and a classy looking, well dressed young fellow, Joe Fischetti, the youngest member of the family. We knew Joe quite well because he was a nightclub habitué and often dated show girls and actresses around town. He turned to Essee and, out of earshot, said: "I want to show you something. It's in my apartment." She hesitated. "You'll be safe."

Essee could never resist getting a possible scoop for me, so she accompanied him to his penthouse apartment where he ushered her into the bedroom. "I want to show you something very important," he said. He went to the bed, pulled down the linens and...he had pink sheets! He was so proud of his elegant lifestyle. Essee said he was like a little boy showing off.

Then he took the gun which he always carried from under his coat, held it in his hand and looked at it. "I'm the only one in the family who hasn't killed anybody," he told her. After saying that, they left and went back to the club.

Once the prohibition era ended and the mobsters lost their main source of revenue, they concentrated on gambling, plus such sidelines as prostitution, usury, kidnapping and head breaking. There were few shootouts in the 1940s and 1950s, but the syndicate was still powerful. The people with whom most nightclub owners did business, for example, were hoodlum-associated in one way or another. Most of the owners had to submit to blackmail, or they couldn't stay in business. They were "forced" to do business with certain companies that provided their meats, towels, the silverware, the insurance—all of which were syndicate-dominated. If you didn't do business with them, you might find yourself in trouble with little mechanical things...like bombs.

When Abe (Franchot) Cohen, company manager of *Mister Roberts*, was in Chicago in the late '40s, he talked of the time hoodlums had a hand in many business enterprises in Chicago. "They even conducted an advertising racket," Cohen recalled, "and once they sent a plug-ugly around to demand some advertising from the show I was managing. This was a new dodge to me and I asked a lot of questions, none of which the hood bothered to answer. Finally, I asked him, *What's the money used for?*"

"To pay funeral expenses."

"Whose funeral?"

"Yours—if you don't fork over."

"That convinced me to increase our advertising budget," Cohen told me.

When TV and changing times put most of the big time nightclubs out of business, the syndicate lost an important source of revenue. So, the mob had to go into even more legitimate businesses, though their methods of making people deal with them were just as illegitimate. In that new era, a good accountant was a hundred times more important than a hired killer. One of the most interesting characters I've ever met was a fellow nicknamed "The Comptometer," Louie (Alexander) Greenberg, once the financial brain of the Capone mob.

One of fate's little tricks was to rub out Greenberg on the eve of what may have been Sugar Ray Robinson's greatest triumph in December of

1955—the rubbing out of Bobo Olsen as middleweight champ. The story going around, which proved to be totally untrue, was that Robinson, along with former heavyweight Joe Louis, supposedly were taken for $100,000 by Greenberg in an ill-fated scam to invade the Harlem brewery market.

But a few days before Greenberg's death, when this reporter saw him in a restaurant near his plush Seneca Hotel, Louie whipped a letter out of his pocket with almost childish delight. It was from a national magazine, abjectly apologizing for saying he'd cheated the two champs, and offering to make a $5,000 contribution to Greenberg's favorite charity. Ray and Joe also told me that they weren't taken by Louie, but were paid well for their investment. The letter meant a lot to Greenberg because, like almost everyone who became rich through racketeering, respectability was what he sought most. It was always hard to come by. But Louie tried harder. He was generous to a fault. He went out of his way to be nice to the "little people" who worked for him. His Christmas gift list cost close to six figures. Again, by eerie coincidence, those gifts that year arrived at the homes of his friends two weeks early as always—but the day *after* he was murdered.

Next to a need for respectability, Greenberg's other sensitive spot was his lack of a formal education. His son-in-law, Nathan Sugarman, was the apple of Louie's eye because he became a scientist, and Louie would always refer to Nathan as "The College Man." But possibly the most poignant little-known story about Greenberg concerns one of his tenants at the Seneca. The man possessed an imposing library and Louie, who could barely read or write and had an alarmingly small vocabulary, would often let himself into the apartment when he knew the tenant was out, just to wander amidst the shelves and shelves of books. "Imagine knowing all them words!" Louie once said to me.

The syndicate today still is alive and the harm it does can never be overlooked or overemphasized. But it is a shadow of its former self, partly because Federal authorities have convicted so many top crime figures, partly because of the trend toward investigative reporting, and partly because the American people are more informed and less tolerant of crime than in the 1920s through the 1950s. A turning point in the downhill slide of organized crime was the Kefauver Commission in the early 1950s. Interestingly, Senator (and later Vice Presidential candidate) Estes Kefauver, despite all his unflagging venom against the syndicate, was one of the worst womanizers I've ever known. Whenever he came to a town, before directing his considerable energies against crime, he let the word out: "Get me a woman!" He would have put Gary Hart to shame.

At the other end of the spectrum was one of his key counsels, Joe Nellis, a close friend of mine from his early days in Chicago. Some of Joe's personal experiences on the committee give an insight into the decline and at the same time the indomitability of the crime syndicate.

In November of 1950, Joe was sent to Cleveland, which he described as "one of the nerve centers of organized crime." The first thing Nellis did, naturally, was to go to the mayor and make him understand that the most important thing was to let no one know he was in Cleveland. The mayor understood completely, as did his safety director, Al Sutton (who worked with the legendary Elliott Ness). Nellis had subpoenas to serve, and you can't serve subpoenas to people who leave town.

The following morning, this was the shocking newspaper headline: KEFAUVER CRIME COMMITTEE LAWYER ARRIVES WITH IN-VESTIGATORS!

Cleveland was one of 14 cities (some of which were far more crime-permeated than Chicago) Nellis visited in the three years he worked at exposing organized crime. The one thing he learned above all was that there was a "remarkable" and "continuing" and "interdependent" rela-tionship between the syndicate and certain private institutions and politi-cians. The proof, of course, was that the high lifestyle of virtually every arrested and rearrested top hood never changed and—in those days—they were hardly ever convicted. And if they were, they seldom served time.

The syndicate tried desperately to get Nellis off the track. He worked round the clock. One morning at four o'clock when he had just gone to sleep a beautiful girl with a bottle of scotch knocked at his door. She tried to get in, but Nellis was too smart. He recognized the old trick or treat. He told her: "I don't know who sent you, but whoever did made a poor job of concealing that mike wire at the top of your bra."

Another time, Nellis had to question a gunman and drug addict named Johnny "Cockeye" Dunne. But first, Joe had to find him. Finally, he did—on a rundown, garbage-strewn street in Brooklyn. "We left our car at the end of the street and walked to the house," Nellis says. "The front door opened onto a hallway and a long flight of stairs. Just as we got near the top, a door on the right hand side of the landing opened and Cockeye came out, his head bandaged and a .38 in his hand. Without a second's pause, he pointed it straight at my head and pulled the trigger."

The gun misfired—and Cockeye was disarmed before he could take a second shot. When the gun was examined, it became clear the second shot wouldn't have misfired. Another half a second and Nellis would have been dead.

One syndicate biggie who did go to jail was Lucky Luciano. Yet Nellis raises a still unanswered question about Luciano's "alleged service to the Office of Naval Intelligence" during World War II, which gave him a parole and enabled him to go back to Italy after he had been sentenced to 15 years in Sing Sing. "Luciano showed up in Havana after allegedly paying a bribe in excess of a million dollars to former Cuban dictator Fulgencio Batista, and was visited by many of his friends and associates, including Frank Sinatra," Joe told me. "Nearly every big-time mobster in the United States beat a path to Cuba to meet with Luciano and Meyer Lansky, making plans to turn the Caribbean island into the greatest gambling center of the world." Fortunately, this was all predicated on Dewey's beating Harry Truman in the '48 election.

Nellis also turned up the fact that Dewey owed his life to Luciano: While Dewey was still a special prosecutor, Luciano had saved him from being murdered by Dutch Schultz (who later himself was murdered on Luciano's orders).

As long as humans are human, there will be cops on the take, and a more than occasional private citizen or politician looking to get rich or more powerful by dealing the cards from the bottom of the deck. I'd be naive to think that it still doesn't happen in Chicago. But it seems to me law authorities have taken a quantum leap in reducing the number of incidents.

17

The Chicago Bears

Of all the sports friendships I developed over the years, none was as dear as the trilogy associated with the Bears—George Halas, the Papa Bear who "invented" professional football; Sid Luckman, the nonpareil T-formation quarterback; and Jack Brickhouse, the Hall of Fame baseball broadcaster with whom I shared the Bears broadcasting booth on station WGN for 24 years.

Let's start at the beginning. I met Halas in 1935, the year I joined the *Chicago Times* as a $32.50 a week sportswriter. My first assignment, obviously because of my football background, was covering the Bears. And from that time until Halas' death 48 years later in 1983, our friendship continued and ripened. During that period, I served as sportswriter, game official, broadcaster and frequent luncheon and dinner companion.

I often have said that George Halas was the toughest person I ever knew, physically and mentally. He seldom knew a day without pain, stemming from a hip injury he suffered as a New York Yankee rookie in 1917 on a slide into third base on a triple he hit off the immortal Rube Marquardt. The injury worsened over the years and there were days when he barely could walk. And not until he had two hip replacement operations late in life was he comparatively free of agony. A lesser man would have folded, but Halas accepted the pain stoically, never flinching, never complaining and continuing his sole dedication to the Bears.

And he had the intelligence and vision to foresee professional football as the game of the future. He refused to be discouraged in those lean years when the Bears seldom broke even. Broke even? One year, early in the Bears history, he had to borrow $25,000 to maintain possession of the team and operate a sporting goods business to make ends meet. But he realized he had turned the corner the day the Bears showed a $300 profit. He was the dominant figure in guiding the National Football League, which he helped found and build into the multi-billion dollar institution it is today, thanks to television and packed stadiums. His own wealth soared accordingly.

After the Bears won the NFL title in 1963—their eighth—by defeating the New York Giants 14–10, Halas, then 68 and one of the oldest active coaches in the game, was the toast of the city. He was urged, at that time, to announce his retirement. He had done it all and was king of the hill. But retirement, even at 68, was not a word in the Halas lexicon. The Bears and coaching were his life. Unfortunately, the team went into sharp decline and the new-breed sportswriters, given more to criticism than applause, started to ridicule Halas. The press went from hagiography to harshness. "He's too old, why doesn't he quit?" . . . "The game has advanced beyond him." . . . "He's too penurious to sign good players," was oft heard as the story of Mike Ditka's classic was repeated. "Halas," Ditka had said while negotiating a contract as a player, "throws quarters around like they're manhole covers."

None of this fazed Halas. He was his own man and would continue to run the club in his fashion. And he gave as good as he got from the media. No man better typified the song made famous by Frank Sinatra, "I did it my way."

Finally, in 1968, at the age of 73, Halas made a momentous decision. He no longer would coach the Bears, but would confine himself to the duties of president. There were tears in his eyes when he broke the news at a private dinner prior to the official announcement. Only his family and closest friends were in attendance—daughter Virginia and her husband, Ed McCaskey; George Halas, Jr., who was to precede his father in death; Jim Dooley, who succeeded Halas as coach; Sid Luckman; and Frances Osborne, Halas' longtime secretary.

George lightened the mood by explaining why he decided to retire: "I no longer have the speed to chase the officials up and down the sidelines." Stomping after the officials and stomping on his hat in moments of anger helped make Halas the most colorful coach in the profession.

Many thoughts raced through my mind on his retirement: How the man some called penurious had contributed a fortune to charity, always anonymously; how he had come to the financial aid of players for health or business reasons; how he had called a gifted halfback, Brian Piccolo, stricken with cancer, and assured him that all his hospital and medical bills would be taken care of by the Bears and added that he was establishing scholarships for the Piccolos' three children.

I recalled how he had turned down a multimillion dollar offer from Chicago industrialist Henry Crown to buy the Bears. Halas had insisted on retaining 51 percent, thus control of the team. That was a deal Crown could refuse. And how Don Maxwell, then editor of the *Chicago Tribune*, had organized a campaign to importune Halas to run for mayor on the Republican ticket. Maxwell arranged for various prominent citizens to tell Halas that "you're the one man who can bring the Republican party back in this city." The Republicans haven't elected a mayor in Chicago since 1931, one of the longest shut-out records in political history. Halas was too smart to buy the blandishments. He punted the suggestion far and away.

I also recalled my relationship with George during my days as an official. Halas took great delight in screaming at officials, berating them with the vilest language known to man, when he felt a decision went against his team. I was subjected to the same belligerent bellowing. Yet after many games we sat down to dinner together, with nary a word passing between us about his conduct on the field. As far as Halas was concerned, his hostility ended with the game.

Halas could be as witty as a professional comedian at the podium. The time I remember best was when my newspaper hosted a civic dinner to commemorate the 25th anniversary of Kup's Column. Halas was one of the speakers and had the blue-ribbon audience in stitches with his roasting of me. The next speaker was Bob Hope. He cast a look of feigned anger at me and stage-whispered for all to hear, "Don't ever invite me to follow that damn Halas. He's too funny."

The friendship between Halas and fellow comedian Hope stemmed from World War II. George had taken leave of his beloved Bears to enlist and was serving as a lieutenant commander on Admiral Nimitz's staff in the Pacific. One day he heard Hope was in the same area on one of his junkets to entertain the troops. He managed to locate Bob by phone and asked him to arrange to entertain the troops aboard his ship. "But I'm dead tired," replied Bob. "And so are my entertainers. We've given a dozen performances in five days and we're headed home." Yet when Hope, as he later related, "recognized the tears in George's voice as he pleaded with me, I knew we had to accommodate him." Hope revised his homeward-bound flight to include a stop on the ship and earned George's everlasting gratitude.

Halas loved to rib me about my officiating career and often told this apocryphal story: "We were playing our bitterest rival, Green Bay, at Green Bay and Kup was working as the headlinesman. It was the usual ferocious game between Bears and Packers. Late in the game, we were marching for the winning touchdown and reached the Packers 10-yard line. It was fourth and one, when Luckman sent Bill Osmanski over tackle. It was a close call, Kup had to conduct the measurement to see if we had made a first down. So Kup handles the measurement and when he sees the Bears made it, guess what he did? He jumped up and down, clapped his hands together over his head and screamed, 'We made it! We made it!' The Green Bay coach, Curly Lambeau, was so incensed that he demanded the league fire Kup immediately."

As I said, the story was apocryphal. I continued officiating for a few more years. And I assure one and all that I was an impartial official, only slightly favoring the Bears on close calls.

A longevity strain runs through the Halas family and the coach had visions of living to 100. Typical of this vision was the comment he made on his 80th birthday, at a party that was an annual affair usually hosted by U.S. Judge Abraham Lincoln Marovitz and attended by only the closest of friends. Halas, rising to speak on this occasion, opened with, "I'm 80 years old today. . .and now that the first half of my life is over. . . ."

He didn't quite make 100. He died eight years later, with his record as the coach with the greatest number of victories, 326, intact, as was his reputation as the man who pioneered and nurtured a new sport into the American conscience. The National Football League was his monument.

Sid Luckman joined the Bears in 1939, fresh out of Columbia U, where he was an All-American. I was covering the Bears at that time and Halas phoned me one day to tell me Luckman was coming to Chicago. He explained that Sid never had been west of the Hudson River "and he thinks only Indians live this far west." He requested that I take Sid in hand and introduce him around town.

I acceded to Halas' request and introduced Sid to many of my friends. A short time later, Luckman was investigated by the league for associating with unsavory characters. How was I to know my close friends, bookies and bettors, were considered unsavory people? Naught came of the investigation, nor did it affect our friendship, which continues to this day. Sid, now a millionaire businessman and widower, resides a few floors above us in the same Lake Shore Drive building and he frequently drops into our apartment for dinner with Essee and me. I often think that's because of our cook, Johnetta Clark, not the Kups. Johnetta is considered one of the finest cooks in the city and has won the admiration of practically every one of our dinner guests. Typical was the offer made by movie director Bill Friedkin, who dined at our home a number of times. Once, half in jest, he told Johnnie, "Come work for me in California." She told him, "Oh, I wouldn't leave here, no way." Bill upped the offer. "Then marry me!"

Of all the games in which Sid starred—and they were legion—the one he and many of us remember best came early in his professional career, in 1940. As previously mentioned, the Bears played the Washington Redskins in Washington for the league championship. It was a game that the experts predicted would be won by the team that made fewer mistakes.

Fewer mistakes? The Bears won by the most improbable score imaginable—73–0. It stands today as the most devastating offensive performance by any football team, especially against a team as good as were the Redskins that year. The chuckle of the day concerned the bettor who took Washington and 72 points.

I was one of the four officials chosen to work that game. (Today, they use seven officials.) Midway in the fourth quarter, word was sent down to the officials to ask the Bears to run or pass for extra points. So many footballs had been kicked into the stands by the Bears for extra points that the home team was running out of balls.

For a football footnote: The lopsided score by a team using the then new T-formation, coupled with the victory of Stanford, another T-formation team, over Nebraska in the Rose Bowl a few weeks later, changed the face of football. Stanford was coached by Clark Shaughnessy, who previously had been on the Bears staff and made many contributions to the new T-formation. Soon every team in football, from high school to college to pro, adopted the T. Gone were the Warner formation, the Notre Dame (Rockne) shift, the single wing and short punt formation. The T was it.

At the end of that memorable 1940 season, Luckman dropped in on Halas to settle his financial matters and request a bonus. "How much are you thinking of?" asked Halas. "How about a thousand dollars?" replied Sid. "One thousand dollars," exploded Halas. "That's outrageous," he exclaimed, whereupon he pulled out a white envelope on which he had scribbled some notes, a custom he maintained through life. "Look, Sid, you threw an interception against Green Bay, you fumbled against Detroit, you called the wrong play against New York, you missed a tackle against Detroit," continued George, reading a list of minor mistakes from his notes in anticipation of Luckman's request. "The best I can do is $250."

Luckman left dejected but a short time later came a letter from Halas, requesting that he report for practice one month early "to learn all the new plays I'm installing." And Halas offered Sid $750 for doing so. The $750, plus the $250 bonus, was Halas' way of granting Sid the $1,000 bonus he requested.

Luckman at that time was earning $5,000 a year, a fair salary in 1940. His highest salary, incidentally, was the munificent amount of $23,500, granted because Halas insisted Luckman deserved the same salary Sammy Baugh was receiving and he felt no other quarterback should be earning more than Sid. Twenty three, five—that's walking around money for today's players. (My own salary with the Philadelphia Eagles in 1935 was $100 a game, the going rate.)

Luckman eventually became Halas' confidante and served for a while as quarterback coach. He once sought to launch a campaign to rename the T formation in honor of Halas. But the coach would have no part of it, saying, "The T belongs to all football, not to any one man."

Luckman and A. N. Pritzker, one of the nation's wealthiest persons, made a bid for the team in Halas' declining years. Halas was a great admirer of Pritzker, who had become a dear friend. Luckman and A. N. reasoned that the coach was getting to the age where he should consider getting his estate in order. So they made an unusual offer: Halas would fill in the price of the team and they would meet it, no matter how much. More, he would remain as president and run the operation at whatever salary he wanted. But even that generous offer couldn't persuade the coach to let the Bears fall into outsiders' hands. The Bears would remain in the founder's family, as it is today. And so, as he had done previously with Henry Crown, Halas said thanks, but no thanks.

The 1985-86 Bears, with their Super Bowl Championship, have regained the glory days they knew under Halas in the 1930s and 1940s...I knew the team would win the Super Bowl that year because of a phone call I received. It was from Richard Nixon, the well-known football buff. He called late in the season to inquire about the team's chances. I responded that they still had a few tough games to play. Nixon remained optimistic, "I'm convinced they'll go all the way because of Walter Payton. He deserves a Super Bowl ring."

"I think you're right, Mr. President," I said with tongue in cheek, "but only if you don't send in any of your special plays." (During his days in the White House, Nixon had sent some plays to Redskin coach George Allen.)

Luckman and I often laugh at what could have been a horrible experience. Sid, then an ex-officio consultant to Halas, and I, as a broadcaster, would fly early Sunday mornings to Bears games away from home. One Sunday, a blistery, snowy day, we were stuck at O'Hare Airport, waiting for the weather to clear so we could fly to Cleveland. Our respective moods were as foul as the weather as we contemplated missing the game.

Finally, however, came word that the plane would take off. As we neared Cleveland, a red light went on in the cockpit, spelling trouble. The trouble: the landing gear was not operating. That would mean a crash landing. I often had wondered how people react in a plane about to crash. I was surprised by the calm atmosphere of my fellow passengers. There was no crying, no shrieking, no hysterics. All remained calm and listened to the stewardesses' instructions. . . place a pillow on your lap and bend over to soften the impact of the crash landing. Ropes were let out of windows for passengers to climb down.

I whispered to Luckman, "Place the pillow on your lap and then bend over to kiss your ass goodbye." Matter of fact, we did kiss each other, not knowing what the end result would be. We could see police ambulances and fire trucks gathering at the runway, which now was being flooded with foam in event of fire.

Then came the good news. Just as we were about to land, the pilot was able to lower the landing gear manually. "So what's the big deal?" asked Luckman, nonchalantly. We both burst into nervous laughter, especially over our goodbye kisses.

And the trip hardly was worth the aggravation. Cleveland clobbered the Bears by some 60 points. Better we should have stayed in bed.

Jack Brickhouse and I teamed up as the radio voices of the Bears in 1959 and for the next 24 years we spent every Sunday during the season together. Jack and I, supported by WGN sports editor Jack Rosenberg, our statistical genius, enjoyed each other immensely. As I often said in speeches, "Brick and I always had fun in the booth. The game we broadcast was not necessarily the game being played on the field, but we had a ball."

It was my assignment to handle the half-time interlude while Brick relaxed from his play-by-play endeavors. Once, while in Los Angeles, Brick told me that if I needed any help lining up interviews for half-time, he would gladly lend a hand because he knew a lot of sports figures in the press box. "I'll be all right," I assured Jack.

And then as the half ended, into the booth came Carmen Basilio, then the hottest fighter in the country because of his recent victory over Sugar Ray Robinson. After Basilio, Bob Hope popped in to add some jollity to the broadcast. And finally, for the coup de grace, in came former president Harry Truman, who had been the guest of one of the L.A. Rams owners and was responding to my request that he say a few words at halftime.

Brick looked at me after Basilio, Hope and Truman departed and exclaimed, "And *I* was going to help *you?!?"*

On the 20th anniversary of the team of Brick and Kup, WGN celebrated with a party. The station surprised us by donating two cub bears to the Lincoln Park Zoo. One was named "Brick," and the other "Kup." At that early age, the gender of the two cubs hadn't been determined. But some time later when one of the cub bears became pregnant, the gender was obvious. The one named "Kup" was preggie.

That gave me the opportunity to use the line that "now you folks know what Brick has been doing to me all these years in the booth."

During our broadcasting career, we had many more lean years than gleam years. But we did have the pleasure of reporting the achievements of three of the greatest football players ever to don cleats—Dick Butkus, the massive and mean line backer; Gale Sayers, who qualified as the greatest ball carrier; and the all-everything Walter Payton, whose achievements on the field were as remarkable as his longevity of 13 seasons, an astonishing career free of injuries. That's one record no running back can equal.

The fun ended in 1983, when WGN was outbid by WBBM for the Bears radio rights and installed its own broadcasting team. Brick and I naturally were disappointed, but I took the philosophical position that enough is enough already. And cried myself to sleep.

18

Causes

Merry Christmas! A poignant letter reached my desk in 1958, when a Chicago mother of six, her husband unemployed, was willing to sell her unborn child in order to keep her family from starving and losing her home. It was Christmas time when she wrote me:

It is with heavy heart that I am offering my baby, due in July, for adoption. I can see no other way out of our financial troubles. My Joe has been out of work since one week before Christmas and we are about to lose our home. Many times my other six children have gone hungry. It's a horrible thing when a mother even has to think of such things, but my unborn child will have a better chance to live a happy life somewhere else. Believe me, sir, it is tearing my soul apart to give up my baby, but what else can I do? We have no one to turn to, except you. We always have been poor and struggling. But never was the situation so desperate. —Mrs. Joseph A.

The big heart of Chicago responded immediately to the letter we printed. Cash donations (which we didn't solicit) and job offers poured in. When husband Joe came to our office at my request to pick up the donations, he burst into tears, astounded that so many strangers would come to his family's aid.

One of those contributors was a woman named Ruth Smith, who wrote:

When I arose this morning things looked gloomy for me. I felt my burdens were heavier than I could bear. I'm living on $30 a week and finding it most difficult. Then I read your column about Mrs. A. and realized I was rich. I'm enclosing $1. It isn't much, but it's more than I can afford. I work part time and I'd like to give Mrs. A. a helping hand in my spare time.

Please explain to her that I am Negro. I don't know what color or faith she is and I couldn't care less.

And then there was this letter from Mrs. A. herself:

I wish I could express how I feel, how grateful I am. You will always be remembered in my prayers. From the bottom of my humble heart, I thank you.

When Richard Finnegan and Russ Stewart asked me to launch Kup's Column, they gave few guidelines. One stood out: A column "must have a heart." One of the first causes I got behind was cerebral palsy, eventually doing the original CP telethon in 1954 with Bob Hope. That was also one of the first times I was given an awesome demonstration of the new medium, television. And I'm not being soapy when I simultaneously say that it similarly showed me how many people *were* reachable and . . . had a heart.

Earlier in the year, we got together with the United Cerebral Palsy Association of Illinois and came up with the idea of a contest with the winner spending two weeks in Hollywood visiting the studios and dining with a favorite movie star, all expenses paid. And all it took was 10 little words or less—a slogan that the CP Association could use in its battle against the ailment. Some stars came up with slogans. Singer Frankie Laine: "Lend part of your purse to lift CP's curse." The Breakfast Club's Don McNeill: "*You* can use *your* hand . . . write a check to check palsy!" The winner was an ordinary Joe, James Hart of 212 Fourth Avenue in Joliet, Illinois: "Your cash—and their courage—can conquer CP."

My readers contributed more than slogans. Because it was important to make people understand that the battle against CP *could* be won, I ran this letter sent to me by Mrs. Philip B. Smith, a grandmother: "My daughter was afflicted with cerebral palsy at the age of eight. Now, at 48, she is the mother of 12 children! She was in third grade when her teacher started scolding her because of her poor handwriting. I discovered she couldn't hold a pencil because of cerebral palsy. She grew steadily worse. Her right side became paralyzed and she couldn't talk. But constant care and attention brought her back almost to normal. And now, as I said above, she is the mother of 12 beautiful children." Mrs. Smith also contributed a slogan—"CP at eight, a mother of 12 at 48"—but wanted someone else to have the trip to Hollywood if she won. She only wanted people to know that cerebral palsy could be beaten.

I also was able to persuade big-name stars to appear on the CP telethons. And those who couldn't come contributed something. One time,

Spencer Tracy gave us the necktie he wore in *Father of the Bride*, Fred Astaire contributed the bow tie he wore in *Three Little Words*, and Clark Gable the scarf he wore in *To Please A Lady*. That first televised show in 1954, on WBKB-TV, lasted 16-1/2 hours, starting at 10:30 p.m. Saturday night until I just about collapsed at 3 p.m. Sunday. It was worth the exhaustion, though, as we raised much more than our goal of a quarter of a million dollars. That doesn't seem like much these days, but it was a record then when telethons were new. A lot of the credit belonged to WBKB-TV's innovative program manager, Red Quinlan, who went all out . . . and to Essee, who poured me, she says, an even hundred cups of coffee in 16-plus hours (which I drank partly because it meant a $500 contribution from Manor House Coffee). She, too, was there for the entire show— in those days she never let me out of her sight.

All the CP telethons didn't run that smoothly, though, as this item in my Feb. 3, 1976, column proves:

> Thanks to the generosity of Bill Veeck, the ill-fated cerebral palsy telethon on Channel 44 last weekend recouped much of the estimated $200,000 loss it suffered when technical difficulties forced it off the air for almost four hours. Veeck donated 25,000 tickets for a White Sox game on May 11, which provided enough revenue to make amends for most of the loss.

Some other early causes included everything from veteran cabbies to police officers' widows to outstanding "anonymous" citizens. One night in early May of '46, I stepped from the Rio Cabana nightspot into the total blackness of the a.m. and, luckily was able to hail a taxi almost instantly. The cab bore no identification, but the driver recognized me and pulled my leg for engaging in so many charitable drives. "Kup," he asked, "how would you like to help a new Veterans Taxicab Company?"

"Anything for a veteran."

"Great!" he replied. "I'm a veteran, and this taxi is owned by Universal Cab Company."

"Who owns Universal?"

"You're looking at him."

"No kidding. How many cabs have you got?"

"You're riding in it."

There was also the Chicagoan of the Year award, which was inaugurated by the column. The 1951 winner, Tim Crocker, was especially memorable because of the depths from which he rose, like a phoenix, to be selected for the honor. To appreciate that, let's go back to Crocker's early days. . . on Detroit's skid row. Tom was at the end of his rope then, an alcoholic derelict, a shred of floating flotsam in the sea of human wreckage. Was it possible to sink any lower? Yes...Crocker was committed to a Michigan state hospital as an "incurable drunk."

Yet when Crocker was voted Chicagoan of the Year he was...Commanding Officer of the Salvation Army's Harbor Light Corps on West Madison Street. "Cap'n Tom" had been responsible for the reclamation of *thousands* of lost souls—alcoholic, dope-addicted derelicts who returned to society, reunited with their wives and families, to lead normal, sober lives. Some of those men were in the audience to cheer as Crocker was honored. Like Tom, they pulled no punches in telling their stories. One was a lawyer from an important Chicago bank, who had ended up in a gutter, filling body and soul only with alcohol until he stumbled into the Harbor Light Corps and met Tom Crocker. Another was a still-young man who stole several hundred dollars from his employer while drunk, took off and wound up on skid row. The law finally caught up with him but, at the pleading of Cap'n Tom, he was turned over to the Harbor Light Corps, stopped drinking, repaid all the money, and his employer took him back.

Where did Crocker find the strength to rise from his oblivion? One big factor was his charming little wife, who worked side by side with him (she was a "lieutenant" in the Army) and never gave up on Tom. Together, their salary was $41 a week. Crocker had turned down offers of large salaries to enter private industry. In the new era of "how much?" and "what's in it for me?" this rare man was chosen by the judges over the other finalists—all of whom were either famous or well-known civic leaders.

Another early cause—and few have been more important—was when I teamed up with a number of actors and actresses to fight blacklisting in Hollywood.

It was in fall of 1947. The House Committee on Un-American Activities (HUAC) was holding hearings on alleged Hollywood Communists.

Some of you may recall the movie *Mr. Smith Goes To Washington* in which Jimmy Stewart portrayed an innocent who was sent to Congress by shyster politicians who expected to boss him. But he got wise to their shenanigans and, before the last reel ran out, made a dramatic plea for good honest government. In many respects, the Hollywood stars with whom I invaded Washington were in much the same boat Stewart was. They, too, were babes in the political woods. They were easily out-maneuvered by the skilled politicians of HUAC. But they were just as determined as was Mr. Smith. This was a comparatively new role for Hollywood stars. The senators, representatives, government employees and bobby soxers who crowded around to ogle them at every turn were seeing serious, intent people instead of the usual actors who flashed white teeth and turned the right profile to catch the photographers' flash. There were some glamor girls among the stars, too, such as Lauren Bacall, June Havoc, Evelyn Keyes and Geraldine Brooks. Glamor, for the time being though, took a holiday.

These Hollywooders went to Washington to protest what they called a threat to their industry and abridgement of the guaranteed rights in the First Amendment to the Constitution. They were not called by the Committee, as were such friendly witnesses as Louis B. Mayer, Jack Warner, Robert Taylor, Adolphe Menjou, Mrs. Lela Rogers (Ginger's mother), Robert Montgomery and Gary Cooper—all on the side of the witch-hunters.

The pilgrimage began when Gene Kelly, Humphrey Bogart, John Huston and a few others were sitting in Romanoff's and bemoaning the fact that a number of the witnesses, particularly Adolphe Menjou and Lela Rogers, were allowed to stamp persons as Communists without verification.

"Why don't we do something about it," asked Gene Kelly, "instead of sitting here in Hollywood and wailing?"

That was the starting point. They decided that if they had any complaints about the method in which HUAC was conducting the hearing, they should go to Washington and raise their voices in protest.

So the stars chartered a plane for $14,000, plus getting together another $8,000 for a Sunday afternoon broadcast. In Washington, they resorted to press conferences in an effort to get their story to the public. The Committee snubbed them completely. Not one was called to testify.

Bogie summed it up: "We fully expected that certain sections of the press would blast us and say we were coming to help the Commies. And we weren't disappointed. We took a real beating in some newspapers. But the last thing we were interested in was defending Communists. Our purpose was simple. We were defending freedom. We were totally opposed to the methods used by the Committee."

The group made a valiant effort, received considerable press coverage for a few days, but in the end made little more than a blip on the nation's radar screen. The anti-Communist sentiment at the time was so overwhelming that moderates were lost in the backlash.

The unbelievable bad taste and sheer stupidity of the HUAC Congressmen would have been laughable if it weren't so treacherous. One day in late October, for example, Congressman McDowell of Pennsylvania referred to Poles as "Polacks." When I questioned him about this derogatory term, he blandly replied, "Sure, people call Poles Polacks. It's common usage." But he didn't amplify on what *kind* of people commonly use such epithets.

A couple of other interesting early crusades were those of Barbara Ann Scott and Craig Rice. Ms. Scott, the Olympic skating queen, turned professional after winning almost every amateur competition including the Olympic figure skating gold medal. She was in Chicago for a two-week engagement. One night she confided to me that she took only a modest salary—the lion's share of her large paycheck went to the St. Lawrence Foundation, which she established to help crippled children in Canada who might never have a chance to skate. I skated aboard.

Craig Rice, Chicago-born queen of the whodunit novels, who earned close to six figures in the late 1940s (which would be about a million now), was an equally humanistic and more fascinating story. Ms. Rice was *practically penniless*. . . because she totally supported St. Edmonds, an orphan home for black children in Selma, Alabama (plus a couple of dozen needy relatives and friends). Her philosophy: "Money is good for only one thing—to give away."

Craig also had the habit of giving away husbands. While I was pushing in the column for the orphan home, Craig gave me a good item on the shelving of hubby No. 4, Henry W. DeMott. I asked her about her numerous marriages and divorces and she replied: "I'm starting another five-foot shelf, Kup—not of books—of ex-husbands."

Most of the causes in which I got involved had a serious tone. But we had at least one light-hearted one. That was the annual Harvest Moon Festival, which my paper launched after the success of the Harvest Moon Ball, sponsored by the *New York Daily News*. Ed Sullivan emcee'd the New York version, I the Chicago counterpart. And for 25 years we filled the Chicago Stadium with a jampacked 25,000 patrons. My assignment was to line up stars from Hollywood and Broadway to join with the amateur dancers to provide an uproarious evening, all for charity.

I made so many trips to Hollywood during that period to beg and coax stars to appear—and practically every big name in show business did respond—that the mere sight of me sent a signal to the comedians and singers. As witness: when I ran into Milton Berle in Chasen's. "Don't bother asking me, he exclaimed. Just tell me the date."

One of the Harvest Moon Festivals still is vivid in memory because the three greatest singers of the day accepted our invitation. We had Frank Sinatra, Perry Como and the late Russ Columbo, all on one bill. It had never happened before.

Missing persons? All you had to do was write Kup's Column:

Dear Kup—I'm a Chicagoan stationed in North Carolina about to go to Vietnam. I don't know if I'll come back, and the one thing that matters to me more than anything in the world would be to learn that my kid brother, Ed, is okay. He disappeared the night before Thanksgiving a year ago when my dad died. He used to read your column all the time, and maybe if you could print a little of this in it, he'd read it and get in touch with our mother or sister. I'd feel a lot better about going overseas if I knew he was all right.

This was a letter I received during the Vietnam War. I've received all kinds of letters from servicemen during three wars. Most turned out happily, but some tragically. In this case, it was both. The boy did read the column with his brother's plea in it and contacted me. I contacted the brother—the day before he was being shipped to Nam. I then called the boys' mother and told her her younger son would be home soon. But the older brother never came home. Still, maybe that GI died with a little more peace of mind because he knew that his kid brother was alive and well and headed home.

And Steve Allen wrote me this note some years back: "Kup—I'm trying to locate an old friend of my late mother. Her name is Alma Russell Morse. She once lived at 1366 N. Dearborn, the last address I have for her. Another clue may be her daughter Betty, who worked for an ad agency in Chicago. If any of your Chicago readers have any information of her whereabouts, please have them contact me at 1313 N. Vine Street, Hollywood, California. Thanks—Steve." As always, my readers came through.

But you didn't have to be a movie star or a GI for Kup's Missing Persons Bureau to go into action. In 1964 a plea to Guy Sanalitro was successful. Twenty-three years old, he had left home and hadn't returned. His disappearance had seriously affected his mother's health. She said he was a regular reader of the column, and could I run an item asking him to please call her. I did. He did.

Now and then the column even played Dan Cupid. Clyde Lawrence of 5664 S. Artesian was a Marine Corporal stationed in Korea. He wrote to me asking if the column would encourage some pen pals (preferably females—a real Marine!) and of course I printed the request. He got 197 letters. One respondent, Elizabeth Ray of 951 W. 35th Place, became Mrs. Lawrence.

Most causes met with success. However, there was *one* that was a notable failure. In the late 1940s, Danny Thomas launched a campaign in Hollywood that should have won the plaudits of most males in the world. It certainly won *my* backing, if not Hollywood's.

Danny thought it was about time that the *ugly* guy. . .wins the girl in the movies.

It was a revolutionary idea. But it happens in real life, so why not in pictures? And Danny was an ideal leader for the cause since, along with your reporter, he had (and has) a nose which definitely qualified him as an "ugly duckling."

The cause was born when Danny was in the midst of negotiations for an important role. He could have the part, the studio informed him. . . provided he submitted to a nose operation.

Danny turned them down flat.

And wisely. He knew, as I do, that if you're going to have a nose, *have* one. One good inhale each morning has always fixed Danny and myself for the day, while poor bob-nosed creatures have to go around panting for fresh air every few seconds.

Whenever I was in for a penny, I was in for a pound. That meant that now and then I supported causes that were unpopular, or where the recipient was even personally despicable to me. One not-too-popular campaign was on behalf of stripper Pinki DeCaro. I've always thought strippers to be okay Janes, but most people tend to dress them down (pun intended) for their mode of making a living. Miss DeCaro, who danced at the Silver Frolics, had been hit in a crossfire during a glass-throwing incident by customers. She was hospitalized and lost an eye. Shortly after, she went totally blind. Her dancing days were over. Though she was in desperate need of financial assistance, Pinki heard nothing from the owners of the night club. Medical bills left her and husband Ted practically destitute. Not only did the Silver Frolics refuse to give her a penny, but wouldn't cooperate in identifying the ringsiders who did the glass-throwing. Fortunately, the readers of the column came to Pinki's help with contributions.

Very few of my readers got behind my effort to support Nazi George Lincoln Rockwell's speaking at the University of Chicago. As he was about to be canceled, and though Rockwell was on my 10 Most Despicable Persons List, I fought for his right to free speech. And frankly, if Rockwell could make any dent in the U of C students' values, then it would be time to cancel not one speech, but our entire educational system. I helped to win that rather unpopular cause, Rockwell did speak, and was greeted—as I predicted in the column—with a derisive laughter more destructive than bodily harm.

When it came down to other minorities, though, I relished the fight in every way. I wrote this personal letter to Senator Theodore Bilbo in the column:

> Last Sunday night Drew Pearson, the Washington columnist and radio commentator, had enough guts and nerve to defy the Ku Klux Klan. Despite threats on his life, he went right into the heart of Klanland, Atlanta, Ga., to do his broadcast, in which he exposed the KKK leaders.
>
> This column is now inviting you, as the chief advocate of "white supremacy," to show as much gumption. We are extending you an invitation to come to Chicago (the North, that is) and address a South Side audience. If you prefer, we can arrange a debate on some interesting subject, say for instance, "Democracy—Is It For Everybody?"
>
> We will do more for you than Atlanta did for Pearson. We will guarantee you protection and your expenses. To make sure you receive the invitation, a copy of it is being Western Union'd to you today.
>
> Just name the date, Senator.

I never received an answer.

Essee's battle for the underdog goes way back, too. When she was at Northwestern University, there was only one Jewish sorority (which she felt was filled with "drips"), and she went to the Dean of Women to start a second one. However, Essee had hardly any chance for success then: There was a 3 percent Jewish "quota" at NU! Some years later, we were more than able to make up for that with our work on behalf of Israel's famous Weizmann Institute of Science. For 25 years now, I have served as president of the Chicago chapter of the Weizmann Institute. Essee and I established the Karyn Kupcinet International School at Weizmann. Each year, we bring the outstanding college science students from around the world to spend 10 weeks in the summer studying with the scientists at Weizmann.

And what is more of a minority than. . .the *young?* Some 25 years before I even began the column, a youthful priest, serving as chaplain at the old Cook County Jail, was accompanying a young criminal on the grim "last mile" walk to the gallows. Suddenly the criminal stopped, broke down and sobbed: "Why do they wait until the rope is around my neck before they do anything for me?"

The young priest, conscious of society's lack of interest in its wayward youth, resolved to devote his energies to helping youngsters, particularly needy youngsters for whom temptation is so great. But being a young priest, he had no immediate means or wherewithal to institute a constructive program. Then in 1928 he was elevated to the episcopacy by the late

Cardinal Mundelein. It had taken 10 years, but it was then that Bishop Sheil was able to realize his long-cherished dreams. He organized the Catholic Youth Organization which became recognized as one of the nation's greatest forces in guiding our youth and combating juvenile delinquency. Each year more than 100,000 kids are benefited by the CYO. Every year, the column was privileged to support Bishop Sheil's crusade.

To the young, a pat on the back sometimes is more important than money. Michele Marcheschi, 11 years old, was one of the students who survived the horrible Our Lady of the Angels school fire in 1958.

The following day, after reading of Chicago car salesman Jim Moran's efforts to raise funds for the tragedy, she walked into his Courtesy Motors and begged, "Please, can I wash windows or sweep up or do anything to show how much I appreciate what you're doing?" I might add that when I happened to tell Joe Kennedy, father of J.F.K., about the tragedy while he was in town on Merchandise Mart matters, he wrote out a five thousand dollar check before I could exhale. And Frankie Laine raised $1,500 selling his albums between shows at the Chez Paree. And this letter, printed on yellow scratch paper in a child's scrawl, came to my desk from Marlene Cannella, 1145 N. Harding, to be forwarded to Santa Claus:

"Dear Santa—My brother was in the terrible school fire and we miss him very much. Please, Santa, come to see my mother. She cries so much that we are afraid that she will get very sick. She calls for our Georgie every day. Can you do something please? I was in the school also."

The Hubbard Street fire on Jan. 28, 1961, was another horrible loss for the city of Chicago. Nine firemen lost their lives fighting the fire. As soon as the story broke, Bill Veeck was on the phone to me with the suggestion that "something must be done for the families of those firemen." The next day we (Bill and I and a few others we gathered) announced the creation of the Firemen's Fund—its purpose to raise funds to guarantee the education of the children of the firemen who lost their lives. The nine firemen had, collectively, 13 children. Within a few days we raised $90,000 for the fund. With the First National Bank serving as our fiscal agent (pro bono publico), we were able to provide funds for the educational needs of all 13 children. In some cases this meant from grammar school, public and parochial, through college and, in a few cases, beyond to graduate school. Then in 1979, our committee, which included Veeck, my attorney Art Morse and Joe Meegan, decided we'd gone as far as possible. Thanks to the adroit investments of the funds by the First National Bank, we had $100,000 in the bank. . . more than we had raised in 1961. At this stage, we turned over the money to the Chicago Fire Department and its chief, Richard Albrecht, to be used to educate children of firemen killed in the line of duty.

Undoubtedly, the cause for which I'm best known is the Purple Heart Cruise. Go back with me, if you will, to June 5, 1945:

> This is the announcement of a Purple Heart Cruise. Wounded heroes who are convalescing in Army and Navy hospitals in the Chicago area, as well as young men and women in our training centers, will be the guests of readers of this column on Saturday, June 16, aboard the S. S. North American, one of the two palatial sister cruisers on Lake Michigan. Through the cooperation of E. J. (Erv) Goebel, General Manager of the Georgian Bay line and owner of the ship, the S. S. North American will proudly sail that day with the most gallant passengers in its history. This will be the first Purple Heart Cruise on record.

> Readers of this column are invited to send in contributions that will make possible this full day of fun on Lake Michigan for these veterans. . . . Checks should be made out to "Purple Heart Cruise," and addressed to this column, care of *The Chicago Times.* The beneficiaries will be the patients at Gardiner, Vaughan, Hines, Marine, Fort Sheridan and Great Lakes hospitals—approximately 500 of them. There'll be veterans who've never sailed Lake Michigan but who sailed the Atlantic and Pacific. They'll be our veterans—out for a full day of sunshine and merriment provided by Chicagoans who already have established their city as the GI haven. Ship ahoy for a Purple Heart Cruise!

Things happened fast after that first announcement. A couple of days later, one of Chicago's biggest radio stations, WBBM, announced it would broadcast the cruise. Leading entertainers volunteered to be aboard.

The response from readers has been so great that we raise the funds to cover the expenses in a matter of days. In addition to a stage show, we have breakfast and lunch aboard the ship, dancing games, contests and strolling entertainers. And every veteran leaves the ship with no fewer than 50 gifts to take home, all neatly packaged in shopping bags. The cruise has become a Chicago institution and no other city provides a similar event for our veterans.

Comedians are always looking for a great finish, and we always looked for a great finish on the cruise. One of the comedians who volunteered for years, Billy Falbo, once ended his act by jumping fully clothed into the lake. Fortunately, we have escort boats for security following us. He didn't tell anybody he was going to do it beforehand. I doubt whether he knew himself until the last minute. He was fished out of the water, but what a finish!

The cruise is now in its 44th year. I had to miss the 1987 cruise because of illness—the first time in 43 years. But I was back in 1988.

The meaning of the Purple Heart Cruise is twofold. First, it celebrates the veterans of all our wars, men and women who put their lives on the line so that the rest of us could live in peace and freedom. Second, it serves to remind the public that we still have veterans lingering in hospitals, some since World War I. At war's end, the public too quickly forgets the veterans. The Cruise serves to publicize the fact that for many veterans, the war isn't over—it merely moved to the hospital.

The meaning and spirit of the Cruise—as in any charitable cause—comes as much from those who give to make it possible. The largest donation last year came from. . . Anonymous. . . the second largest from Oprah Winfrey. But maybe the most meaningful contribution came many years ago. It was fifty cents from a little girl with this note: "Here is my money. My daddy was killed in the war."

There are so many more causes that space doesn't permit me to mention. But as you can see, I've gotten a thousand times more in return than I've ever given.

19

J.F.K.

It has been said that almost everyone remembers exactly where he was when first hearing President John F. Kennedy had been shot.

I was in the office writing a column that memorable Friday morning when the phone rang. "Turn on the TV," Essee exclaimed breathlessly. "The president has been shot."

I told her to calm down, that the first reports of any tragedy invariably were exaggerated and this could be another example. Then I put down the phone—and watched Camelot die.

"Why?" asked our cabdriver as we drove through a downpour in a dark and deserted city. As the rain splattered against the windows of the cab, I couldn't help but recall the unparalleled tragedy that ran in the Kennedy family. Joseph Kennedy, Jr., the oldest brother and the one Joseph Kennedy, Sr., favored to be president, killed in World War II. Sister Kathleen's husband, the Marquess of Hartington, killed in the same war. Kathleen then dying in a plane crash. A son born to J.F.K. and Jacqueline dying shortly after birth earlier in the year. Another sister, Rosemary, institutionalized for mental retardation. And little did we know how much more grief was to come.

Memories of J.F.K. flashed through my mind. Strangely, the one which kept surging to the surface was a conversation I'd had with Newton Minow shortly before. He had suggested that John Kennedy join our then three living ex-presidents—Herbert Hoover, Harry Truman and Dwight Eisenhower—on my TV program to discuss the presidency, a unique historical happening. Kennedy took to the idea immediately.

"Who would think," Newton and I would say to one another later, "that Jack Kennedy would be the first of that foursome to pass on?"

A few days later, along with millions and millions of other Americans, I watched the funeral on TV, amazed at the strength and spirit of Jacqueline Kennedy. As Chief Justice Earl Warren spoke of "the hatred that is finding its way into the mainstream," I glanced at my desk. On it rested a recent edition of a hate newspaper bearing a vicious headline about the president. Also on my desk was a huge stack of letters, postcards, telegrams and poems, from everywhere, expressing the world's grief. The one I recall best was from Rabbi William Sajovitz of Chicago's South Shore Temple:

> And now we mourn—Now we cry aloud—
> The bullet which ended his life—
> Entered our hearts, for he was part of our family.
> We, too, were wounded.
> Harken, all ye deluded fools—
> You have but killed a man—not a dream;
> You have but stilled a body—not a soul.

As somehow seemed almost inevitable, the aftermath of the assassination produced a Chicago connection: Lee Harvey Oswald had purchased the fatal rifle from Klein Sporting Goods in Chicago via mail order. Then. . .a second connection: Oswald's slayer was a former Chicagoan, Jack (Sparky) Rubinstein, who shortened his name to Ruby when he moved to Dallas.

I knew Ruby when he was a one-time organizer for the Waste and Material Handlers Union, run by Paul Dorfman. I finally located Dorfman in Palm Springs.

"Not Sparky!" he gasped. "Sparky worked as an organizer for three or four months after I took over the union, but he didn't have what it took, so we let him go. He's the *last* guy you'd think would do this. He was a nebbish kind of guy."

Kennedy's name first appeared in my column on July 3, 1953:

> Senator John Kennedy (D-Mass.) was one of the speakers at the Business Hall of Fame, hosted by his father, the former Ambassador and owner of the Merchandise Mart. John Kennedy received the evening's heartiest response when, in commenting on the Democratic support President Eisen-

hower was getting from Congress, he said: "If the Republican President can get two more Democrats elected, he'll have control of the Senate."

In 1956, I predicted that he would be president four years later. He had come to Chicago that March for a St. Patrick's Day dinner sponsored by the Irish Fellowship Club and had sparkled: "Tell the folks in Chicago to continue voting Democratic—so they can continue living like Republicans." After the '56 Democratic Convention it was obvious to many that Jack Kennedy was the rising star in the Democratic Party. His nomination speech for Adlai Stevenson and dramatic contest against Estes Kefauver for the vice presidential nomination—climaxed by his urging the delegates to put Kefauver on the ticket by acclamation—thrust him head and shoulders above all future democratic candidates. "In racetrack parlance," I itemed again about J.F.K., "tab this one for '60."

Actually, I had a little help with that prediction. A year before, Eunice Kennedy Shriver had phoned me. "Do you want to interview the future president of the United States?"

"Do you mean your brother?"

"That's right."

That was my first recognition that the family was going for the gold.

Eunice and Sarge Shriver were ardent liberals with a long record of not just talking, but doing something about their beliefs. There was the time, for instance, when I was told that they of all people had been dropped from the exclusive Saddle & Cycle Club for non-payment of dues. I couldn't believe it, and investigated. The truth was that the Shrivers had hosted a party at the club and invited a number of blacks, for which a number of other members roundly criticized them. So Eunice and Sarge simply dropped the club, rather than the other way around.

No doubt the sisters of many a presidential hopeful throughout our history have said the same thing. But I was close to Eunice because of her marriage to Chicagoan Sarge, and knew her to be tough-minded...and the Kennedy family to be uniquely ambitious and wealthy enough to fulfill those ambitions. In 1953, John Kennedy was barely old enough to legally be a presidential candidate, but even then you could sense that he had it all, virtually every attribute for an American president. In the best sense of the word, he was *bred* to it as few had been before or since.

Moreover, the times were becoming right for his special amalgam of boyishness and manliness, direction and dream. A new generation had grown up during a suffocating depression and terrifying World War II. We were an energetic, youthfully restless and ambitious nation. We were ready to be on the move again—ready for an energetic, youthfully restless and driving leader.

Though J.F.K. was "bred" to the presidency and had all his father's millions, it is little realized how strongly Jack had to oppose Joe Sr. to fight his way to the top. To begin with, Joe was an ardent conservative who'd gained power and riches by sometimes combining free enterprise at its best with dubious methods at their worst.

I got to know Joe when he made one of his little acquisitions: No less than the Merchandise Mart, then Chicago's biggest and most expensive building. When the elder Kennedy met Harry Doherty, head of the Merchants and Manufacturers Club in the Mart, Joe asked him: "Haven't I met you somewhere before?" Doherty nodded. Shortly after Joe had been appointed Ambassador to England, he spoke at the Union League Club which Doherty then managed. After the speech, Doherty went up to Kennedy and, unaware of his wealth, offered him a six hundred dollar fee. Kennedy politely refused. "Lord, how embarrassed I am meeting you now," Doherty told Joe. "*Me* offering *you* six hundred dollars—when you've got 19 million to buy this building!"

Yes, six hundred dollars was pocket change to Joseph Kennedy. But when it came to fighting over real money, he took a back seat to no one. In 1949, for instance, he came to Chicago to argue with Mayor Kennelly about the taxes on the Mart, which had almost doubled from the $430,000 paid in '45. And when, during J.F.K.'s campaign for the presidency, Jack went to his father for more money, Joe's reply was the oft-quoted: "I promised to finance your campaign—but *not* to buy a landslide!" After J.F.K. was elected, Bobby was appointed attorney general, and Teddy was assistant district attorney in Suffolk County, Massachusetts. I asked Ambassador Kennedy what he thought of his family. "Well," he snapped revealingly, "my boys are all working."

The election of John F. Kennedy was one of the closest in history, and there was no doubt that the TV debates—particularly the first one held in Chicago—helped turn the tide. That confrontation at CBS' TV studios was held in a room which I knew all too well. It was the same room from which I did my weekly late night TV talk show that had begun a year and a half earlier and would continue for 27 years.

The "debate"—nothing more than a glorified press conference—was won by J.F.K. for several reasons. Probably the least important was that he seemed a little better prepared. More significant was that he had begun to generate that feeling of "Camelot" which would sweep across the country.

Yet the metaphoric "horseshoe nail" which has turned the tide of history many times was the key: Nixon was the victim of a poor makeup job. I saw him coming into the building, then saw him coming out of the makeup room. "He looked a lot better *before* they put on the makeup," I commented to another reporter, who agreed.

After congratulating Kennedy on his performance in the debate, I joined Nixon in his dressing room while he was changing shirts. We chatted for a few moments. I asked him if he'd come back to that same room where he'd just debated Kennedy and appear on my show. He promised he would—*after* the election.

"Win *or* lose?" I asked.

"Kup, *please*," he joked, "don't mention *that* word."

Nixon removed his makeup and looked much better—though tired. Somehow, Jack Kennedy even when totally exhausted and drained by severe back trouble, never looked tired.

Vigor, or, as he put it, 'Vigah', was a byword by which we came to know J.F.K., and I think one of his outstanding qualities indeed was his stamina. One Secret Service agent moaned to me about the new hours he had to keep after Kennedy was elected: "He got up at six o'clock this morning and has been going at breakneck speed throughout the day and night attending conferences and parties. Now, here it is 3:30 a.m. the next day and he finally signaled us that he's ready to go home. But he'll be up at six again tomorrow to attend early Mass. I don't know if I'll last."

At times he might have had a little too much vigor. J.F.K. was far from a perfect person. As I noted in the chapter on Marilyn Monroe, it was common knowledge among those who covered him that Kennedy was one of our more promiscuous presidents. Jackie bore up beautifully under Jack's infidelities—and under the Kennedy family's fidelity to a touch-football way of life for which she was totally unsuited. Immediately after the inauguration, Jack sat down with Jackie and recited a long list of things in which he felt a First Lady should become interested. She looked at the list in silence for a few moments, and then said, "Oh, Jack, can't we please bring back Eleanor Roosevelt as First Lady?"

Jackie dealt with the public and press with the same sharp yet lady-like humor. During an always secluded vacation at Hyannisport, a newspaper photographer used a long lens to snap pictures of Caroline and John-John playing. When the photographs appeared in print, Mrs. Kennedy ripped out the page and pencilled a note to Press Secretary Pierre Salinger, saying: "Pierre, can you please get away from the bar long enough to make sure this doesn't happen again?"

Jackie told me a wonderful story about Caroline that had international ramifications. It revolved around Kumjo Chumbi, a Nepalese official who visited the White House during the end of Ike's administration.
Chumbi was treated so nicely that, upon returning, he dispatched his vil-
lage's greatest gift to Eisenhower—the tail of a yak. The gift was misplaced
and later found by none other than Caroline Kennedy . . . who used it for
swatting flies. One day Mama and Papa Kennedy became suspicious of
Caroline's new toy and sent the staff checking into it. They finally discovered the source of Caroline's unusual fly-swatter, which was immediately
packaged and sent to former President Eisenhower who in turn instantly
sent a belated thank-you note to Chumbi—thereby saving a social rift between the U.S. and Nepal.

The Kennedys may have been the most charismatic and powerful en-
tourage ever to lead the country, but their tough, pragmatic Irish background didn't always allow them into the highest echelons of so-called
society. A few years after the brouhaha with the Shrivers and the Saddle
& Cycle Club, actor Peter Lawford and wife Pat were actually rejected as
tenants in a snooty New York apartment building. At the Oscars that
year, Lawford told Sidney Poitier of the rebuff they'd suffered. "I can certainly sympathize with you," said Poitier, the first black to win an Oscar
for best actor. "But tell Pat that you and she can move into *my* neighborhood any time."

The genesis of the Kennedy affinity for movie stars and vice versa was
father Joe. He always liked beautiful show girls. I recall when a friend of
his, Tony Curtis, introduced Joe Sr. to Hugh Hefner. The two immediately became buddies. Kennedy helped Hefner with some sound business
suggestions for the Playboy Club operations and Hefner in turn . . . did
some favors for Joe Kennedy.

In a way, Jackie was above all this. It was she who gave to Jack that
extra touch of class.

After the assassination, Jackie became estranged from some of the
Kennedys. As much as he could, the old man smoothed things over. But
without Jack, inevitably she became less and less involved with the family. Her marriage to Aristotle Onassis, who had some of the enthusiastic
qualities of Zorba the Greek and much more money, turned off the Kennedy family and left the public with a far different opinion of Jackie. She
was called a money-grubber, marrying the short and dumpy, rough-hewn
and elderly Onassis for his wealth. At least that was the general impression. And the Onassis ardor cooled when Jackie's spending sprees caught
up to him. Even a man of his wealth was startled. There's little doubt, as

Kennedy watchers maintained, that Onassis planned to seek a divorce, but his death intervened.

Jackie's sister, Lee Bouvier, who characteristically married a Polish prince, Radziwill, had some of her class. Lee, at the urging of her mentor, Truman Capote, tried mightily for an acting career. Truman was convinced he could do as much for her as Professor 'Enry Higgins did for Liza Doolittle in My Fair Lady. Unfortunately, Capote never got around to exclaiming, "By gosh, she's got it." And Lee gracefully bowed out of the theater.

The moment I remember best about Lee was the night Capote and she and Maria Tallchief Paschen were dinner guests at our home in July of 1967. Lee was appearing in The Philadelphia Story at the Ivanhoe Theater. I used the wrong fork for the first serving. And Lee, sitting on my left, graciously made the same mistake, rather than embarrass me. Now that was class.

One of the things that made Jack Kennedy—and his family—so special to me was that he was a contemporary, just a few years younger than myself. I was even closer to Truman and admired no president more. But Roosevelt, Truman and Eisenhower were more like father figures. Kennedy was the first president I'd known who was at the same stage of life as I was. This was true of most of the press, and it intensified his relationship with them.

Still, as a reporter, I couldn't let this stop me from taking him to task when necessary. When he made an historical slip regarding Abe Lincoln, I corrected him and he took it with good grace. But not so in March of 1963 when I itemed:

> The time has come, we believe, for President Kennedy to issue a "white paper" on the Bay of Pigs fiasco. The American public is entitled to a full report, instead of the piecemeal stories which have been leaking out. Most of the confusion is due to the fact that this was a Central Intelligence Agency operation, and the CIA operates in cloak-and-dagger secrecy. Not until the President issues a white paper will the public's right to know be satisfied. . . .

Another columnist put it this way: "The Kennedy rocking chair is indeed the symbol of the New Frontier. You get the feeling of moving—but you're actually not going anywhere."

J.F.K. was shocked and angered that the honeymoon with the press seemed over.

After a few months, however—unfortunately, only a few months before his death—a rapprochement began. The honeymoon may have been ended, but the marriage lasted. You couldn't help but love him.

Like every notable president, side by side with his seriousness was a sense of humor. Chicago's powerful Mayor Daley, for example, was a stylistic opposite to Kennedy—Daley the rough and ready, old-time political boss, Jack the smooth, movie star-like politician who seemed to be anything but a wheeler-dealer. Yet Daley threw his crucial weight behind Kennedy for the nomination. The two Irishmen hit it off at that 1956 St. Patrick's Day dinner where Daley saw that J.F.K. was both witty and a winner. And, thanks to Daley, J.F.K. became a winner. Kennedy's victory over Nixon was razor-thin. And nowhere was that razor's edge thinner than in Illinois. Kennedy won by a nose, some 8,858 votes. And the consenus at the time was that Daley "stole" enough votes to make the slim difference. I can't vouch for that, but the relationship between the Kennedys and Daley became exceptionally close. And various investigations failed to turn up any election fraud. But as one of Daley's local pols explained, "What's the big deal? We didn't steal any more votes in this election than we do in others."

When Rabbi Maurice Eisendrath of New York, winner of the 1961 Gandhi Peace Prize, later presented a Torah to Kennedy, Labor Secretary Arthur Goldberg kidded the president about "accepting the Holy Scriptures of Judaism without wearing a hat."

"You forget, Art," said the always hatless Kennedy, "I'm *reformed*."

One of the great bonds between Jack and Jackie was this sarcastic yet never slashing wit. Sensitive to the charges of a "Kennedy dynasty," Jack was unhappy with sister Eunice, for example, for talking about Bobby's qualifications to run for the presidency someday. The next time Jack and Eunice were together, she further fueled the furnace by telling the president that he'd do better if, like Bobby, "you put more fire into your speeches."

"And you, my dear sister," replied Jack, "would do better... to put your speeches into the fire."

A Kennedy dynasty certainly was in the offing, though. After Jack's death, when the press asked Bobby whether he was going to run for president in '68 (which, of course, he did), he deadpanned: "I have no presidential ambitions. If you don't believe me, ask my wife, Ethel Bird."

And it was true that Bobby had a rare passion, and as much energy as Jack—Bobby's all on the outside. In 1959 when he was counsel for the Senate Rackets Committee, he was threatened with two libel suits in two successive TV appearances for speaking out against Chicago insurance man Alan Dorfman on "Meet The Press" and Jimmy Hoffa on "The Jack Paar Show." Bobby was Essee's favorite. But he had a mean streak, and did all Jack's dirty work. When Ethel was pregnant with their last child, he announced that they were going to call her Ruth . . . "So they no longer can call me ruth-less."

Later on, when he visited Poland, Bobby did something which characterized him best: He leaped on top of an auto to greet the huge crowd which assembled to catch a glimpse of him. What is little known was that an African student in Warsaw then jumped on top of the car while Secret Service agents froze. Bobby just smiled . . . as the African handed him a bouquet of flowers "to show our appreciation for your efforts in behalf of civil rights in America."

Whether J.F.K. forged a "new frontier" politically and economically is very debatable. What he did was to create a new *spiritual* frontier. Because of him, the nation—both those backing J.F.K. and those in opposition to him—were moved to an energetic rededication of values.

He brought a young, "perfect" wife into the White House, and then children. When was the last time that happened? At great risk to charges of nepotism, he brought brother Bobby into the cabinet as attorney general. And Bobby didn't let Jack down. He injected the Justice Department with a new found zeal and determination. He even did what previous attorneys general feared to do. He took on J. Edgar Hoover, who, as head of the F.B.I., was one of the most powerful figures in Washington. He let Hoover know that the F.B.I. was subservient to the Justice Department, which it seldom had been before. And he persuaded Ed Murrow, the most respected broadcasting figure of the day, to leave CBS to become head of the United States Information Agency, which brought world-wide respect to the USIA.

The charge of nepotism for appointing Bobby as attorney general was handled by Kennedy with his usual aplomb and humor: "Bobby plans to be a lawyer and where else can he get the experience?" That was almost as sharp as the comment by Mayor Daley, when he too was charged with nepotism for favoring his sons with city contracts. Said Daley with a straight face, "What's wrong with nepotism, as long as you keep it in the family?"

It was natural that celebrities would surround J.F.K. far more than any administration before or since. Camelot drew the brightest stars of show business to its inner circle and none more so than Frank Sinatra. Old Blue Eyes and J.F.K. became fast friends—so close, as later developments revealed, he even provided young ladies for Kennedy's vast sexual appetite.

The President assigned the task of staging an all-star show for the inaugural to Sinatra. And Frank did a remarkable job in lining up top performers for that snow-swept, stormy inaugural night when D.C. practically came to a standstill in hip-deep snow.

Sinatra, who had been a lifelong Democrat, later switched to the Republican party when J.F.K. cooled on their relationship, allegedly because of Frank's unsavory associates.

Anyway, Sinatra convinced Sidney Poitier to halt his movie in Paris and fly in. He was able to get a night off from their Broadway shows for Ethel Merman, Sir Laurence Olivier and Anthony Quinn. And that morning, Frank was at the airport to greet one of the night's performers, Milton Berle. The comedian took one look at Sinatra, dressed in all of his Don Loper sartorial elegance at 6:30 a.m., and asked, "Do we bury you now, Frank?"

J.F.K. enjoyed his appearances at public affairs more than anyone. He'd take his turn, right along with the pros, with ad lib after-dinner entertainment. I recall his once yodeling "When Irish Eyes Are Smiling" like a regular Morton Downey.

With or without celebrities, the Kennedys always were surrounded by "star" aura. Joe Sr. had an idyll with Gloria Swanson, among others. The former Patricia Kennedy had married actor Peter Lawford long before J.F.K. was president. Lawford, the suave leading man of the movies, took a lot of ribbing over the fact that he was so nervous he forgot to kiss the bride. I asked Lawford about it and he said he wasn't nervous: "The kiss wasn't included in the rehearsal," he answered, "and so I didn't do it in the ceremony."

J.F.K. became known for a number of statements that have now become American truisms. One of the least known, though, is a small inscription which adorned his desk: "Oh, God, thy sea is so great... and my boat so small." And one of the best known is that "On this earth, small and flawed though we may be"—and he was more flawed than many—"God's work is truly our own."

I agree with Rabbi Sajovitz: His truth still marches on.

NEW HERALD STAFF

Here's the staff of my high school paper. I'm in the first row, second from right.

I made the college All Star Football team in 1935 as quarterback. I'm No. 29. No. 40 went on to even bigger things — he became *President* Jerry Ford.

Essee and I married in February 1939. This Sixta cartoon ran in the *Chicago Times* to commemorate the event.

My Cookie—Karyn Kupcinet—her death is a loss I feel every day.

Opposite page, top. Benny Goodman and I were honored together as prominent alumni of Harrison High. Here Superintendent Ben Willis presents plaques to us.

Opposite page, bottom. Diana Barrymore—the sister Essee never had.

Late in 1952, just before he moved out of the White House, President Harry S Truman invited my family there for a ''presidential'' tour. It's a day Cookie and Jerry and this reporter never forgot.

August 1963—Our last family photo on our last vacation together.

My granddaughter, Kari, with Essee and Ann Landers celebrate the 40th anniversary of Kup's Column in 1983.

We're all gathered in Las Vegas before the 1986 Jerry Lewis Telethon that my son, Jerry, directed. Left to right is Jerry's wife, Sue, Jerry, Essee, me, Kari, and grandson, David.

Above, left. Bing and I go casual at his Elko, Nevada, ranch. *Above, right.* Diana Barrymore sent this photo of herself and Tennessee Williams to Essee in 1959. Tennessee's inscription: ''The roof is hot, but the cats are cool. Love—10.'' *Right.* Nat King Cole gives me a private interview.

I don't know who's on first, but I wish Abbott and Costello would quit kissing Essee.

Here I am with Cookie, Leslie Caron, Hedda Hopper and Joshua Logan at a Warner Bros. party.

Goosing Frank Sinatra—hey, he seems to like it.

I guess I thought Louis Armstrong and Ella Fitzgerald would put me into the act if I showed them how good I looked in a hat.

The Andrew sisters, Bob Hope and me.

Here I am with Burt Lancaster, Mark Hellinger and an unidentified lady columnist.

All in a day's work—here I am in Rome with Gina Lollobrigida.

Jimmy Stewart shares a story with me.

I'm gazing at the stars while sitting with them. Frank Sinatra and Janis Paige at the Harvest Moon Festival.

Eddie Cantor was always a favorite of Essee's. He and his wife, Ida, join us here. *Below.* ''As comfortable as a pair of old shoes'' was John Wayne's favorite way to describe a friend. Russ Stewart, my good friend and editor, and I were both members of the Duke's *Old Shoe* club.

Three intelligent, beautiful Hollywood stars—Jane Wyman (top), Dorothy Lamour (center) and Paulette Goddard (bottom). Essee wonders what they see in me.

Sid Luft, me, Essee, Buddy Rich, and Judy Garland.

Essee, Adlai Stevenson, and I visit backstage with Melvyn Douglas, who then was starring in *Inherit the Wind.*

Essee's favorite actor friend, Clark Gable, turned
women's heads at our parties more than anyone.

Opposite page, top. Harry Belafonte tries to put one over on me.

Center. A wonderful, gentle man—until he got in the ring—Joe Louis.

Bottom. I guess I'm the winner and champion . . . sleeper. Bob Hope's
open eyes prove it.

Backstage at the Chez
Paree with dear friend
Joe E. Lewis.

My body language says
I'm having trouble
digesting one of Walter
Matthau's points.

I've never seen a better picture of the
Marilyn which almost all America wanted
to think she really was.

Essee and I emceed the opening of the picture, *My Fair Lady*. Arthur Godfrey is to her right, Jack Warner and Audrey Hepburn to her left.

Pals Carol Channing, Zsa Zsa Gabor, and Essee at the Palmer House.

And you thought kids today wear crazy get-ups. Sonny and Cher stopped by my office in 1967.

Marlene Dietrich in 1971.

Above. A close friend for many many years now, Danny Thomas hugs Essee.

And his daughter Marlo *(below)* has all her father's best points. Essee and I joined Marlo and then soon-to-be-husband Phil Donahue at their engagement party.

Truman Capote was a perfect guest on Kup's Show.

Backstage in New York with Lauren Bacall—she could whistle for me any time. *Below.* No question—the jokes are good when Sammy Davis, Jr., and Bill Cosby get together.

Three of Hollywood's most notables — Henry Fonda *(above)*, Katharine Hepburn *(below, left)* and Bette Davis *(below, right)* give interviews to me.

I came to know the Wabash Avenue bridge as well as any part of Chicago, walking across it each day to the newspaper where I've worked for more than fifty years. When it became, officially, the Irv Kupcinet bridge in June 1986, I was deeply honored. Left to right is Cook County Board President George Dunne, *Sun-Times* Publisher and President Robert Page, me, Essee, and Mayor Harold Washington.

Essee and I join Mary Ella Smith and Mayor Harold Washington at the 60th anniversary of the Goodman Theater in October 1985.

Chicago Bears' 1986 Super Bowl quarterback, Jim McMahon, with agent Steve Zucker in the background and wife Nancy at his side at the opening of Jim's restaurant in 1987.

All five Chicago River bridges rose in unison the first time ever for the 1982 Purple Heart Cruise.

Left. Bill Veeck, former White Sox president and owner and dear friend, was one of the best prepared guests on my TV show.
Right. I loved the man that made the Chicago Bears and the NFL what they are today—George Halas.

Our Town is not short of superstars. Oprah Winfrey and Roger Ebert presenting Governor's Award to Essee at the 1986 Emmy awards.

Left. Essee and Sir Georg Solti in April 1984 at the Chicago Academy for the Arts first Academy Honors for distinguished Chicago artists in art, music, dance and theater. *Right.* Danny Glover with Essee at a press party to announce the Academy Honors for 1986.

I started my career as a sportswriter. Here I am interviewing the Brooklyn Dodgers' Woody English in 1937.

In 1947 I made my first trip to Israel (then Palestine) with this group of prominent Chicagoans.

Above. Lewis and Martin could have been big stars if they'd only kept the talented guy in the middle in the act. We're working a cerebral palsy telethon here. *Below.* And I'm working the CP telethon here, too —taking pledges from generous folks who helped us break records year after year.

Writing a story at the 1969 Academy Awards. Best Picture—*Midnight Cowboy.*

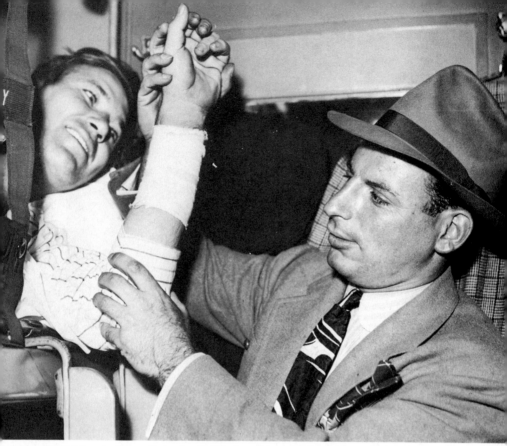

I punched him during a fight in 1938, but Dizzy Dean and I patched it up and became buddies.

I always tried to provide an open forum on ''Kup's Show''—and Reverend Jesse Jackson was a frequent visitor. Here he joins me in October 1983.

President Napoleon Duarte of El Salvador joined us on the show in 1985.
A big part of my job—meeting people.
Here we're at the famous Fritzel's.

Above. Julie, Pat, Tricia and Richard Nixon join me for an interview. Where's Checkers?

Left. I didn't always agree with his politics, but Richard Nixon always made himself available to me.

Below. Henry Kissinger passed through town in July 1976 and I get a few moments with him here.

After emceeing the Variety Club Celebrity Ball . . . a quiet moment.

20

Who Killed Karyn?

In December 1963 I wrote a column about my daughter.
It was infinitely the hardest column I ever had to write:

...Two Sundays ago I sat at my typewriter, groping for the words for a Monday column to portray the majesty that was Mrs. Jacqueline Kennedy in her hour of travail. Now it is Sunday again. And again I am groping for words to describe the majesty of another young lady, my very own. The newspaper stories reported she was strangled. That may suffice for the authorities. But those who knew and loved her scoff at the official findings. No one could stifle the gaiety and laughter and ebullience—"effervescent enthusiasm," we called her—that were her trademarks. That is how we remember Karyn, our beloved "Cookie," and that is what we are clinging to as fervently as a shipwrecked sailor at sea clings to his lifeline.

Oh, the memories that now dance amidst our groping. How she twirled a pirouette before our last dinner together in Hollywood where she was pursuing her career as an actress. And how, laughing and running, she led me up the stairs to her new apartment, modest in circumstance but rich in the art and literature of the Renaissance period. Irving Stone's "The Agony and the Ecstasy" had introduced her to Michelangelo and now she had adopted him as her very own, with Michelangelo prints dominating walls and bookshelves. Strange that the ecstasy she brought to Essee, her brother Jerry and her father, as well as hosts of others, should turn so quickly to the agony.

The memories are too many to capture at this macabre moment. Rallying friends have spared us the solemnity of solitude. But still we cannot keep from our mind the critical acclaim of her last performance in Chicago and the accolades, including a West Coast editor's editorial, for her *Miracle Worker*. And now the farewells from such friends as Earl Wilson and Bob

Considine and Leonard Lyons and Dorothy Kilgallen in New York; Reverend Ted Hesburgh, president of Notre Dame; Hedda and Louella and Mike Connolly in Hollywood; and the inspirational eulogies of Russ Stewart and Rabbi Louis Binstock here.

Lt. George Walsh of the Los Angeles County police, in charge of the investigation, provided comforting words when he told the press: "This girl had more friends than anybody I ever heard of. And not a knocker in the bunch. They all loved her." In a sense, this may have been her undoing. She saw only good, never evil, in her uncomplicated view of her fellow being. She related with one and all, young or old, joyous or sorrowful. This, in her naivete, could be the answer to why she opened her door to a knocking at midnight.

The mail, piled high at office and home and bearing postmarks from such distant points as Tokyo, Rome, Jerusalem, Frankfurt, Paris and London, has barely been skimmed. Yet it has brought solace, like the note from the Rev. Edward F. Murphy: "It is night here in Newburgh (N.Y.), but I seem to see a star shining fresh and new and serenely beautiful above the summit of Storm King Mountain across the Hudson River. I have given it a name—Karyn."

An ancient proverb tells us that there is grief enough when a child buries a parent, but that grief is monumental when a parent buries a child. The mail indicates the vast number of parents who have experienced our torment. There is no surcease from the anguish. Do we stand indicted as parents for cutting the umbilical cord too soon to let Karyn seek her place in the world? Or should we have hovered over her and held her close to our breasts, as we so wanted? Each parent who has suffered such an abysmal loss must find the answer in his or her heart. But our heart can't answer. It is shattered.

* * *

It's now 25 years later, a quarter of a century of agony, and the question still haunts us, "Who Killed Karyn?"

What disturbs us most was the failure of the Los Angeles Sheriff's police to pursue the evidence that Essee and I thought pointed directly at David Lange, who had been a friend of Cookie's. But he was best known in Hollywood as a heavy drinker, a hanger-on, and a go-fer. One day he told Cookie he was looking for an apartment and asked her if she knew of any availabilities. She inquired in her building and learned an apartment was vacant. It was on the first floor and he moved in. Cookie lived on the second floor. This juxtaposition became important on the night her body was discovered by two of her dearest friends, Mark and Marcia Goddard.

They became alarmed when their repeated phone calls to Cookie went unanswered. They decided to go to the apartment to see if she was all right. Instead, they found her body.

Lange's behavior that night made him suspect. He was in the bedroom of his apartment with a girl friend, who later told police that they "heard some sort of a commotion outside the apartment and it sounded like a lot of people were running up and down stairs." Lange, she said, ignored the excitement and did not leave the bedroom to see what was happening. She also added that a short time later someone knocked on the door. He answered it, she said, "and came right back to the bedroom and made no comment." Police suspect the unidentified caller had informed him of Karyn's death, but he chose not to appear on the scene because he already knew what had happened. That enabled him to stay clear of the authorities.

If that behavior was suspect, there also was a "confession." The police report includes a statement from a friend of Lange who reported that he told her that he was the person who killed Karyn. Essee and I pressed the sheriff's police to pursue such a revealing statement, but their response was that they had tried with no success because Lange by this time had moved into the home of his sister, Hope, and she had retained attorneys who refused to let him answer any questions.

That didn't satisfy us and I now realize what a colossal blunder I had made. Essee wanted to retain a private investigator to complement the police effort. But knowing how police generally resent the intrusion of a private eye, I thought it best to ask for their approval. "No," we were told, "That would only hamper the investigation." How wrong I was not to insist on a private eye. Instead, I called on J. Edgar Hoover, head of the FBI and a person I had met on many occasions. He wrote a warm letter, in which he urged the police to be aggressive in their investigation. Since it was not a crime that crossed state boundaries, the FBI officially could not get involved.

One who did get involved was Walter Winchell, then the reigning columnist of the day. Winchell happened to be writing his column from L.A. at the time and was determined to help solve the case. "I promise you I'll find out who did it," he told me. "And this will win a Pulitzer Prize for me." Winchell meant well, but he began to pepper the police with questions and suggestions day after day. Sheriff Walsh finally called me and pleaded, "Please get Winchell off our back. He's interfering with the investigation." Winchell, to his everlasting credit, tried mightily, but in vain.

Essee and I made countless trips from Chicago to L.A. to confer with the police and lend what assistance we could. And each time we were assured by the top man—the officer in charge changed many times with the passing years—that "this is one case we are going to crack." But the police failed for some inexplicable reason to pursue the lead.

In our desperation we sought aid from psychics as far away as London and throughout our country. One of these was the famous Peter Hurkos, a practitioner of extra sensory perception (ESP). Hurkos, now dead, confirmed our worst fears about the man we considered the prime suspect.

The police subjected Lange and another suspect, Andy Prine, to polygraph tests, which proved inconclusive. But no follow-up was done.

John Austin, in his book, *Hollywood's Unsolved Murders*, included a chapter on Karyn's death and concluded with these prophetic words: "Perhaps one day the sheriff's police will come up with a lost clue, a dropped word, a deathbed confession that will lead to the murderer of Karyn Kupcinet." That's our only hope at this late date. When the sheriff's police, in their frustration, pointed out to two embittered parents how many hundreds of murders they're working on, Essee exploded, "So our daughter is now only a statistic to you." As far as the Los Angeles sheriff's police are concerned, that's what she remains to this day.

But even though the police were unable to obtain an indictment, Essee and I think we know who murdered our daughter.

* * *

In browsing through our scrapbooks, as well as our memories, we selected a few column items to include in this chapter.

7/10/56

Pardon our parental pride, but here's a good luck wish to daughter Cookie, who bows in Drury Lane's *Picnic* Tuesday night in the role of Millie, the brat sister. Her brother Jerry's "good luck" wire from Camp Interlochen: "Typecasting!"

7/18/56

We got scooped by our daughter Cookie on Jack Eigen's TV show Monday. She revealed that Darren McGavin (with whom she was appearing in *Picnic*) and his wife have dated the stork.

7/22/58

Pardon this point of personal privilege, but here's a good luck kiss to daughter Cookie. She opens in *Chalk Garden* at Drury Lane Tuesday.

9/17/58

We personally can vouch for this one: It costs as much to get a young lady ready for college as it does to buy a star college halfback. Our daughter Cookie departs Wednesday for Pine Manor College in Wellesley, Mass. (It seems like only yesterday—oh, well!)

10/1/59

Personal to Pat O'Brien: You'll be usurping my role for the next three weeks in *Father of the Bride* at Drury Lane by playing father to daughter Cookie.

1/11/62

Memo from daughter Karyn: "Don't forget the Gertrude Berg Show switches to its new time this week. Thursday at 8:30 p.m. on CBS." (We'll be glued to the watching machine to watch you, darling daughter). . . .

And other, more objective, viewers prove it wasn't just fatherly pride speaking. After seeing Cookie perform on the West Coast in *The Miracle Worker*, the critics were enthusiastic:

Karyn Kupcinet *is* Annie, devout, patient, tough, and inspired. . . . — *Laguna Beach Post*

Karyn Kupcinet. . .gives an impact-perfect performance. . .masters a difficult role in a veteran's style. . . —*Southland News Service*

Miss Kupcinet [gave] a warm and moving performance which left small doubt of her ability as a rising actress of considerable stature. —*Variety*

And the laudatory words of the noted Lee Strasberg, with whom Cookie once studied, come to mind: "She's an excellent actress now, but someday she will be outstanding.

Cookie's career in Hollywood got off to a promising start when she was selected in 1962 as a "Deb Star," then an annual event to find outstanding young actresses. She was one of 23 that year who was depicted as a "future star." In her brief life span, Cookie appeared in 41 TV shows, including the Gertrude Berg series, "Mrs. G. Goes to College," in which she was a cast member. She also had 14 stage plays to her credit. And her most devoted fans were her grandparents, Joe and Doree Solomon, who never missed one of her performances in Chicago.

* * *

From the moment she was born on Mar. 6, 1941, Roberta Lynn Kupcinet (later changed to Karyn, but always Cookie) had "star" written all over her. She was vivacious and intelligent and with every passing year an increasingly stunning beauty who obviously possessed true acting ability.

At age 15, the Chicago critics pointed out she "stole the show" from John Mills and Cathleen Nesbitt in *Chalk Garden.*

Hollywood beckoned in 1960, when Jerry Lewis cast her in *Ladies Man.* Her grandmother accompanied her to Hollywood and they lived together at the Hollywood Regency. Then, in 1962, a young actor, Andy Prine, entered her life. He moved in with her. We heard from friends on the Coast that he wasn't the most desirable young man, but Cookie was infatuated with him.

The relationship was a stormy one. She began taking pills. She was the same captivating Cookie in public, but privately she was troubled. Essee still talked via long distance to her practically every night. But sensing trouble, she insisted Cookie come home for Thanksgiving. She would be a delightful and surprise addition to the Thanksgiving Day party we annually hosted for all the actors who were far from home.

"It's more important than the party," Essee maintained, with a sense of foreboding. Let's call her and see if we can work it out." But Cookie resisted.

On the evening of November 30, we were attending the opening of a new Sara Lee plant in suburban Deerfield. In the midst of the gala, I was summoned to the phone. It was Russ Stewart, editor of the *Sun-Times* and my dearest friend on the paper. The tone of his voice was ominous. He had been trying to reach me for hours by calling my usual haunts. How he found me in far away Deerfield is still a mystery. And his next words shattered the lives of Essee and Irv Kupcinet and our son Jerry. Cookie had been found dead in her apartment, cause unknown at the time.

I ran to find Essee who was mingling with the guests in a distant part of the new plant. She had but to look at me to know something horrible had happened. It was the first time she saw me in tears. I don't know how either of us survived that moment. Part of us didn't.

The news of Cookie's death had been flashed on television while we were attending the Sara Lee opening. And dozens of friends had rushed to our apartment, even before we arrived there.

I left immediately for L.A., accompanied by my brother Joe and my attorney, Arthur Morse. We arrived at 2 a.m., and found another dear friend, Sid Korshak, awaiting us at the airport. The following morning police asked me to identify the body. It was more than I could handle. Korshak offered to do it instead. It was Cookie.

* * *

She was found unclothed on a couch in the living room, her robe folded neatly on a chair. The killer had obviously folded the robe, because Cookie would leave clothes wherever they fell. The police figured she died on November 28. She was found on the 30th. Because semen lives only 18 hours, they could not determine whether she had been sexually assaulted. But what was determined was that the hyoid bone in her throat had been crushed, resulting in death. Police theorized that a powerful person, possibly left handed, had seized her from behind and had applied such tremendous pressure that he broke the hyoid bone.

At one point a sheriff said to us, "We've talked to about 500 people and can't find one person to say a negative thing about her. But by that same token, we don't know what the hell we're looking for."

Yet, while the passage of time moved us further and further from finding her killer, it locked us more and more suffocatingly into our unconscionable, incomprehensible loss. "If there's a God, Irv," Essee would sob, "how could He ever take the child before the parent? How could He. . . do a thing like that?"

We never spoke of it to each other, but every day we both thought of suicide. We were overwhelmed by her death. We still are. Essee was a zombie. She started to drink, and she doesn't drink. She took pills—in the morning to pick herself up, at night to put herself to sleep. She temporarily turned to Catholicism because of its teachings of life after death. . . and the subsequent belief that we could join Cookie eventually.

I couldn't help her. I could hardly help myself. It was all that I could do to awaken each day and go down to the paper. And each day, when I walked across the Wabash Avenue Bridge to my office—a bridge that ironically would bear my name—I invariably would pause, look down at the murky water, and think of throwing myself into it. "What the hell!" I thought to myself. "Why not? What does life matter anymore?"

* * *

We're still here.
What saved us?
Our son Jerry. He was a tower of strength.

And the constant love of our real friends. There were many. I remember best what Sidney Poitier said when he first phoned after hearing of the tragedy. "My heart is broken with yours."

One of the saving graces, especially for Essee, was a letter from Rose Kennedy, who wrote to us after columnist Ed Sullivan told her of Essee's turmoil. It read:

> It was with great sorrow that I heard of the sad passing of your beloved daughter. . . I know how very difficult it is for us parents to understand and to accept these tragedies, for it is unnatural for youth to precede age on the final journey to our Eternal Home. But if it is God's will to send us this heavy cross, we must trust his goodness and wisdom in respect to our lives . . . and most important, we must carry on and work for the living. We can work indefatigably for a charity and see the faces of orphans or cripples or the aged become bright with new hope because of our efforts. God created that strong bond of love between children and parents. He did not intend to have it severed. He gave us hope that we could by prayer communicate with our beloved ones even after they had left us. So pray to her when you cannot sleep, and pray when your heart is heavy and you can find no solace. I shall pray for you, too.

The letter was postmarked Palm Beach. It was dated Jan. 26, 1964. . . two months and four days after Rose Kennedy had lost her own beloved son, John Fitzgerald Kennedy.

That letter showed strength such as Essee had never known. It touched a place in her that even she did not know she had. It inspired her to go on living, as Cookie would have wanted, even though Essee wanted to die with her.

With Karyn's death, Essee decided to dedicate herself to helping youngsters interested in the performing arts. She became the moving spirit of the Academy of the Arts, a private school where high school students interested in acting, dancing and music could learn their skills, as well as receive a normal high school education. The school, similar to the one TV made famous with the series "Fame," has started many of its students on the way to personal fame. In the same vein, Essee became active in the Joe Jefferson awards, judging and rewarding excellence in Chicago theatrical productions. And with every outstanding performance by an actress, Essee had visions of Cookie.

And in our daughter's memory, we established the Karyn Kupcinet Gallery at Francis W. Parker School, from which she was graduated. There also is a Karyn Kupcinet Center at Little City, in Palatine, Illinois, a home for mentally retarded. And in Israel, we established the Karyn Kupcinet International School for Science at the famous Weizmann Institute of Science.

* * *

Our son Jerry attained maturity in a hurry. He was 19 when Karyn died. He immediately sensed his responsibility and, as I mentioned, became a tower of strength for his parents. I was constantly conscious of how difficult it was for him to be the son of a father who arrived with everyone's morning newspaper. I made sure he knew he didn't have to follow in my footsteps: "You don't have to play football, you don't have to be a newspaperman—just do whatever you do best and be yourself."

And what he did best was television. After attending Bradley University and Columbia College in Chicago, he joined the ABC station in Chicago, WLS, starting as cameraman, stage manager and then director. He was chosen to co-produce and direct the station's 30th anniversary show, for which he won a local Emmy. But after 12 years at WLS, Jerry decided to broaden his scope by going to Hollywood. The first show he directed there was the Richard Simmons series, for which he won a national Emmy. That was tantamount to hitting a home run with the bases loaded in your first time at bat. He since has directed any number of TV shows, including the Jerry Lewis telethon, "Entertainment Tonight," "That's Incredible," and was selected as one of the directors on the world-wide fundraiser "Live Aid."

But TV isn't his proudest achievement. He and his beautiful wife, Susan, are the parents of two children; Kari, 17 (named for the aunt she never knew), and 10-year-old David. Both have brought sunshine into our lives. Kari has all the qualities of Karyn, including her exuberance and her love of the theater. Essee and I, looking at her, often say maybe there is something to reincarnation. She has written, directed and starred in plays in her high school and qualified for Northwestern University's Cherub program for gifted high school students.

And David is all boy, a rough and tumbler with a brilliant mind. As I mentioned, when he turned 10 in the summer of '88, I invited him to join my group on our annual deep sea fishing week in the Bahamas. He was accompanied, of course, by his father. And I "kvelled" to see how well he conducted himself with the adults, "man to man." We have high hopes for the futures of both our grandchildren, who have filled our lives with joy.

As for me, I gradually regained the zest for a scoop, the daily deadline and the reward of putting one more column to bed.

And when I come home at night, there in our living room is a large portrait of Karyn, painted by longtime friend LeRoy Neiman. Essee and I often just sit there, in silence, "visiting" with Cookie. I know no better way to end the day.

21

The Funniest Man

Some years ago Hollywood scriptwriters, most of whom earned huge salaries, were threatening to go on strike. I asked Bob Hope what he thought about it. "I don't understand those guys," he replied. "What are they going to strike for—shorter hours and longer swimming pools?"

In times of tragedy, or simply during our problem-plagued daily lives, the ability to laugh is sometimes a matter of survival. The man who has made me laugh the most during my life is Bob Hope. He also happened to be the first celebrity I met on my beat. Mack Millar, his press agent and an old friend of mine, introduced me to Bob in '44. Bob's been my closest Hollywood friend ever since. He should be—I tell everybody I write his material.

People can't understand why Bob and I are still friends, because he constantly complains that I print all his punch lines before he gets to do them. He started the story himself and he delights in keeping it going. The truth is that he invariably tries out his gags on me before his TV shows. Then, to promote his show, I print the ones I like best—even before he is on the air.

But some of Bob's best stories have never been aired. Like the time he found himself sitting in a Paris bar next to the most delicious woman he'd ever seen. "What do you call *this?*" Bob asked, putting his hand on her left knee.

"Zat ees Christmas," she replied.

"Well, what do you call *this?*" he asked, moving his hand to her right knee.

"Zat ees New Year's."

"I'll see you between the holidays," Bob quipped.

The punch line was that "she" had more than her holidays mixed up. The gorgeous gal was a female impersonator.

Paris is just a pit stop for Hope. He's logged more miles to make people laugh than any other performer. I remember when he was in London way back in 1945 for the opening of his picture, *The Princess and the Pirate* at the Leicester Square Theatre. While riding by the theatre in a cab, he saw hundreds of people lined up waiting to purchase tickets. Instantly, he ordered the cabbie to drive back and forth in front of the theater. Each time the cab passed, Hope would stick his head out the window and shout, "You'll love that picture—it's wonderful!" Finally, the patrons recognized that the Bob Hope fan was none other than Bob Hope himself and almost started a riot in an effort to corner his cab.

That closeness to his fans is one of the things that has made Bob the Top Banana of comedy for almost six decades. A couple of years later in London, for example, he was in his Savoy Hotel suite when he received a transatlantic phone call. It was from a Jack Lindquist of Cleveland. "I don't recall the name," Hope told the operator, "but if he's calling me from Cleveland, my home town, put him on."

Thereupon, Lindquist began talking and explained he had never met Hope. He just felt like talking to him. And so talk to him Bob did.

I started out writing about Bob's overseas Christmas junkets to entertain the troops, but in short order I was accompanying him. There was the time I went with him to Korea and Japan. He sent Essee a gift—a washcloth from a geisha house with a note that. . .he and I were staying "very, very clean."

The trip to Japan was my first and I was startled by the night life on the Ginza. I had covered night clubs in this country for years, but Tokyo was an eye-opener, with bars, private clubs and ultra-fancy (and expensive) night clubs. Hope and I caroused every night into the wee hours, drinking, eating and whooping it up in general. I returned home weighing 235 pounds, the most in my life. I had gained 25 pounds in two weeks in the land of the Rising Sun, which never set for us. I immediately went into a rigid diet and exercise routine to regain my svelte figure. Hope, remarkable man that he is, didn't add an ounce.

And then there was the Alaska trip in December of 1956. The seats in the Military Air Transport Service plane that flew Hope, his troupe of traveling troubadors and your reporter from Los Angeles to Anchorage... faced backward. It was a safety measure to reduce casualties in the event of a crash. "This," quipped Hope in his finest form, "is the first time I ever backed into Alaska." Naturally, Hope had been at Uncle Sam's northernmost outpost several times previously to entertain GI's.

Before landing, Bob began to warm up by warning his troupe what to expect in the way of weather: "It will probably be so cold that Betty Furness will open the door of our plane. And when the natives tell you the temperature is 20 below zero, be sure to ask what it is *outside*."

Actually, the weather on our arrival wasn't too bitter, at least not for someone who has lived with the wintry blasts off the plains of North Dakota and Lake Michigan all his life. We were told it would be 20 below, and we were bundled in fur-lined parkas and heavy boots. It was a delightful 10 above, however. Indian summer.

Hope never traveled light. The plane we were on was only one of four which brought almost two hundred persons and 18,500 pounds of equipment to Anchorage, including entertainers, press, TV technicians, movie cameras, lights, cables, films, et al. Shows being staged for the GI's, of course, were filmed and later reduced to one hour for Hope's NBC-TV specials. Some of the biggest names in sports and show business were on our plane, from Ginger Rogers to Hedda Hopper, Mickey Mantle to Carol (Miss Universe) Morris, Les Brown and His Band of Renown to the 56-voice Purdue University Glee Club.

Chicago was mainly represented by this reporter, but I too was well equipped. In addition to cashmere longies from my everlovin' Essee (with a note: "Don't freeze your typewriter up there") and a pair of electric socks, Fanny Lazzar, the famed Evanston restaurateur, gave me a St. Christopher's medal for survival and Mayor Daley gave me a Chicago flag bearing the inscription: CHICAGO—FRIENDLIEST CITY IN THE WORLD, to plant in Anchorage. I also took a gigantic cake with a multicolored frosting of our city's skyline, from Chicago's USO Club. Last but not least, I carried a note from a reader asking: "Haven't we got enough blubber up there already?"

For one show in Alaska, Bob worked your reporter and Hollywood columnist Mike Connolly into a scene. We did all right, even without Gregg Sherwood Dodge. It was in a barroom, and Hope called it typecasting for Connolly and me. In it, I got slapped by Ginger Rogers, but I also had one line: "Gold!" I delivered it with a silver tongue.

When Bob wasn't entertaining the GI's, we spent most of our time in downtown Anchorage which, speaking of typecasting, was just one long line of bars at that time. There were about 40 or 50 on each side of the main street. Naturally, Bob and I visited every one—just to drink in the local color.

Anchorage is a beautiful place, facetiously known as the "Banana Belt" by the natives because the temperature is mild by comparison to the Alaskan interior (which at that time of year ran about 45 below). The sunrises and sunsets are unequalled. "Unfortunately," according to Hope, "they come at the same time." As a result, it's not unusual for golfers, weather permitting, to start playing at 2 a.m. with the sun shining brightly.

On the plane going home, Bob and I—probably the world's two champion sleepers—found a rival in Mickey Mantle. Bob and I always had contests when we were together to see who could fall asleep faster. The one who took longer than a couple of seconds lost. But Mantle, the most relaxed member of the troupe during the 10-hour flight, was timed sleeping nine hours and 28 minutes. When he finally roused himself, Hope was hovering over him. "Back to sleep," ordered Hope. "You've been awake for a full minute now."

As I said, I've never known a performer—and I've known quite a few—who could keep up with Bob's schedule. After one whirlwind tour, for instance, he entertained troops in Germany at breakfast and in England for brunch. Then it was the troops in Paris at dinner, after which he flew to the Azores to do a show at 3 a.m. for the GI's there (who had to be awakened for the occasion), then to Washington, D.C., for breakfast at the White House and back on the plane for California for an appearance at the Rose Bowl game (where the crew of the plane were all Bob's guests).

Hope is still following almost the same kind of schedule while in his mid-eighties. Needless to say, sometimes he works sick. I recall when he was confined to his Drake suite in Chicago for couple of days because of sunburn poisoning, which he acquired on a rare non-working cruise from Central America to New York. His doctor wanted to put him in the hospital, but there was little chance that Hope would do that. Bob compromised with his physician, went back to work, but stayed off the golf course until his seriously infected blisters were better. As he left Chicago, he said to me: "I guess I'm just not cut out for vacations." Then he was instantly back to his hectic schedule—an itinerary so demanding that once, when he alighted from a plane, Hope said that he was surprised to be greeted by a roaring crowd that was already laughing. "I'd unfastened the wrong belt."

When you travel as much as Bob, some close shaves are inevitable. Yet Bob's closest shave may have been in his own den, on one of his infrequent overnight stays at home. Among Bob's most prized possessions, next to a few thousand awards and documents and prizes which themselves could fill a small-sized home, is a German luger pistol. Bob showed it to me with a few other friends there. One warned him to be careful as he fondled the gun. "Don't worry," replied Bob. "It's not loaded"— whereupon the gun went off, missing a guest by inches and drilling a hole in the woodwork. Hope later painted a large arrow on the woodwork pointing to the bullet hole, above which are these words: DON'T WORRY—IT'S NOT LOADED.

Though it would seem he travels almost too fast for trouble to catch up with him, Bob occasionally has had his problems. The traveling itself is one, threatening his relationship with his wife Dolores. But his marriage traveled through the turbulent times and endured. . . as he has.

Bob survived the usual career goofs, too. Early in his radio career he thought he was off the air one Tuesday night when he spotted a friend and said, "Didn't it stink?" Unfortunately, that comment went coast-to-coast. When he was making the movie *Sorrowful Jones*, in which five-year-old Mary Jane Saunders played a role made famous by Shirley Temple, he had trouble concentrating because of an impossible schedule, and repeatedly blew his lines. At the end of one scene, little Mary Jane turned to director Sidney Lanfield and remarked: "Can't Mr. Hope be replaced?"

Hope acknowledges that he doesn't knock 'em dead every single time. "I've laid enough eggs in my day to have my own harbor," he once said in Egg Harbor, Wisconsin, while on a holiday with his wife and son Kelly.

Bob is human—though he acts like an indestructible machine. His four children were adopted from Evanston's famed Cradle ("I wasn't home long enough to have them myself"). Along with Bob and Dolores, stars such as Wallace Beery, Gloria Swanson, Barbara Stanwyck, Fredric March and Al Jolson had their homes immeasurably brightened by the Cradle.

Bob will lend a hand to anyone in need. Shortly after I met him, I was talking to John Garfield in the Pump Room. "Do you know why Hope is so beloved in Hollywood?" Garfield said. "I'll give you just one example. Before I left Los Angeles on this trip, I tried to contact him to get some comedy material for a USO tour. I missed him, but left word with his secretary. I never expected an answer. Then the other evening I got a long distance call from Hollywood. It was Hope. He had just gotten the message and had sent me special delivery just what I needed." And in 1955, when Hope's closest friend and agent, Charlie Yates, died, Bob was so affected that he announced his retirement from TV. But as you'd expect, he bounced back from the grief and was soon on the road again.

Bing Crosby called him Ski Nose. His folks called him Leslie, his name until he entered school in the U.S. after emigrating from England. The first day he answered the roll call in approved British fashion: "Hope, Leslie." Immediately, his school chums dubbed him "Hopelessly." And immediately, he became Bob Hope.

His kids refer to him as Pops. His associates nicknamed him "The Atomic Kid," since he wears down business managers, directors, gag men, writers and fellow actors with a literally endless supply of energy and enthusiasm. His idea of a good vacation once was to organize and rehearse a troop of performers, charter two planes and play 32 engagements in less than 30 days, from Seattle to Mobile.

The fifth of a stonemason's seven sons, Leslie Townes Hope was born in Eltham, Kent, England, and first wanted to become a boxer. His career, under the name of Packy East, lasted just a few fights: "There had to be an easier way to make a buck." He then decided to be a tap dancer and formed a team with a pal named George Byrne: "It was an easier way to make a buck, but we didn't make many."

Bob's first professional break came in Chicago. In the early 1920s, he discovered he could get audiences laughing by telling them jokes. He sensed that's where it was at for him, but when he came to my town, he literally almost starved before landing a job. For more than a month, Bob subsisted on a nickel's worth of beans a day.

Then he met agent Charlie Hogan who at that time was booking shows for small vaudeville houses. Bob cornered Hogan one day and told him of a master of ceremonies who was simply wonderful. Hogan's ears perked up.

"I am telling you about this man only because you are wonderful, too," he told Hogan.

Hogan was impressed. "Who is this fellow you are raving about and where can I find him?" he asked.

"Right in front of you."

The novel approach sold Hogan and he offered Bob a contract—$50 a week at the Stratford Theater on the South Side. For six consecutive months, he worked the Stratford. There he learned almost every trick of the trade. His Chicago success encouraged him to try New York. After appearing in a flop called Ballyhoo, he landed in the musical Roberta, and was an instant click with his rapid-fire comedy routine.

After his performance each evening, Bob would visit a nearby night club to listen to a charming young lady sing. Her name was Dolores Reade. He eventually contrived to meet Miss Reade. She asked him what he did for a living. "Who me?" he stammered. "I am a chorus boy in *Roberta*."

She visited the theater the following night hoping to spot him on the line. Instead, she discovered he was one of the stars. It didn't take long for their friendship to blossom into a romance which led to marriage, now, as I write this, in its 54th year.

Bob's next big break came from Rudy Vallee, who engaged him for a guest appearance on the air. Major Bowes was listening in that night and decided Hope was the man for the Sunday morning hour at the Capitol Theater in New York. By this time, Hollywood was sitting up and taking notice. Paramount executives got there first. They wanted him for "The Big Broadcast of 1938."

After that, everyone wanted Bob. He became not only the biggest comedian of the day—and stayed the biggest for years—but the top entertainer. They come and they go, but only a few stand the test of time. No one matches Bob for staying at the very top for more than six decades and almost four generations. I remember attending the '71 Academy Awards which Bob emceed, and thinking: "How does he keep it up?" It marked 30 years he'd been participating in the Oscars. He opened with a variation of the theme he first used in 1941: "I'm very happy to be here for my annual insult." Who would think that I'd be seeing him there, fit as a fiddle, participating three decades later?

In the pre-TV 1940s, the Awards were broadcast on radio. So some of Hope's visual gags were missed. But on TV in '45, as Buddy De Sylva approached the stage to accept the Oscar for best film, *Going My Way* (starring Bing Crosby), Hope got down on his knees as if to kowtow to greatness, then plucked a handkerchief from his pocket and began shining De Sylva's shoes. As he later stepped to the mike in Grauman's Chinese Theater, Hope looked longingly at the assembled Oscars on the nearby table, realized again that there wasn't one for him and, in mock seriousness, stuck out his tongue at them. In '46 he opened with, "I just came down again to see how long they could ignore me." In '53: "I like to be here in case they have one left over." In '58: "I just returned from Moscow. They didn't recognize me there, either." In '67: "I don't mind losing, but I hate to go home and explain to my kids how the actors I've been sneering at all year beat me out." In '68: "Welcome to the Academy Awards—or, as it's known in my house, Passover." In '70: "Welcome to the Oscars—or, as it's known in my house, 'Mission Impossible.'"

Hope on the movies is always good material. Of *A Clockwork Orange* in the early 1970s he said, "It has murder, robbery, rape, mugging and sadism. New York considers it a musical comedy." And another along the same line, "With the type of movies being made today, you can win an Oscar without getting out of bed."

One reason Bob is king is that he has always employed several of the best writers of the day and keeps every joke he's ever told on file—the largest file in show biz history.

And one of Bob's continuing targets was the most famous singer of the 1940s and 1950s (and whose "White Christmas" is still our No. 1 song), Bing Crosby. Bing had a reputation, along with Perry Como, for being the most relaxed performer in show business. Crosby was also among the few performers who had more money than Hope at the time.

Crosby was unflappable with Hope. But stuttering comic Joe Frisco could always break up Bing. Hope told me of the time Crosby took Frisco to a nightclub to catch another up-and-coming comic. Throughout the new comedian's act, Frisco simply buried himself in a huge steak, eating away and paying absolutely no attention to the performance. Finally, the comic became annoyed and began to heckle Joe from the floor. Frisco kept eating. The comic tried harder—and harder. Finally, Frisco looked up from his dinner and stopped the show by commenting: "*I g-g-g-gotta* eat. I ca-ca-can't take you on an em-em-empty stomach!"

Crosby and Hope both loved golf. While Crosby made a profession of recreation, golf was about Hope's only recreation. One time, shortly after he had retired from the ring, heavyweight champ Joe Louis was golfing with Bob. Joe had a powerful drive, but not always accurate, and his putting sometimes was terrible. "Joe," Bob said, because they always played for money, "I don't mind you giving up boxing. But, please, *never* give up golf."

Crosby had his opponents spooked, even Hope. There was the time Bob checked into the Blackstone Hotel in Chicago for a charity golf match against Bing. As soon as he got to his room, a package containing three bottles of liquor was delivered. There was no card. "This," said the suspicious Hope, sniffing one of the bottles, "is another Crosby gag. 'Lard' is trying to slip me a Mickey Finn to get me off my game." As the other members of Hope's party protested vehemently in vain, the comedian opened the bottles of expensive liquor and poured them into the toilet. A short time later, a friend phoned Hope and asked: "Did you get those three bottles of imported Scotch I sent to your suite?"

At one Academy Award ceremony, the big question was: "What happened to Bing Crosby?" He was scheduled to play a key part in the ceremonies by presenting a miniature two inch Oscar to Bob, who had never received the coveted award. After the show, the head of Paramount hosted a party in honor of Hope and Crosby. Again, Bing was a no-show. "It was a black tie affair," was the way in which Hope sympathetically explained the absence of Crosby, who detested anything formal.

Sometimes Crosby was a little too relaxed, which led to this humorous incident. Bing was driving home from a late date at four o'clock in the morning when he had an accident. When Bob told his very religious wife about the incident, she said, "Oh my, poor Bing. He must have been driving to church."

Hope had too much style to ever kid Bing about personal problems. But when it came to anything else, their friendly rivalry knew no bounds. Bob particularly chided Bing about his money (Hope is today the largest real estate tax payer in the state of California, and long before Bing died, had passed him in personal wealth). Once, when Bob was entertaining the troops in a suburb of Berlin, he was greeted with this huge sign 50 feet square placed directly behind the stage: WELCOME—TO THE WORLD'S NUMBER ONE COMEDIAN. Hope was all smiles until he saw the rest of the sign . . . a picture of Bing Crosby. To begin the show, he seized a brick and threw it at the picture, feigning anger. At intervals throughout his entire time on stage, he'd pick up another brick and throw it at Crosby's countenance. At the end, the picture was ripped entirely to shreds except for a small portion of Crosby's forehead which Bob then ripped off by hand.

Bing always seemed to even things out, though. Once he was presented with a beautiful new convertible by a media magnate. Unfortunately, the vanity license plates had been screwed up. Instead of reading BC-88—of all things, the C had mistakenly been made into an H. With perfect elan, Crosby quipped: "I don't mind your putting Bob Hope's initials on my license, but did you have to put his age on it, too?"

But, again, some of the best Hope stories come from his trips to entertain our troops. Once, during World War II, Bob and his troupe arrived in Algiers and the Nazis flew over on a bombing mission—their first raid in a week. When Hope arrived in Palermo, the same thing. And the day he arrived in Bizerte, the Nazis bombed again. Quentin Reynolds pointed this out to General Eisenhower at a press conference, saying: "General, all you've got to do is order Hope out of the area and the Nazis will stop bombing us. I'm convinced they're after him." To which Eisenhower laughingly replied: "I wouldn't be surprised, after listening to his last show."

But the one-up on Hope that gave Bob the biggest kick was years later when he was entertaining at an army camp in Tampa. A GI broke through the MPs waving a telegram and shouting, "I've got to deliver this to Mr. Hope!" He thus made his way back stage and handed Hope, surrounded by more MPs, a wire which read: PLAY IT STRAIGHT. I JUST WANT TO GET A SEAT ON THE STAGE.

Flabbergasted at first, Bob quickly gave the soldier a knowing wink and told the MPs, "Don't let this boy get away. I want to answer the wire right after the show. In fact, keep him right up on the stage with me." After the show, Hope threw his arm around the GI and congratulated him on his ingenuity. "What possessed you to do it?" asked Bob. "It's like this," the GI answered. "I bet a bunch of my barracks mates that I could get you to invite me to sit on the stage during the program."

When Gary Hart pulled out of the Democratic presidential race the second time, Hope was right on target: "Hart wanted to throw his hat back in the ring a third time, but forgot where he left it." Though a staunch Republican, Hope has spared no presidents. Despite being closer-thanthis to Vice President Agnew, he zinged him, as well as Nixon many times. And at Toots Shor's 65th birthday party, Hope got the biggest laughs when he turned to former Chief Justice Earl Warren, and exclaimed: "You were replaced by a Burger. Now you're here to pay tribute to a meatball." And: "Toots looks great for a man whose liver died 15 years ago."

Another topic close to Bob's heart is money. No one makes better investments than Hope, no one makes better deals with sponsors or networks. When in '55 he picked up a whopping $100,000 for one hour's work as MC for a General Motors show on NBC-TV, he called the fee "the greatest larceny job since Willie Sutton." Then he added, "When Sutton reads that I'm getting 100 G's for one hour, he'll probably start writing me fan letters." And when he was the guest speaker at a dinner with a bunch of biggies including the secretary of the treasury at a private luncheon, he began: "I'm so close to the secretary of the treasury that I can actually touch him, and I like that—because he's touched me so often." In the late 1960s, Hope was thinking of paying ten million dollars for the hapless Washington Senators baseball team. "It's a lot of money to pay for comedy material," he laughed. And in '76 during one of the familiar stock market declines, he wired me: "My stocks have slipped off the financial page and onto the want ad section."

As I write this, Bob has just completed his longest trip ever to entertain the troops—traveling around the world in eight days—at the age of 84. He began in the Persian Gulf, but couldn't resist stopping off in Honolulu, the Philippines, at Diego Garcia in the Indian Ocean, the aircraft carrier USS Midway, and you name it. The last stop was to be for the servicemen in the Azores, but winds of 51 knots kept Hope's C-141 Starlifter transport from landing. So he did the show by radio from the plane. "We had a lot of wind jokes ready for the Azores," he told me. "I never saw wind like that. I didn't know the presidential candidates were here."

Presidents change, but the king of comedy is still on top after 60 years.

Long live the king.

22

Frank . . . Sinatra

When Ava Gardner began dumping Frank Sinatra for a bull fighter and the great romance of his life plummeted downhill landing with a divorce in 1957, so did his career. For the first time in his meteoric career, Sinatra was depressed and desperate. The type of bookings to which he was accustomed no longer were forthcoming. His despair showed in his voice. He wasn't singing well. His popularity had dwindled. The "chairman of the board" was on the rocks.

That was the ominous picture when Frank passed through town and joined Essee and me for lunch in the Pump Room. No sooner had we exchanged greetings than Frank posed a question to me, "Do you know Harry Cohn?"

I replied that I had a fairly pleasant relationship with Cohn and only a week earlier I had contacted him about getting one or two of his stars for the Harvest Moon Festival.

"Then you've got to do me a favor," continued Frank. "He's making *From Here to Eternity* and there's a part in it—the role of Maggio—that's perfect for me. I've got to get it, and money is no object. I'll work for whatever he wants to pay me. So would you call him and put in a plug for me?"

The first thing I did when I got back to the office was to call Cohn. The head of Columbia Pictures had the reputation for being Hollywood's leading son of a bitch and a ruthless user of people. Moreover, Cohn reveled in his reputation. When a son was born to him, he was asked why he didn't name the boy after himself. Cohn answered: "And have him go through life being called Son-of-a-Bitch, Jr.?"

But as his ability to make fun of himself reveals, Harry had a warm side and, of course, didn't become the boss of a major studio by being a cream puff. I asked him if he had cast the part of Maggio yet, he said no, and I told him that I really thought Sinatra would be perfect for it—and that Sinatra thought so, too. I'm sure I was only one among dozens of friends whom Frank urged to call Cohn. Yet the bottom line is that he got the part, won an Oscar, and permanently turned his career around.

Some years later, Sinatra and Dean Martin came to play a weekend gig in a Chicago suburb—for a whopping fee. The only way the owner could come out with a small profit was by charging the unheard of sum at that time of one hundred dollars per person. The suburbanites gasped at that price and stayed away accordingly. A few days before the opening, the owner, Arnold Mazzarelli, called me in tears. "I'm gonna lose my ass on this one. The advance sale is slow because of the hundred dollar tab."

I ran the item as legitimate news. Even biggies like Sinatra and Martin can't command that size tab, I wrote. Frank read the item and literally blew a gasket. He left no doubt about his reaction when I came backstage, as I do after most performances, to visit with him. This time I was stopped at the stage door by Mickey Rudin, then Frank's attorney. "He's not seeing anybody, especially you," Mickey declared.

Such incidents come and go in Frank's mercurial life. And he apparently forgot all about the night club incident when a few years later we again were together in the Pump Room.

While we were chatting, I received a phone call at our table from the wife of an old high school friend, who was at the end of her rope. Her husband, who'd had a bad heart for about 10 years, was at death's door. As I talked to her, I noticed Sinatra listening intently, reading the one-way lines in the conversation. The minute I put down the receiver, without a word he picked it up. "Operator," said Sinatra, "I want to make a long distance call to Dr. Michael DeBakey in Texas." Before we'd finished lunch, Frank had set up an operation for my pal with the most famous heart surgeon in the world—the tab to be picked up totally by Sinatra, of course. Then he turned to me: "This is just between us, Kup."

One of Frank's dear friends was Joe E. Lewis, the night club comedian non pareil. Sinatra played Lewis's life in the movie, The Joker Is Wild, which heightened the mutual love for each other. When Lewis suffered a stroke and was in intensive care in New York's Roosevelt Hospital, Frank dropped everything and flew to New York to be at his side. A little over a week later, the beloved Joe E. died. The one notable figure missing from the funeral was . . .

Frank Sinatra.

I first met Frank way, way back in the 1940s when he was king of the bobbysoxers. He was coming to Chicago to record at CBS and we struck up a friendship through his press agent, the late George Evans. Forty-five years of knowing a man is enough time to have some stories to tell that few people have heard. Yet so much has been written about the enigma of Sinatra that there's no room for still another chapter painting Frank as all black or all white.

To understand this man who one moment softheartedly saves the life of someone he doesn't even know and the next moment attempts to capriciously crush a career, you first have to go back with me those forty-five years. Frank, only in his mid-twenties, had suddenly skyrocketed from anonymity to the very top. That's not unusual today in an era of overnight rock stars and immediate media sensations. In 1943 it wasn't that easy. Yet Frank had something more than the great set of vocal chords and good looks most other leading singers had, something probably unrivaled until Barbra Streisand—he totally understood the lyrics of a song and creatively conveyed it clear and certain. And he chose lyrics that meant something, particularly to him. His unique phrasing, his special control that always left his audience wanting more, his durable "style," all stemmed from Sinatra's grasp of a song's meaning.

I got along famously with Frank at the outset. He'd call me on my birthday. Or send a gift, like the solid gold lighter I still cherish. Or send a telegram such as the following:

DEAR KUP—TRIED TO REACH YOU BY PHONE. WILL TRY AGAIN. IF DO NOT SUCCEED, HAVE A FEW FOR ME. AND A HAPPY BIRTHDAY. MUCH LOVE AND KISSES—FRANKIE.

In fact, when Frank was elected one of Hollywood's "most uncooperative stars," I treated it with feigned shock and ran the following item:

OUR FRANKIE DO ANYTHING WRONG? *IMPOSSIBLE!*

The Sinatra I knew at that time returned from a seven-week USO tour where at one engagement in Italy he'd entertained some 30,000 GI's. The show was scheduled to start at 7 p.m., but the soldiers were so eager that they began congregating at four in the afternoon. Frank arrived a little early himself, and was told how long the GI's had been waiting.

"Let's start the show right now," Sinatra said. He was informed that it couldn't begin until the commanding general and his party arrived.

"We're not waiting for the general," snapped Sinatra, "not after these boys have been sitting out there for almost three hours." That was pure Sinatra, resisting authority. And despite the protests of the officers, Sinatra started singing right away . . . about half an hour before the general and his party arrived.

During that same stint, Frankie "adopted" 12 Italian orphans whose parents were killed as political hostages. Through the Red Cross, he provided funds to feed, clothe and educate the kids, whose ages ranged from two to six, until each was 18. A year later when Frank was coming through Chicago, he picked up the paper and read the pitiful tale of Mrs. Charles Womack, who gave birth to a daughter some 30 hours after the funeral of a five-year-old son who had died of burns. He immediately sent her a dozen roses and enclosed a huge check. A few days afterward in an engagement at the Beachcomber in Miami Beach, Frank failed to draw the anticipated crowds and almost made the owner faint when he returned a large chunk of his paycheck.

In 1971, a 13-year-old St. Louis girl lost her sight in both eyes. When Frank heard it on the news, he instantly sent her family a check to pay the hospital expenses and then got in touch with her doctor and helped find a donor to restore the girl's sight. Just a few months ago, Sinatra found a small item in the morning paper about an out-of-work laborer in Texas who had a run of bad luck, couldn't feed his family and was on the verge of suicide. Frank picked up the phone, finally reached the man (who couldn't afford a phone) and told him to express mail all the bills to him.

Sinatra's good deeds hardly need verifying, however. For every one I know of, there are doubtless dozens I don't. And these are people who can't help Frank in any way . . . except possibly the one way that no amount of success or riches can give. Shrinks, of course, might say that Frank does these things to pay his dues.

Another incident to which I was a witness occurred at the Chicago Theater long, long ago. Just before he was about to perform, two teenagers, a black and a Nisei, walked on stage with a large basket of flowers. Frank's hand shot up, stopping them in their tracks: "And what, pray tell, have we got there?" They told him, "We represent Bishop Sheil and the Catholic Youth Organization. We read what appeared in the papers about your singing for kids who had it tough. We want you to know that we're for you and what you're fighting for."

Sinatra was speechless for a few seconds, then gave an impromptu and remarkable rendition of the most appropriate song for the occasion, "The House I Live In"—a musical plea for better understanding between the races. Afterward, he rushed from the stage, shut himself in his dressing room, and burst into tears.

His relationships with people in the business are equally as mercurial. Rags Ragland, once the vaudeville partner of Phil Silvers, was a close friend of Frank's. Silvers and Ragland were about to play the Copacabana in New York. Shortly before the engagement, Ragland died. Sinatra called Silvers to express his sympathies and learned that Phil was calling off the engagement. Immediately, Sinatra said: "How would it be if I flew in and volunteered my services? It's the least I can do for Rags." Silvers was happily stunned and Sinatra made good on his promise—saving Phil a big engagement.

On the other hand, there was the time that Frank "saved" Shecky Greene's life. Shecky is one of the more talented comedians of the day. He once revealed to me, "Two nights a week I attend Alcoholics Anonymous, two nights a week Gamblers Anonymous, and the rest of the week Weight Watchers." Shecky was a man of tremendous versatility...with a drinking problem which he then couldn't control. When he was working on the movie *Tony Rome* in Florida with Frank, while under the influence, he began heckling Frank and they got into a bitter argument. Afterward, a couple of the tough guys always surrounding Sinatra called Shecky outside and began to beat the hell out of him. They were almost beating him to death, in fact, when Frank appeared and "saved his life" by saying "that's enough fellas."

Nor did Frank spare his "Rat Pack" which, at his behest, made movies, played clubs, visited the White House, tore up a few towns together and were supposedly inseparable. Angie Dickinson and several others were part of the pack for a time, but the real nucleus was Sinatra, Dean Martin, Sammy Davis, Jr., Peter Lawford and Joey Bishop. Yet in an interview in Chicago, Sammy said something critical in jest about Frank. As soon as Sinatra heard of it, he threatened to cancel Sammy out of his next picture. When Kitty Kelley wrote her scathing book, *His Way: The Unauthorized Biography of Frank Sinatra*, she had a willing source of negative material in Peter Lawford, J.F.K.'s brother-in-law. And therein lies this story: Frank added his one-time chum, Lawford, to his drop dead list after President Kennedy canceled his announced plans to vacation at Sinatra's Palm

Springs home. Frank had gone to considerable expense in preparing for a presidential visit, even installing a helicopter pad on his estate for the president's use. But the FBI and brother Bobby caused Kennedy to change his plans, allegedly because of Frank's association with mobsters, including Sam "Momo" Giancana. And to add to Sinatra's embarrassment, Kennedy further zinged him by vacationing at the Palm Springs home of another singer, Bing Crosby.

Sinatra was livid: "I was good enough to stage the show for Kennedy's inaugural, but I'm not good enough for his vacation." And Sinatra never forgave Lawford for not using his relationship to convince the President to keep the Sinatra appointment. Lawford immediately was put at the top of Frank's "drop dead" list and he never heard from Frank again. Little wonder that he was a willing "collaborator" on Kitty Kelley's book.

Incidentally, the quip at the time was that Sammy Davis, Jr., was a member of three minority groups—he's black, he's Jewish and he's a friend of Peter Lawford.

Even Dean Martin, whom Frank truly loves, hasn't escaped. I think if anything happened to Dean, Frank would find it as difficult to take as if he had lost a brother. But I do remember that in '68, before Sinatra had completed that 180-degree turn from dedicated Democrat to rabid Republican, Frank was backing Hubert Humphrey, and Martin didn't show for a Humphrey rally spearheaded by The Leader. As a result, Sinatra immediately reversed field and refused to grant Martin permission to rerun their TV Christmas special of the year before, showing the Martin and Sinatra families spending the holidays together. Later, Frank and Dean patched it up. When Martin recently played Chicago, Frank made sure the occasion would be a total success by flying in for a surprise appearance and bought at least a hundred tickets for "friends."

In March of 1988 the Rat Pack—Frank, Dean Martin and Sammy Davis, Jr.—reunited and played the Chicago Theater. On opening night, Martin was far off his form and slowed the show considerably. Shouting later was heard in their dressing room and my sources reported that Frank, a perfectionist, criticized Martin for his performance. I reported that Martin opened the show by bringing it to a sudden stop.

The item apparently incensed Frank, who called me on the phone from his suite in the Ambassador East and declared, "Stop writing that bullshit. There was no argument and we love each other. Whatever happened to our friendship?" Click.

As I put down the phone, I thought to myself. Here I've printed maybe five hundred complimentary items about Frank and his super performances. I went to bat for him in the column and on TV, criticizing parts of Kitty Kelley's biography about him. I defended him innumerable times when I thought my fellow members of the press were clobbering him unnecessarily.

Never once did he pick up the phone and say thank you. Nor did I expect him to. I was merely doing my job as best I could. Yet one or two items in the column that he considered negative could rupture our friendship. Not that Sinatra was unique in that regard. It's common for many stars to do the same. Yet Frank does it in a way that is unique. All in a day's work, I guess.

One of Sinatra's "hot spots" is his background. As far back as '48, for example, Frank leaped into the anti-Communist fight with both tonsils, wiring Secretary of State George Marshall that he'd assembled a group of Americans of Italian descent to combat the Red threat in Italy. Among them were Joe DiMaggio, Arturo Toscanini, writer Paul Gallico, and director Frank Capra. And in 1971, he waged a one-man campaign against the making of the movie, *The Godfather*. It was Sinatra's influence that resulted in Vic Damone's withdrawing from the cast of what turned out to be the most successful picture of the year. And when *Godfather* author Mario Puzo tried to introduce himself to Frank at Chasen's restaurant one night, Frank not only refused to acknowledge the introduction but gave Puzo a verbal beating "for writing such crap about Italian Americans." At least it was only verbal and Frank didn't have to "save" Mario's life as he'd "saved" Shecky Greene's.

When the House Select Committee wanted to talk to him in '72, Sinatra said they didn't even have to send him a subpoena—he'd appear voluntarily to refute the charges by convicted hoodlum Joseph Barboza that Frank once was "a front for the mob." A week later, when Frank's attorney learned that they wanted to discuss other related matters as well, Sinatra did an about-face, ducked out and went overseas.

The syndicate enjoyed "adopting" one of their boys when he made it big. So they naturally wined and dined Frank. Sinatra in turn felt they were part of his roots. As a youth, Sinatra idolized members of the mob, as did many young Italians. But later in life, he realized it was injurious to his career and he tried to cut those ties. As he discovered, it was not easy to do.

Sinatra, in applying for a Nevada license as a casino owner, appeared before the state's gaming commision and was asked if he ever permitted Sam Giancana, then on the state's black list, to visit at Frank's Cal-Neva Lodge. Sinatra looked the commissioners straight in the eye and declared he never saw Giancana on the grounds. That gave Essee and me a chuckle. We just happened to be at Cal-Neva at the same time Giancana was there with his ever-lovin', singer Phyllis McGuire, and we dined at an adjoining table.

Phyllis McGuire had a deep hatred for Sinatra because she felt Frank had turned on Sam Giancana, her lover. Once on my TV show, Phyllis was a guest along with Buddy Rich and Johnny Carson. Johnny, by the way, was delightful and proved to be as good a guest as he is a host, with a tremendous grasp of a number of "heavy" subjects which he seldom discusses on his own program. But the exciting moment came when the inevitable subject of Sinatra was raised. Buddy, then one of Frank's closest friends, defended him. Phyllis, because of Frank's treatment of Giancana, verbally blasted Frank as seldom is done on a TV talk show. In a last-ditch effort to defend The Leader, Buddy told of all the wonderful things Sinatra had done without publicity. Phyllis shot back: "If he wants to keep them quiet, how come they always turn up in the newspaper?" The minute they began the argument, Carson sat mute, apparently enjoying the verbal fireworks.

The only exemptions to Sinatra's storms are his daughters. Son Frankie, Jr., hasn't had an easy time with Frank as a father. But when Robert Wagner broke off his romance with daughter Tina, Frank dropped everything and took her on an extended tour of Europe. And, of course, the sun rises and sets on daughter Nancy "with the laughing face."

Frank's wives and lovers get a different treatment. When his romance with Ava was getting shaky, Frank brought her to our house for dinner, greeting Essee with a big kiss. But the dinner was strained—you could tell Ava wasn't giving Frank any big kisses. I filed the first story on their breakup:

> Miss Gardner, as her Hollywood friends well know, is insecure, and she has been trying to overcome her insecurity with regular visits to a psychiatrist. It is an insecurity that takes as one of its shapes a constant demanding of proof of love. Ava, throughout her romance with Frank, is forever challenging him to prove his love for her. While she was in London filming *The Knights of the Round Table*, she demanded that he fly there to be at her side. When she was filming *Mogambo* in Africa, she wanted him at her side. When she visited Spain, she demanded he fly to her again. These were challenges she issued, according to the psychiatrist, to Sinatra to constantly prove his love.
>
> In the early days of their romance, when Ava was still the reigning queen of the films and Frank was trying for a comeback, he readily accepted the challenges—he did the chasing on the merry-go-round of love. But with his

splendid performance in *From Here To Eternity*, Sinatra emerged as a big star himself. With this new success, he was no longer able to do the chasing. The constant proof she demanded of his love was not forthcoming. There were two careers in their family. The end of their marriage was in sight when he failed to meet the plane on which Ava arrived from overseas, and she purposely stayed away from his opening at the Riviera Nightclub in New York.

Interestingly but not surprisingly, Ava's career and life began to go slowly but inexorably downhill afterward. On the other hand, Sinatra has taken all the blows, survived and prospered. In 1961, Joe DiMaggio was carrying a big torch for Marilyn Monroe. Marilyn welcomed Joe at her side during one of her many pill-induced illnesses, but told him no about reconciliation. DiMag finally decided to file for divorce and I learned that the Los Angeles County grand jury was thinking of indicting Sinatra and DiMaggio as well as a couple of private detectives "for allegedly conspiring to break into and enter an apartment" while seeking evidence against M.M. for DiMag's divorce suit. Yet guess who was sweeping Marilyn off her feet two months later? None other than Ol' Blue Eyes.

The romance with Marilyn was brief, with Frank moving on and leaving her to Bobby Kennedy. Sinatra's next marriage was to Mia Farrow, young enough to be his very young daughter. Frank swept Mia off her feet, then dumped her. She arduously attempted a reconciliation with him and even went down to the Fontainbleu Hotel in Miami Beach where he was appearing to plead for him to take her back. His answer?

He hummed her a few bars of "I Get Along Without You Very Well."

I was the one lucky enough to get the scoop on the next Sinatra marriage, to Barbara Marx, tipping it in the column of May 20, 1976, when Frank presented her with a whopping diamond ring between shows at the Sabre Room in Chicago. Typically, Frank's official announcement of the wedding caught Barbara herself by surprise. After she received the ring, I asked her: "Does that mean you're engaged?"

"Don't ask me, ask Frank," she replied. I went with the story.

When Frank hosted a dinner the night before the marriage, a stranger was spotted mingling among the guests. Sinatra immediately signaled for Jilly Rizzo. "Looks like we've got a gate-crasher over there," Sinatra said, pointing to the stranger. "Get rid of him." Jilly sidled up to the party and started to give him the bum's rush. "Hold on!" exclaimed the man. "If you kick me out, there won't be a wedding." The gate-crasher was California Judge Tom Walsworth, who had been invited to perform the ceremony.

There's one facet of the Sinatra saga that never has been mentioned in the press. That's the bitter feeling between first lady Nancy Reagan and Sinatra's wife, the blonde and beautiful Barbara. Frank endeared himself to President Reagan and Nancy and for a time he was the darling of the White House. During this period, Nancy and Frank were especially close, much to Barbara's annoyance. At many White House social functions, Frank was placed next to Nancy, while Barbara was allocated a seat "out in left field." This even happened at the annual New Year's Eve party hosted by Walter Annenberg at his Palm Springs estate. This time Barbara threatened to leave. Only Frank's entreaties kept her at the party. Whether the Nancy-Barbara bitterness was a factor, I don't know, but Frank's relationship with the White House eventually turned cold.

Frank hates growing older and abjectly fears death. He has retired and un-retired more than anyone in show business. I remember in '71 he called me and said, "I'm getting out while I'm ahead." That lasted about a month. Now, borrowing a leaf from President Reagan, Frank uses teleprompters (not visible) to help him remember the lyrics to his songs. He has gained weight, his hair isn't his own. And though the phrasing and timing are still perfect, the voice is not the same.

But the temperament *is* the same. Sinatra has not mellowed. The two sides of him are still at war, sometimes with each other, always with those around him. He does it his. . . way.

23

The TV Show

Early in October of 1964, the following article was featured in *The New York Times:*

M'NAMARA WARNS
ON A-BOMB SPREAD
Says 'Tens of Nations' Will
Have Nuclear Capability
Within 10 to 20 Years

Washington, Oct. 6—The Pentagon made public today the transcript of an interview in which Secretary of Defense Robert S. McNamara forecast that in 10 to 20 years "tens of nations" would be capable of having usable nuclear weapons.

Not only will the cost of production go down dramatically, but the cost of the delivery systems, such as planes and missiles, will also go down, the Defense Secretary predicted.

The proliferation of nuclear weapons, Mr. McNamara said, "is one of the most important problem's [sic] we face."

The interview was broadcast Saturday by station WKBK-TV [sic] in Chicago. Irv Kupcinet, who conducts a regular interview program, was the interviewer.

That was one of many headlines that Kup's Show made in its 27 years

on the tube. I can't take all the credit—Essee was especially helpful in as-
sembling guests and putting them in the proper mood in the "green"
room. The weekly program enabled me to engage in what we called "The
Lively Art of Conversation" with presidents and kings, Nobel Prize winners and revolutionaries, movie stars and literary giants. Moreover, the
show's 27-year life span represents a real reflection (and often an omen) of
notable events, people and ideas in the 1960s, 1970s and first half of the
1980s. Names like John Lennon and Yoko Ono (whose appearance on the
show in May of 1972 catalyzed the campaign to allow them to remain in
the United States), Warren Beatty, Kate Webb (the UPI correspondent
who was imprisoned in North Vietnam), Margaret Mead, Norman Rockwell, Ed Murrow, Alger Hiss, Malcolm X, Milton Friedman—these represent just a fraction of the variety of views and "eras" the program covered.

A few individuals carried the show all by themselves. Mel Brooks certainly needed no help. Nor did Steve Martin, who broke me up with his
story of accepting an invitation to visit Terre Haute, Indiana, after describing it as "the most nowhere city in America." They gave the wild and
crazy Martin the red carpet treatment, and he thus rescinded his rap on
Terre Haute. . . but not until he'd been taken on a tour of one of the city's
largest firms—a fertilizer plant. "Any city that can make so much shit
can't be all bad," he deadpanned.

Robert Redford was his ever-charismatic self, with a prepossessing
concern for saving the environment. He not only was a great guest, but
he helped get other guests from time to time. I remember in February of
1976, after checking into my New York hotel, a palpitating telephone operator rang the room and said, "Robert Redford is trying to reach you!
Please put the call through right away! I want to hear his voice—even if
it's just for one second." A couple of minutes later, Redford was on the
phone from Warner Bros.' studio, where he was finishing *All The President's
Men*. But he wasn't the least bit interested in talking about the film.

"I'm calling for a favor," Redford said.

"You name it."

Bob then outlined his involvement in opposing unsafe nuclear
plants. "You heard about Robert Pollard, who just resigned his job as
safety official in protest against an unsafe nuclear plant in New York?"
asked the actor. "Well, I'm working with the Union of Concerned Scientists to bring this to the public's attention. We want a moratorium on nuclear plants until their safety is assured. And I'd like to arrange for Pollard
to appear on your show."

"Fine. But what about *All The President's Men?*"

"That can wait a day or two," said Redford. "This can't. How important is a movie compared to the safety of a nuclear plant?"

Pollard, by the way, was a good guest...but there's only one Robert Redford.

And, of course, only one Marlon Brando and Muhammad Ali. Each made some interesting stipulations before he would appear on the show.

Both appeared several times. In April of 1963, Brando made news by declaring that he was going to retire from movies in two years. The scoop turned out to be an *Oops!*, of course, but happily so—Brando is probably unsurpassed as an actor. A year later I did a show originating in Hollywood where Marlon appeared and stipulated that he be allowed to devote a certain amount of time to the mistreatment of the American Indian, his pet interest, and I wholeheartedly agreed. Unfortunately, his efforts on behalf of the Indians also haven't materialized the way he'd hoped.

An interesting sidelight came when Brando corrected an error about his background. Lee Strasberg was given credit for first teaching Marlon his profession. "Absolutely erroneous," Brando said. "It was Stella Adler. She taught me all I know. She took me under her wing and was responsible for any acting ability I had. Lee Strasberg? I visited his classes for only one reason—to meet pretty girls." Marlon was watching a syndicated version of our show in Hollywood one afternoon in '76, picked up the phone and almost floored my secretary, Stella Foster, when he said, "Just called to tell Kup I'm watching his show out here and enjoying it immensely." At first, Stella didn't believe it was Brando. She thought it was one of the kibitzers who disguise their identities to throw me off balance. But Brando it was.

One of Ali's stipulations was also a scoop of sorts. Mine was the first show on which he insisted beforehand on publicly being called Muhammad Ali instead of Cassius Clay. On a previous visit to the show, the problem was money, not his name. Cassius came up to me before the show, and said I had to pay him three hundred dollars. I replied that the purpose of the show was to give people a chance to air their views and espouse their causes, and for that reason we had never paid anyone.

"Well, there's always a first time," he answered, "and this is it."

I didn't want to discuss it in front of the other guests, so I asked him to step out to the hall with me where the discussion became more and more heated. I told him that I hadn't paid former presidents of the United States and Nobel Prize winners, so why did he deserve a fee? Clay wouldn't budge. "Three hundred dollars or I don't go on," he demanded. Finally, I gave in. A good deal of advance publicity had promised our viewers that they'd see Cassius Clay/Muhammad Ali, and I didn't want to let them down. So Clay/Ali became the first and only guest on Kup's Show that we paid to appear.

Ali was a scintillating guest, needless to say, though all of his clever remarks were not of his own making. He got ample assistance from other sources. Yet as with all great humorists (he could have been one if he hadn't taken a more serious turn), his delivery was the key. Essee and I were saddened in recent years when that rat-a-tat-tat poetry became muffled and stumbling, the victim of Parkinson's Disease and the ravages of the perennial "one more fight."

Clay/Ali's name change was among the first signs of the division among black militants, which occasioned two of the show's hottest arguments. One was between playwright Lorraine Hansberry and producer Otto Preminger, when she came close to actually hitting him because of his portrayal of blacks in *Porgy and Bess*. The other was between Malcolm X and, of all people...your usually imperturbable moderator.

Kup's Show was sympathetic to the cause of blacks and was among the first to afford them a TV outlet, a fact that Reverend Jesse Jackson often substantiates. I had witnessed the number of indignities heaped on blacks, even on top performers like Lena Horne, Harry Belafonte, Sammy Davis, Jr., Ethel Waters and others too numerous to mention.

When Elijah Muhammad, leader of the Black Muslims, appeared on the scene, I was determined to get him on TV to expose his theory of black separatism and his theory that "the white man is the devil." I finally managed to get his approval for an appearance, but it would have to be at his huge South Side mansion. Under no circumstances would he go to the studio.

He lived like a monarch, with a retinue of servants and numerous bodyguards, known as the Fruit of Islam. Muhammad was in his sixties at the time, but he spoke like a much older man, slow and deliberate, low key and with poor command of the language. We engaged in a lively exchange over his policy of black separatism and his "white man is the devil" philosophy. But on other issues he was progressive. He forebade use of alcohol or drugs, he encouraged blacks to start their own businesses and he insisted his female members dress in long white gowns to emphasize their virginity. Minister Louis Farrakhan, the outrageous anti-Semite of today, was and is a disciple of Elijah Muhammad's teachings.

Another disciple of Elijah Muhammad was Malcolm X, who made a number of appearances on my show. In his first visit, he espoused vicious anti-white propaganda, which led to a bitter exchange between us. Finally I was so angy that I exclaimed: "I'm a better black than you are." But with each succeeding visit, Malcolm X mellowed, until he finally broke from the Black Muslims. Shortly before his last appearance on my show, Malcolm made a pilgrimage to Mecca, holiest of the holy shrines for Moslems. There, as he later recounted, he saw blacks, browns and whites in close association. He came full cycle and now believed, as he told our audience, that "black separatism" was not the answer and that black and white must live together in friendship.

It was on this show that Malcolm told me of the threats on his life for changing his views. And he made the frightening prediction that he was marked for assassination by his Muslim enemies.

Two weeks later, on Feb. 21, 1965, he was assassinated while delivering a speech in New York. Farrakhan was questioned about the murder, but there was no evidence to link him to the plot.

Mayor Harold Washington of Chicago and Jesse Jackson also had problems with how to deal with Farrakhan. Washington sidestepped the issue, while Jesse went back and forth—but he'd done that more than once with me when I'd questioned him both on the show and off. In late 1979, for instance, the Reverend Jackson took a cheap shot at Israel's Menachem Begin, calling him a racist for refusing to see him. Jesse knew the real reason Begin declined a meeting was because of Jackson's pro-PLO posture.

Shortly thereafter, the Reverend Jackson named this reporter, along with colleague Roger Simon, the *Tribune's* Bob Greene, and Channel 2's Walter Jacobson as "Jewish members of the media" who criticized his Middle East journey. But the following Sunday, Jackson was on the telephone, assuring me that he had no intention of disrupting our long relationship. For the record, (1) We never criticized Jackson's visit to the Middle East, and we salute anyone who can make a contribution to the possibility of its peace, (2) We *had* corrected a number of Jackson's erroneous statements about the Middle East, which indicated his lack of knowledge on the nuances or the complicated situation, and (3) His attack on only "Jewish members of the media," while ignoring the black newsmen who had criticized his trip, smacked of racism.

More memorable than any individuals on the program, though, were the groupings and interactions of the guests. One of the most inspiring was when we had the Reverend Martin Luther King, Jr., Percy Julian and Isaac Stern. One of the funniest of our shows had to be when Danny Kaye got together with Victor Borge, Pat O'Brien and Phil Foster. A unique program was a show featuring the four Eisenhower brothers. Dwight, who was ex-president at the time, came to Chicago to make a speech and was joined by the three other Eisenhower brothers. I in turn arranged to tape the show with all of them from the hotel where Ike was speaking. He was obviously the major domo of the family, but by far the most intelligent of the quartet was Dr. Milton Eisenhower, who had been a college president (as had Ike). One of the two lesser Eisenhowers, not incidentally, was a candidate for a minor county office, for which he later was defeated. What I found most delightful about this particular program was the warm relationship among the four brothers, with due deference to the former president of the United States. But I couldn't help but note that brother Milton spoke eloquently, while Ike still garbled his syntax.

The man Dwight Eisenhower twice defeated for president, Adlai Stevenson, was a member of still another singular set which included astronomer Harlow Shapley, Sir Julian Huxley and Sir Charles Darwin. The program created such a stir in academic circles that an entire transcript of the show was printed in book form by the University of Chicago Press. It was the highest level of conversation I was ever fortunate enough to bring to my audience.

Adlai, of course, was the master of the bon mot. I asked him about a study by Sheldon Cherney which was done on the use of humor by presidential candidates in which it was found that Stevenson employed humor in 84 percent of his speeches, compared to 78 percent by Franklin Delano Roosevelt, 67 percent by Harry Truman, 54 percent by Wendell Wilkie, 46 percent by Eisenhower and only 29 percent by Tom Dewey. Stevenson's comment: "I wish Cherney would conduct a study to determine if they were laughing *with* me—or *at* me."

But Adlai's finest moment on the show was during an ardent discussion about progress. Sir Julian stated that he thought manmade machines eventually would best man, and added that the day wasn't too far off when a machine would be able to write poetry. Sir Charles quickly replied, "Yes, but the type of poetry the machine will write will be appreciated only by another machine!" And when the conversation turned to the college curriculum, Sir Julian kiddingly predicted that a good course might be pickpocketing. "Oh, but they teach that already," interjected Stevenson. "They call it business and finance."

The Darwins, Huxleys, Stevensons and Eisenhowers were class acts. Often, however, the interaction between guests was more visceral. I enjoyed the heated arguments as much as the high-level humor and philosophizing, and frequently found it surprising who came out on top. Jimmy Hoffa, for example, got the best of no less a mind than Mortimer Adler.

Adler spoke in lofty, philosophical terms. Hoffa was down to earth in expressing his differences with Adler. His concern for the bread-and butter issues made him a clear winner that day.

And in another appearance on the show, we asked Hoffa about newspaper stories that indicated he'd sailed through his four years, nine months and sixteen days at the Lewisburg, Pennsylvania, jail without incident. "Don't let anyone kid you," Hoffa shot back. "Every person in jail is doing *hard* time," and then went into some prison stories that made everyone's hair stand on end.

Kup's Show also was the catalyst for a bitter split in the ranks of women's lib. In February of 1972, I thought Betty Friedan and Gloria Steinem were going to pull out each other's hair. Gloria always created tension on the show—I recall one time when she and John Wayne committed conversational mayhem—but with Betty the fur really flew after she charged Steinem with "ripping off the women's movement for private profit." Not incidentally, the show with Wayne had taken place just a month before and the angriest point between Duke and Gloria was Wayne's attacking the women's movement and Friedan in particular, whom Gloria then stoutly defended. But Gloria had all she could do to defend herself against Friedan who got the last word, castigating Bella Abzug along with Steinem, but adding that a rapprochement with Abzug was possible—but not with "female chauvinist" Gloria!

In a lighter vein, I once invited exiled King Peter of Yugoslavia and the celebrated fan dancer, Sally Rand, with other guests. Before Peter and Sally arrived, I sat around with the other guests, wondering how to address King Peter. Was it Your Highness, Your excellency, or what? The King arrived a few minutes before Sally and she threw courtesy to the wind by walking up to him, shaking his hand and exclaiming, "Hi ya, King."

Sally gave an even bigger shock in August of 1964 to author Irving Shulman, biographer of Jean Harlow. Irving began talking about Paul Bern, the movie exec who was Jean's second husband and had committed suicide, according to Shulman, because he couldn't consummate the marriage. This apparently infuriated Sally, who gave the author a dirty look and exclaimed, "You're wrong about Bern." Shulman, who didn't like to be questioned or corrected, demanded, "And how would you know?" Sally didn't flinch as she replied, "Because I dated him. . .and slept with him."

The next day, *Variety* headlined the story FAN DANCER SALLY RAND FANS UP A CONFESSIONAL ON 'HARLOW' TELEPANEL and went on:

Sally Rand must have shocked the viewership out of a half-sleep at 1:30 a.m. Sunday morning when she testified to having slept with the late director, Paul Bern. Not only was the intimate confession startling in itself, it also pointedly refuted Shulman's allegation in the book that Bern committed suicide after his marriage to Jean Harlow because he was unable to consummate it.

When that point was made about Bern on "Kup's Show," Miss Rand blurted out suddenly, "That's not so. I know because I. . .dated him." Then realizing what she had said, she added she was 19 at the time and anxious for experience and deeply attached to Bern, who had been her mentor. She said that there was nothing wrong with him and that she knew that a number of other actresses could have vouched for that too.

Another humorous moment on the show occurred when Ann Landers, the celebrated advice columnist, was scheduled as a counterpoint for porn star Linda Lovelace, who then was in the news because of her performance of oral sex in the movie, *Deep Throat*. At that time Ann admittedly was a square about unusual sex and had no idea what *Deep Throat* was about. I doubt that fellatio was in her vocabulary. But to be safe on such treacherous ground, she decided to contact her daughter Margo, who also had been a Chicago columnist and now is married to actor Ken Howard.

Margo filled in the blank spaces for a startled Landers. Now fully prepared, Ann wasted no time once the cameras started rolling. She looked directly into the camera and explained for the audience exactly what Linda did in the movie. I almost fell out of my seat. That segment proved to be one of the most discussed of our many programs.

There were innumerable great arguments on the show—too many to name—but it would be an omission not to mention the time Bob Hope got on the subject of Vietnam. Hope, a hawk partly by political persuasion and mostly because of his love of American fighting men, had employed British actor Robert Morley in more than one of his movies and TV shows. The two had gotten on quite well, no doubt because they hadn't discussed Vietnam. But when Morley, a dove, joined Bob on the show and strongly espoused his views on Nam, Bob dropped a barrage of verbal bombs on Robert which made even Hope's joke-a-second delivery pale in comparison. All that a weary Morley could say to me after the show was, "Well, I guess I'll never get a job from Bob Hope again."

And last, but certainly not least, there was William Buckley. . .who would argue about anything with anybody. I seldom agreed with him, but he was always a wonderful guest and I'm frankly proud that we were the first to invite him on this kind of show when he was just starting his *National Review*.

You might wonder, with such frequently contrapuntal pairings, whether anyone walked off the show. There were a few. Only one time did I dis-invite someone. Hjalmar Schacht, the German financial wizard who first supported Adolf Hitler and later broke with him, was invited to appear in 1964. He wanted to be accompanied by an "aide," and stipulated that there should be no "uninhibited conversation"—which meant nothing about his association with Der Fuhrer. I told him to forget it.

In 1970, actress Sharon Farrell cordially asked us at the taping session if she could leave after one hour because she didn't feel she could cope with the conversation dealing with sexual permissiveness and religion and "besides, I haven't had a chance to mention my movie." I bid her adieu. On the "Johnny Carson Show" shortly after, she said she walked off the program "after two hours because I was ill." Next, she long-distanced Hank Grant of the *Hollywood Reporter* and said she "stalked off the show and would sue Irv Kupcinet if he syndicated the program." Quaking in my boots, I allowed it to be syndicated anyway.

And then there was Shere Hite, author of the recent book *Women and Love: A Cultural Revolution in Progress*. She walked off many years ago because she didn't like the way I was questioning her. "You're getting too personal," she exclaimed, and left the set in a huff. What she meant by "too personal" was that I wanted an actual conversation about ideas and not a plug for her book every 30 seconds.

Raquel Welch threatened to walk out. One of the actresses who is as beautiful off-screen as on, she is also one of the many actresses who can be childishly temperamental. When she strolled into the studio, there were a dozen newspapermen and TV people waiting for her. Her reaction? She blew up. "If you don't get them out of my way, get rid of every one of them, I will not do the show!" Fortunately, Essee was at my side and hustled Raquel into the makeup room where she was able to calm her down. On the show, Raquel was so sweet she made Pam Dawber and Barbara Mandrell look like Cagney and Lacey.

It wasn't the first time that I'd known Raquel to have a similar problem. In July of 1976, there was a mysterious cancellation of her engagement at the Condesa Del Mar, a supper club in Alsip, Illinois. However, it was no mystery to Steve Gianakis, owner of the club. "I canceled her, she didn't cancel us," he told me. According to Gianakis, busty Raquel was a bust at the box office. "We sold only thirty reservations at $30 a head for her engagement, so I called her agent and said she'd be embarrassed if she came here. And that was that." The Condesa Del Mar did fine with their next engagement, Wayne Newton, by the way. Raquel also was linked romantically with "Broadway Joe" Namath in the early 1970s, and supposedly dropped him. The truth is that Namath didn't request a second date with Raquel after escorting her to the Academy Awards. Shortly before, Raquel was asked what she thought about some of the fine actresses of the day who were not as well endowed as she. "I'm not about to exchange my equipment," meowed Raquel, "for what Sandy Dennis has." All Ms. Dennis has, of course, is talent. And it's not hard to understand, therefore, what the talented James Mason said about Raquel after appearing in a movie with her: "She's the most inconsiderate actress I've ever had the displeasure of working with."

And then there was Abbie Hoffman.

Rarely, there were subjects we couldn't or wouldn't discuss for legal reasons. One was the Chicago Seven Conspiracy Trial which was ongoing in Chicago when I invited Abbie Hoffman on the show in February of 1970. He had just written a book, *Woodstock Nation*, which had some revolutionary ideas that I wanted to talk about. Once on the show, though, he instead started to express his feelings about Judge Julius Hoffman, before whom he was appearing. This could have prejudiced the trial and I stopped him short.

I told him flatly that we couldn't discuss the trial, and he responded in that case he wasn't going to stay on the show. Before leaving, though, Abbie decided to have a cigarette. It wasn't one of your name brands. He lit it, took a big drag, then passed it around to the other members of the panel—Arlo Guthrie and George Carlin. They each took a drag, and then returned the joint to Abbie, who finished it, stood up and left.

I had Abbie and some of the other members of the "Chicago Seven" on the show some years later. They had undergone quite a change. Jerry Rubin, whose motto once was not to trust anyone *over* thirty, now said he didn't trust anyone *under* thirty. Tom Hayden, of course, had married Jane Fonda and was following a political career. Lee Weiner was in education. And so the world turns.

With guests like these, the lively art of conversation prospered. The one fear that I always had was that people *wouldn't* talk. Silence reigned only twice during the show's tenure. The first time was when Alfred Hitchcock was on with Jack Paar. Hitch was a good friend and I expected some droll and incisive conversation from him. Paar had incredible emotional swings—Essee says he breaks into tears over a bad weather report. Paar, of course, had the "Johnny Carson Show" of its day and walked off when NBC blipped the phrase "water closet" out of one tape. He chose two columnists to "grill" him on the air about that. Hy Gardner of the *New York Herald Tribune* was one, I was the other. It turned out that Jack didn't really want to be grilled at all, and he cooled toward me considerably after the interview. Later on, I wrote one of my tongue-in-cheek "Damon Runyon" columns about a headline-making show he did in Berlin, as follows:

In Mike Fish's the other night, members of the Damon Runyon set were discussing the refusal of NBC-TV's "Meet The Press" to schedule Jack Paar for a guest appearance. "I do not think Paar should be angry on account he cannot get on 'Meet The Press,' " exclaimed Society Kid Hogan. "He would be much better on a show called 'To Tell The Truth.' I would like to see the real Jack Paar stand up."

"You've got the wrong show for Paar," offered Morose Artie. "He should by all means appear on 'What's My Line?' Nobody seems to know the answer to that one."

"I do not wish to argue with my closest chums," cut in Silk Hat Harry, "but to me the show for Paar is 'I've Got A Secret.' He could tell the audience his secret is that it is not so tense in Berlin and what's all the excitement about, anyhow?"

Five-Star Final could hold back no longer. "The trouble with you guys is you don't understand Paar. If he wants to guest on a show, the one for him is 'Yout' Wants To Know.' He is very good with the yout's of our nation on account he has nice, easy answers for everything."

When Paar read the column, he released a vitriolic outburst against me on his show. Hugh Downs, formerly a Chicago broadcaster and Paar's sidekick on the show, criticized Jack openly for his personal attack on me. We Midwest boys stick together. Seriously, though, Downs, who went on to a distinguished career, tried to restrain Jack on many occasions and was about the only one who sometimes could do it.

With the passage of time, though, Paar warmed up and was more than happy to be on my show. Little did I know that Hitchcock was very *un*happy to appear... with Paar. Alfred didn't say a single word on the show. I kept trying to draw out the famed director in every way I knew how. But *nothing.* He wouldn't comment on *anything* Paar said. He wouldn't answer any questions I asked him directly. It was embarrassing as hell. Finally, during a commercial break I motioned Alfred aside. "Why aren't you *saying* anything?" I implored.

Hitch looked up at me and answered: "I *detest* that man."

And didn't say a word for the rest of the show, either.

But, at least, Paar was willing to talk. There was *one* show I did where *no one* was willing to talk.

I had assembled what I thought was the most distinguished panel of newsmen possible. There was Walter Cronkite, the patriarch of television news, Walter Winchell, the god of gossip columning, and Edward R. Murrow, the most famous journalist of the day. And for good measure, they were joined by none other than the leading educator of the day, University of Chicago President Robert Maynard Hutchins.

This had to be the fastest group of talkers ever. But they also were an impish lot and, beforehand, decided to play a little joke on me.

I began what I thought was going to be one of the best shows ever by throwing out a powder puff question just to get the conversation rolling. Then I sat back and relaxed. This was going to be great.

But no one talked. *No one said a single word.*

Rattled, I turned to Cronkite who, probably for the first time in his life, didn't have an opinion. I posed the question a different way. He *grunted.*

I turned to Ed Murrow and did the same. "I don't know," he said.

I went to Winchell. I'd known Walter longer than any of them. He'd save me. He could do 20 non-stop minutes *without* a question. "No comment," he commented.

I looked at Hutchins—but by that time I began to realize it was a gag. Before Hutchins could refuse to say anything, Murrow burst out laughing and related they had entered into a conspiracy of silence, "just to have some fun at your expense." Laugh, I thought I'd die. I felt like I'd aged 10 years and my forehead was covered with "flop sweat." After that first couple of torturous minutes, though, it did indeed turn out to be a great show, with this unparalleled quartet talking more in an hour and a half—and saying much more—than a lot of politicians do in an entire career.

However, when it came to non-stop talking, no one could outdo Vice President Hubert Humphrey. He was on the show a number of times and my main task was to make sure the *other* guests could get a word in edgewise. I recall during one program, with just a few minutes left, I turned to him and laughingly said: "Hubert, I have time for one more question . . . but not time for one of your answers."

Because of the free swinging nature of the show, and the late hour at which we were on, things could be said on Kup's Show that weren't heard on prime time TV. Guests often came just to say things they couldn't say elsewhere. Very early, author Lillian Smith (*Strange Fruit*) appeared mainly to level a charge of censorship against NBC. Ms. Smith, a southerner who had been fighting segregation for more than twenty years, had been invited to appear on Dave Garroway's "Today Show," but apparently tremendous pressures were brought to bear on the network to prevent her from airing her views there. She aired them with us. In those days we were live, but never had a problem. Later on when we were taped and some guests knew they could be edited, we had to do some of our own "censoring." Richard Pryor, one of the funniest and one of the dirtiest mouths in show business (or out), once uttered a comment about Richard Nixon that we actually had to bleep five times.

There were warm and poignant moments as well. On the 25th anniversary of the show, Essee brought together three Chicago mayors at one time. We kept them in three different rooms until the program went on. But more important than getting the three unfriendly mayors to sit together was Essee's ten-strike. With the help of old friend Jim Hoge, formerly of the Sun-Times but now publisher of the New York Daily News, she was able to get tapes from four presidents—Ronald Reagan, Jimmy Carter, Gerald Ford and Richard Nixon—to air on the show. Each of the presidents enjoyed throwing in some humorous jabs at the anniversary boy.

Incidentally, Nixon was a long time friend, even though I disagreed with his politics. He never let opposing views interfere with friendly relationships. And once, while he was speaking in Chicago, accompanied by a half dozen of his cabinet members, he spotted me during a break and summoned his cabinet members to his side. "I want you all to meet Kup," he said. "And whenever you are in Chicago, you should go on his show. It's the best of its type." I was floored. I didn't expect such a recommendation from a president I often criticized in the column. But he fondly remembered his four or five appearances on Kup's Show, and never hesitated to tell me so when we met.

Another president who remembered was Carter. He had just left the governorship of Georgia and was making his first appearance in Chicago on his presidential campaign. Everybody said, "Carter, who?" at that time, but his name was fresh in my memory because show business friends of mine had appeared in Atlanta and told me what a nice gent he was. Hence, I extended an invitation to appear on the show. It was his first introduction to Chicago and apparently it was a good one because Jimmy never failed to thank me during the many times our paths crossed later, including in the White House.

In 1983, Eubie Blake appeared. His long career had ranged from a bawdy house piano player to a famed Broadway composer, and he appeared on our show as he turned 99. Still lively and alert, he told me,

"I've got one more Broadway musical in my system. If I just live to 100, I can get it out." Unfortunately, death intervened.

On one of the first shows we had Ed Logelin, a vice-president for U.S. Steel, and actor Richard Carlson. The two had never met before. As successful people are apt to do, they began reminiscing about a tiny town, in Chaska, Minnesota. Lo and behold, it turned out that Carlson's granduncle was the sheriff in Chaska, and Logelin's grandfather was his deputy. The sheriff and deputy had "distinguished" themselves by playing cards all night with a stranger, who was as shrewd a poker player as they had ever met. Two days later, a bank in Northfield, Minnesota, was robbed—and the stranger turned out to be the culprit. His name: Jesse James.

Looking back, there were so many other unforgettable moments on the program. A few highlights that come to mind:

MOST TRAGIC PREDICTION

—Martin Luther King's sad prognostication of an assassin who would soon end his life. He said: "But I cannot let the fear of death turn me around. Nor will I let it deter me or go into hiding because of what is coming."

MOST MARITAL MOMENT

—One of my favorite theatrical couples, Hume Cronyn and Jessica Tandy, appeared on the program a number of times. On one show, they discussed the romantic days of their long ago youth. Suddenly Jessica blurted out to Hume, "Come to think of it, you never proposed to me." Whereupon Cronyn, ever the gallant, got down on his knees in front of Jessica and pleaded, "Darling, will you marry me?" I don't recall that she accepted him.

MOST OSTENTATIOUS GUEST

—Rev. Ike. I like his philosophy of "joy"—but I was a bit taken aback when he brought his own very expensive silverware, napkins and wine glasses and placed them on the coffee table in case we served anything. We served only coffee, but Ike still told the viewers: "Get your pie in the sky now, not in the by and by!"

MOST UNUSUAL GUEST

—Paul Crump, a convicted murderer who was seeking a parole after serving a record number of years, appeared on the show with his defense attorney and the prosecuting attorney. I received permission to originate the show in Cook County Jail, where Crump was incarcerated at the time. It was a "first" in that era.

MOST POPULAR SHOW

—The "My Fair Lady" special with Audrey Hepburn, Rex Harrison, Jack Warner and Arthur Godfrey. We asked Audrey how she got the role when she didn't sing and Julie Andrews, who created the role on Broadway, did sing. Before Audrey could answer, Warner cut in sharply, "I paid millions for this story and I'll cast whoever I want."

BEST INFORMED GUEST

—Bill Veeck—who would call me before the show and ask who else was on. If it was an author, he'd read that writer's books. If it was an astronomer, he'd brush up on astronomy. If it was a baseball owner, he'd pick up a couple of comic books.

MOST REVEALING INTERVIEW

—Truman Capote, ever a fascinating guest, discussed his homosexuality and sex life in one of his appearances. He went so far as to reveal he made love to four-legged, as well as two-legged partners and even, once to a fire plug.

MOST BITTERSWEET MOMENT

—Astronaut Alan Shepard appearing after our great space accomplishment, while prejudice and poverty still abounded at home. "We conquered the heights, but not the hates," he said.

WHEN YOU GOTTA GO

—Bette Davis and her then husband, Gary Merrill, were in town doing a play based on a Carl Sandburg story. Hence, we put all three together for a stimulating discussion about the theater. But in the midst of the conversation, the elongated, white haired Sandburg stood up and announced, "I've got to pee," whereupon he left the set for the nearest men's room and then nonchalantly returned.

Originally called "At Random," the show became the longest running of its kind and won dozens of Emmys and a Peabody Award. When I went to New York to accept the Peabody, I paraphrased a line from my old Illinois patron saint, Abe Lincoln: "If you can fool some of the people all the time and all the people some of the time—don't press your luck." I think the accolade of which I was most proud, though, came when *Variety* said: "Kup's prowess in obtaining the top show biz and political names is legend, sometimes to the frustration of the other video talk shows which must often do with the leavings."

The guests in 1985–1986, our final year, showed how times change and, at the same time, how some things never change. Bob Hope was there, discussing how old age and forgetfulness take over and told the story of an elderly couple in Florida. The wife sent her husband out for ice cream—and told him to be sure it was covered with nuts and chocolate sauce. Forty-five minutes later the husband returned with six bagels. "And where," asked the wife, "is the cream cheese?"

New era writer Sydney Sheldon and director Bill Friedkin revealed how to write bestsellers and make successful movies. Controversial minister Louis Farrakhan vented his hate, while Dr. Benjamin Spock aired his love.

The relatives of three Americans held hostage in Lebanon—Mrs. Jerry Levin, John Jenko, brother of Reverend Lawrence Martin Jenko and John Weir, son of the Reverend Benjamin Weir—tugged at our heartstrings. Judy Blume told us about *Smart Women* and Mort Sahl and actor George ("Cheers") Wendt tickled our funnybone.

Former President Carter came on and predictably ripped Ronald Reagan for the budget deficit and his visit to the German cemetery where SS men are buried. President José Napoleon Duarte of El Savador gave us an exclusive interview. Gary Hart discussed his aptly named book, *The Double Man.* Jim McMahon stopped off on his way to the Super Bowl.

It was a very good year.

24

Oops! What—Me Mortal?

A not-so-funny thing happened to me in 1980.
For 37 years, I had never missed a column. I had developed
an "iron man" reputation and was the envy of many of my colleagues,
who demanded, "What's your secret?" There was no secret. I was just
blessed with good health, followed a daily workout program at home, and
loved what I did. Then, all hell broke loose and hospitals became my
home away from home.

It started mildly enough, just before Christmas of 1980. I had asked
Santa Claus for a Cadillac. I got a cataract instead. I consulted the father-
son opthalmologist team, Drs. William and Michael Rosenberg, who performed the operation at Columbus Hospital, removing the cataract and
implanting a permanent lens in my right eye. The rule of thumb on cata-
racts is that the other eye will require the same surgery in a year or so, and
the next Christmas I was back in Columbus Hospital. The nurses assured
me I had nothing to worry about. Cardinal John Cody had occupied the
same room a short time before and blessed it for future occupants. So with
one cardinal and two Rosenbergs, what's to worry? The two operations
were eminently successful and the Rosenbergs once again proved the
hand is quicker than the eye. They also assured me that on a clear day I'd
be able to see their bill.

Then in 1983, I was headed back to the office after a Christmas-New
Year's vacation with Essee to see our son Jerry and his family on the West

Coast, when I experienced chest pains. The pains passed, but when I mentioned them to my internist, Dr. Eddie Newman, he rejected my explanation that watching Dallas lose to Minnesota on Monday night football could cause angina pains. The next thing I knew, I was watching TV in Chicago's Michael Reese Hospital, where my heart specialists decided my angina could be treated with medication and shorter hours. I took the medication.

A year later I again was covering my beat from a hospital bed, humming "Nearer My God to Thee." Dr. Newman, who still makes house calls, believe it or not, had rushed to my home because of the severity of the chest pains. Before I knew what was happening, he ordered an ambulance to rush me back to Michael Reese. "Rush" was the laugh word. The two operators of the ambulance performed like they were the Frick and Frack of Futility. First, they had raced their ambulance around the Near North Side because they couldn't locate my residence, while I sat in the lobby, trying to act nonchalant. Did you ever try to act nonchalant, clad in pajamas and robe while sitting in the lobby of your building in the wee hours?

I kept thinking what a hilarious skit it would make for Second City.

Frick and Frack, huffing and puffing, finally managed to stow me into the ambulance, but then they had trouble strapping me onto the stretcher. Even with Essee's help it wasn't easy. An ambulance ride may not be as smooth as imagined, especially on a bitter, snowy night. Every time the van hit a bump, the restrainers slipped loose. And a sudden stop had me sliding off the stretcher. The bumpy ride on icy streets made it almost impossible to get the oxygen hose to the nose, despite the size of the objective, with Frack screaming at Frick to slow down.

Even arrival at the hospital added a comedic touch. The emergency door used for such cases was bolted tight at that wee hour, sending Frick and Frack into convulsions. They finally located another door and managed to get the stretcher, with the patient half in and half out, into a corridor deep in the bowels of the hospital. Then came a mad dash through a forlorn area to the proper site, but not before the speed with which they wheeled me caused us to lose Essee, who was running as fast as she could to keep up. She became lost in a maze of corridors, which branched off every which way.

I kept recalling one of Danny Thomas' lyrics, "Nothing is more unnerving/Than to lose track of Irving."

By the time a breathless Essee came racing into the room, the doctors and nurses had begun their work. In a matter of minutes, an IV needle was inserted into my arm for intravenous feeding. Another needle was inserted to extract blood. A nurse was taking my blood pressure. Another was applying electrodes, two above the ankles, two above the wrists and six more across the chest for the electrocardiogram. I was also attached to a computer, which monitored every beat of the heart. Residents and interns were applying stethoscopes, first to the chest to hear the heart, then to the back for the lungs.

Then came consultations with Dr. Richard Langendorf, the heart genius, and Dr. Mukesh C. Jain, a native of India and authority on angiograms, joined by Dr. Newman. They patiently explained the workings of the heart and were most thorough and gentle in their dialog, assuring the patient that while they thought nothing serious had occurred, medical diligence dictated every precaution be taken. They proposed two immediate procedures—a myocardial scan and an echocardiogram.

I kept thinking of the play, *Whose Life Is It Anyway?* and the late comedian Joe E. Lewis' line: "My doctor says I'm in perfect shape—every artery is hard as a rock."

One more procedure was required before the doctors would feel assured. That was the angiogram, or cardiac catheterization, in which a small incision is made in the groin after a local anesthesia. Then two flimsy flexible tubes are inserted, one into the vein, the other into the artery, both of which the doctor maneuvers to your heart. The patient, feeling little pain, can observe the procedure on an overhead TV screen and carry on a conversation with the doctor. This is the definitive test to determine where the problem is located and the treatment necessary—surgery or medication. I told Dr. Jain that I'd seen better TV shows, like "Hart to Hart." "But," he added, "never one with a happier ending. All *your* heart needs is medication."

The nurses again welcomed me back to my room after the angiogram with this cheerful earful: I was the "reigning in-house celebrity." That lasted about 15 minutes, or until Donald O'Connor was wheeled in for an emergency appendectomy. I lost my honorary title as quickly as you could lose a fortune shooting dice with Nick the Greek. I was released from the hospital several days later with nitroglycerin tablets in my pill box and at the ready.

Then on a Sunday in the fall of 1985, I was at my office, batting out a Monday column, when suddenly I started to shake, rattle and roll. I became feverish and weak, and my immediate thought was, "How am I going to finish this column?" I began to sweat profusely and a classic comment by Red Smith, the famous New York sports columnist, again came to mind. He once explained that writing a column is easy. "All you do is sit down at your typewriter, roll in a blank piece of paper and then watch the blood drip on it." How I managed to finish the column that day still mystifies me. I felt a fatigue I had never known before. But complete it I did, and was in bed at home immediately thereafter.

The day remains vivid in my memory because I was able to watch the Bears, in one of their finest performances of that Super Bowl year, demolish Dallas 44–0. I also got the news from Dr. Newman—hepatitis! Fortunately, it was Type A. Type B hepatitis can be fatal. So for the next nine weeks I remained in bed, cursing my luck, reading a few books, watching TV and doing more cursing. And finally, I began this book—when I could lift the pen.

Dr. Newman did give me permission during my convalescence to break the monotony by writing my traditional Christmas column, in which I facetiously present gifts to the high and mighty. This a brief sample:

Santa Claus, Superstar!

With visions of the Super Bowl Shuffle dancing through his head, your reporter once again hitches up Dasher, Dancer, Prancer and Vixen, Comet, Cupid, Donder and Blitzen (plus William "the Refrigerator" Perry for protection) and off we go on a sleigh ride to deliver these appropriate "gifts" and wishes to the following VIPs:

President Reagan—Enough Grecian Formula to last him through his retirement. (And maybe some left over for a real Greek.)

Mike Dukakis—A gift of a book, *The Making of a President*.

Ayatollah Khomeini—A sanity claus from Santa Claus for the Grinch who stole Christmas.

Johnny Carson—A new show, "The Best of Carson."

Dean Martin—Give him anything, as long as it's bottled.

First Lady Nancy—A charge account at K mart to see how the other half shops.

Mikhail Gorbachev—A bottle of champagne with which to join Ronald Reagan in a toast: "May the Iron Curtain rust in peace."

Joseph Cardinal Bernardin—The Nobel award for his noble aspirations for peace on Earth and goodwill to men.

Bob Hope and George Burns, disciples of Methuselah—The biblical allotment of 120 years, inasmuch as they're almost there now.

Lech Walesa—May all Poland adopt his theme song, "Look for the Union Label."

Frank Sinatra—A case of Geritol to keep up with the Pepsi generation.

Stella Foster, my assistant—The Lois Lane award for devotion to a mild-mannered reporter.

For all of us—A typical American Christmas, with a tree from Canada, ornaments from Hong Kong, bulbs from Japan and the idea from Bethlehem.

The hepatitis left me weak and my record of consecutive columns was kaput. I did get a lift, though, when I received this letter:

Dear Kup;

Word has reached us that you are not feeling up to par lately and Nancy and I want to encourage you to keep your spirits high. So many people must be pulling for you, and so are we.

Our best to Essee. You both have our prayers and warm regards.

Sincerely,
Ronald Reagan.

I did keep my spirits up, but my doctors recommended that I give up one of my activities. They insisted I needed more rest. Certainly, I wouldn't give up the column. And surrendering the three-times-weekly appearances on Channel 2 wouldn't provide the required extra rest. That left but one choice—Kup's Show, which I had conducted for 27 years.

The work connected with the TV show, including the lining up the guests, doing the research, reading the authors' books and then the taping session, added up to more than 20 hours a week. I loved every bit of it, especially the association with many of the most important figures in our nation, if not the world. I was reluctant to terminate the show, but my doctors were looking over my shoulder, awaiting a decision. So I bade a tearful farewell to Kup's Show.

Now I'd be able to spend more evenings at home with Essee. But hold on—it was early in 1987, I was kibitzing, as usual, in the lobby of my building with my two morning companions, former State Senator Bernie Neistein and Frank Casey of Warner Bros., before we drove downtown. Suddenly, or so they tell me, I collapsed. Casey took it calmly. "There goes Kup, falling asleep again."

This time Casey, who could have qualified as an Indianapolis 500 race driver, rushed me to nearby Northwestern Memorial Hospital's emergency room, where Dr. Neal Stone, a young and brilliant cardiologist, joined my medical team. It didn't take long, after the invariable series of heart tests to come to a conclusion. A valve had to be replaced and an artery bypassed.

But hold on again. We were making plans for the big cut when, another morning in spring as I was getting ready to leave the office, I began to bleed rectally. It was so voluminous, I couldn't stop it. So I just stuffed in as much toilet paper as possible, called my doctor and took a cab to Northwestern Hospital. This time Dr. Robert Craig, chief of gastroenterology at Northwestern Hospital, was added to the team. The prediction was gloomy. The doctors ordered a biopsy, which they said indicated the polyps in my colon *could* be cancerous. And in keeping with good medical practice, they explained in detail all the possibilities while awaiting the results of the biopsy. They listed one, two, three, four hypothetical eventualities—and the fifth, a colostomy. Inwardly I was frantic. Outwardly I forced a weak smile.

And so Essee and I waited and waited and waited for the results of the biopsy. It was nail-biting time. Finally, the doctors marched into my room all smiles. The news must be good. And it was. The biopsy was negative. But there was a "but" in their report. The biopsy only confirmed that the *tops* of the polyps were benign. The *bottoms* still could be cancerous and surgery was the only sure solution.

Now Dr. Stone and Dr. Newman, joined by Dr. John Sanders, the heart surgeon, and Dr. Gerald Ujiki, the abdominal surgeon, went into a huddle. I was an innocent bystander. It was only my life at stake. They had to determine which operation should come first, the heart or the abdominal to remove the possibly malignant polyps. The decision: The weakened heart might not withstand major colon surgery. And while the doctors all agreed the polyps should be removed as quickly as possible lest the cancer spread, the decision nevertheless was to do the heart first.

Heart surgery is so commonplace today that the patient need have little fear. And Dr. Sanders, in his pre-operation pep talk, filled me with so much optimism that I went into the operating room singing, "You Gotta Have Heart." It's the post-operative period that gets you.

I had been told that a period of depression usually follows heart surgery, but I wasn't prepared for what happened to me. Heart surgery is, of course, a physical trauma. Let me not make light of it. But even more disconcerting, at least in my case, was the psychological effect.

For a week or so, I wasn't sure where I was. For some unfathomable reason, I thought I was in L.A. So you know what hell I was going through. Actually, in my mental fog, I wasn't sure I was going to make it. I kept thinking of a *Sun-Times* in the sky, where I could continue columning.

And it was much more difficult for Essee, who had to put up with my bizarre behavior. How she didn't crack under the strain remains a mystery. Sleep escaped me. I would awaken at 2 a.m. and, unable to fall back asleep, I would walk the floors, back and forth, back and forth, oftimes sitting on our 10th floor patio, overlooking Lake Michigan, until daybreak. At times I imagined I couldn't breathe. Finally, Dr. Stone decided to put me back in the hospital for a few days, assuring me I'd overcome whatever demons had been released by my brain. That did the trick and I returned home, there to convalesce and regain my strength until I was ready for the abdominal surgery. Back-to-back surgery. Is that any way to treat your body?

Once again I was in the hands of a superb surgeon in Dr. Ujiki. This time the operation was made difficult because the polyps were deep in the abdomen. What I thought would be a breeze turned into an ordeal. But to coin a phrase, all's well that ends well. The operation not only was successful but the fear that the bottom, or hidden parts of the polyps, might be malignant, proved false.

The two operations and the convalescence periods kept me out of the paper for three months. My one satisfaction was extracting a promise from my two surgeons—they would use the same stitching pattern so that I would have the exact design from my collar bone down to the soft underbelly. I'm proud to exhibit the stitching, if anybody is interested.

One problem remained. Dr. Sanders used a pig valve in replacing my damaged one. Now I have an uncontrollable urge to go "Oink, oink." It's very embarrassing when I attend services in my synagogue.

25

Scoops

You never know *where* scoops come from.

One that caused an international ruckus occurred when Princess Margaret visited Chicago. The year was 1979. One of the parties in her honor was hosted by Abra Prentice Wilken, a Rockefeller heiress, in her penthouse duplex. Among the guests was Jane Byrne, then mayor. Margaret, oft criticized back home for putting foot in mouth, had recently suffered the loss of her uncle, Lord Mountbatten, blown up by a bomb that exploded as he stepped foot aboard his yacht. The IRA was suspected.

In the course of her conversation with Mayor Byrne, the princess blurted out, "All Irish are pigs!" She apparently didn't realize she was seated alongside the No. 1 Irish figure in Chicago. The mayor ignored the remark in deference to the status of the princess, but inwardly she was burning. And a few hours after the incident, the mayor's husband, Jay McMullen, a former newspaperman and a friend, was on the telephone.

The item was picked up by the wire services and was a 48-hour sensation. British radio, TV and press kept my phone ringing, as did calls from around this country. Byrne graciously tried to cover up for Margaret at a news conference the next day by saying, "Oh, it wasn't 'all Irish are pigs.' She said 'all Irish love to jig.' " Obviously, it didn't wash and Margaret was subjected to intensive questioning on the remainder of her U.S. tour and even more so when she returned home.

Another scoop that made the front page came while I was in a hospital bed.

On Monday, Mar. 16, 1987, the headline of the *Sun-Times* was:

PROBE HOOKS
12 BIG FISH
U.S. Indictments Due Today
In City License Fraud Cases
By Art Petacque

A former alderman, a former state legislator and an ex-official in the City Health Department are among 12 people expected to be netted today in a federal investigation of city licensing corruption. The dozen are to be named in indictments stemming from the FBI's Operation Phocus Probe.

Information about the charges was given to Chicago *Sun-Times* columnist Irv Kupcinet, who is in Northwestern Memorial Hospital for removal of a benign growth.

I phoned the story to my city desk, which assigned Art Petacque, the city's leading crime reporter, to handle the writing. In 45 years of writing the column, I was bound to get some scoops in some strange places—but that was the first time I ever did it from a hospital bed.

My first "prime scoop" was more than 40 years before that. It happened when William Heirens' slaying of six-year-old Suzanne Degnan was making headlines across the country. He then cut up the body and wrapped the different parts in grisly packages which he hid in sewers around the city. KUP REVEALS BILL HEIRENS TRIES TWICE TO END LIFE! was another headline.

This was in July of '46, and I still can't reveal the source. But immediately after the story broke, reporters made a beeline to State's Attorney William Touhy's office, demanding to know if it was true. "All I can tell you," replied the State's Attorney, "is that I took Heirens' 'notes' home for safekeeping. The only person who knew was Mrs. Touhy. If Kup got a scoop from those notes, my wife has to have given it to him." P.S. It *wasn't* Mrs. Touhy.

In late 1950, 22-year-old bandit Robert Luttrell gave himself up to this reporter after being the object of a police search for months. This was a classic example of how you can find a story anywhere.

A little less than a year before, I was on a tour of Israel. A top-ranking army officer, learning I was from Chicago, took me aside and asked if he could tell me an "off-the-record" story. No matter where I am, someone invariably has an "exclusive" for me. Ninety-nine percent of them don't turn out, but I listen. I was glad I did this time.

Luttrell, one of the many non-Jews who volunteered his service for the Israeli cause, had cracked up in a plane and was under treatment in a hospital. He tried to leave, but was halted at the door by an orderly. Luttrell whipped out a gun from his belt, shoved it into the orderly's chest and pulled the trigger. Fortunately, the gun jammed. Luttrell made his escape from the hospital anyway, but was captured a few blocks down the street. "He's a brave boy, that Luttrell," explained the officer, "but he's not all there upstairs. He needs psychiatric treatment badly." After I heard the Luttrell story in Israel, it made an interesting paragraph in my column, but little did I know that some day it would make a major scoop.

I didn't hear about Luttrell again until late in October the following year. I had printed a small item about him after my trip to Israel and now I was talking to a frantic voice at the other end of the phone...who identified herself as Mrs. Mayme Luttrell, Robert's mother. Her son was in trouble—serious trouble—and she sought help. She told me briefly of his career in crime. Police had warned her he might be shot on sight. She feared that Robert would be badly beaten, if not killed, were he to be captured.

It was a plea any mother would make to protect one of her brood. She wanted her son to give himself up, and realized he had to pay for his mistakes, but she couldn't stand the thought of his being mauled because of a police vendetta. Could I give her assurance, if Robert did give himself up, that he would be treated fairly? I told her that I would make sure he'd be dealt with fairly—but first I wanted to speak directly with him.

This was arranged, and I contacted Robert at his hideout in Milwaukee. He promised to come clean—"to get the whole horrible mess off my chest." He understood that he'd go to jail and pay for his mistakes. "Jail would be better than this life of a fugitive," he said. "Some of the police have it in for me. I want to make it to jail." The bottom line is that because of my conversation with the Israeli officer, I had that extra insight into Luttrell which made the difference.

A car was dispatched to Milwaukee to pick up Luttrell and bring him to Chicago, where I met with him, joined by Luis Kutner, a leading attorney I had asked to represent Robert. Together, we drove to State's Attorney John Boyle's offices in the Criminal Courts Building. There, I explained Mrs. Luttrell's fears about police brutality. I extracted a promise from him that Robert would not be subject to the "third degree." With Boyle and his two top aides, Edward Breen and Police Captain Dan Gilbert, listening, Robert then told his story—a story every youth with wayward tendencies should hear. It was more than the usual "crime does not pay" lesson.

Luttrell admitted to between 40 and 50 holdups in a whirlwind career of crime which had lasted merely three months. He had nothing to show for it—except a frenzied mother, a dead sidekick (Jerome Zeidman, slain the week before), another cohort in jail facing a long sentence, and mental anguish such as I've seldom seen.

Money? Robert figured if he'd devoted the same energy and time to a law-abiding job for just $50 a week, he would have been much further ahead. Whatever sums he had stolen were dissipated quickly in leading the hunted life, ever on the move for fear of attracting police attention.

Toward the end of the session, Robert actually felt relaxed for the first time—so much so that he told a humorous story, at which the rest of us couldn't help but grin. It was about the time he and his gang decided to stick up a North Clark Street bookie's messenger. Daily, around noon, the messenger delivered five thousand dollars in cash, carried in a large brown bag, to the bookie. Luttrell had the messenger's path "cased" and a system of signals was set up to warn of his approach. As the man neared a certain building, he was to be shoved into a hallway and relieved of his precious brown bag. The operation went according to plan, except the messenger refused to be shoved into the hallway. So Luttrell and his cohorts pulled their guns and there, on Clark Street, with hundreds of persons milling around, they pleaded with him to enter the hallway!

Finally, in desperation, they just grabbed the bag and scrammed in their getaway car, eager to cut up the loot. Lo and behold, instead of money, the bag contained only two ham sandwiches and coffee...the bookie's lunch.

And where there are criminals, can politicians be far behind?

In 1976, there was the brouhaha about Congressman Hayes' affair with Elizabeth Ray. Really, this signaled the beginning of an era in which politicians' affairs went public. Shortly after, Ms. Ray, a la Donna Rice and so many others of recent years, capitalized on her "fame." She came to Chicago to star in *Will Success Spoil Rock Hunter?* at Pheasant Run. The show was not only attended by Chicago critics, but the Associated Press, the United Press, and just about everybody else.

Actingwise, as the saying goes, Elizabeth should've stayed in bed, one of her favorite locales. At the same time, some of the lines she delivered in the play were food for thought. The biggest gag of the night came when she sat down at a typewriter and, in an exaggerated hunt-and-peck style, proved that what she said in Washington about her typing was true.

We later met with her in Washington, D.C., for lunch at Duke Ziebert's and she opened up even more. "Notoriety came so suddenly that I just don't know how to cope with it," she said over a corned beef omelet.

"One day I was nobody, the next day—wow! My phone doesn't stop ringing, my picture is on Page 1. I had to change my number, so many people
are calling me that I don't want to talk to anyone. My lawyers are warning
me to keep quiet, and everyone is criticizing me for being a 'kiss-and-tell'
broad. I can't handle it."

That Elizabeth was near suicide was confirmed by Duke Zeibert, colorful owner of the restaurant, who joined our luncheon session. Also
present was Essee, who told me she came along "for your protection, Irv."
Duke was Miss Ray's closest and perhaps only real friend in Washington.
He confided, "Elizabeth called me at 3:30 this morning—frantic. She was
hysterical, as she has been so many times since this story broke. She said
she couldn't take it any more and wanted to jump out the window. I had a
helluva time trying to calm her down. And me, I'm not a psychiatrist. I
just sell boiled beef and matzo-ball soup. What do I know from psychia-
try?" Miss Ray nodded her head in agreement as Duke went on about her
threat to end it all. "I really have been on the verge," she said. "Everything has been closing in on me, and I have nowhere to turn—no family,
no friends." Yet Elizabeth didn't look as desperate as she sounded while sa-
shaying through the restaurant. She gave the appearance of a cool, blonde
beauty, wearing a slinky halter-neck white jersey dress, no bra and a large-
brimmed straw hat.

She wasn't completely comfortable with this reporter, at first, since
she was under orders not to discuss any phase of her relationship with
Hayes. But I knew she'd open up with Zeibert there. They had struck up a
friendship some six years before in his restaurant and ever since, Duke (a
divorced man) had been her father-confessor, escort, lover and adviser.

I tried to lighten the heavy tone of the discussion by quoting some of
the lines political humorist Mark Russell was using in his act at the
Shoreham Hotel. Mark interrupted his show to bring "the latest results of
the primary. Congressman Hayes not only won Sodom, but Gomorrah as
well!" Later, the comedian allegedly quoted Hayes, saying: "Why make a
big fuss over the fact you can't type?"

Miss Ray, suicidal thoughts notwithstanding, had a neat sense of humor and didn't really resent the quips making the rounds. But she found it
hard to laugh with financial problems aggravating her plight. What about
the sale of her book, *The Washington Fringe Benefit?* I asked. Dell was reportedly publishing one million paperback copies. "Money from the
book?" she repeated. "That's a laugh. First, my ghostwriter, Yvonne Dun-
leavy, worked some kind of deal. She gets 50 percent of the measly
$25,000 I signed for. Then I had to hire lawyers and an agent. And my

real psychiatrist—not Duke—costs me a fortune. So where am I? I had one chance to make some real money. *The National Enquirer* offered me a small fortune for an interview. But they told me, 'You've been quoted enough, but you haven't named any names. You name these people you slept with, and the money is yours.' I don't want to do that. Hayes was the exception, and *The Washington Post* did that. So I told *The National Enquirer* people to get lost. But would you believe they're parked on my doorstep and won't give up?"

Elizabeth Ray fancied herself as a movie actress a la Marilyn Monroe. "She was always my idol. Oh, she was so lovely. Perhaps with all this publicity. . . ."

"Do you really think you have a future as an actress?" I asked.

"I must be pretty good," she replied. "I made Hayes think I was having a good time!"

Of all the other lighter political scoops to which I was privy, maybe the most memorable was the first time I interviewed a mayor in the nude. Come to think of it, it was the first time I interviewed anybody in the nude. Before your sexual fantasies run rampant, this was Detroit's Mayor Coleman Young. Both of us were being pampered at La Costa Spa in California (otherwise known as "The Fat Farm"), where patrons seeking to shape up had access to such delights as steambaths, whirlpools, sauna baths, facial and body massages, and a diet menu. There, all modesty disappears. I could have interviewed a number of other celebrities who were there at the time, such as Bill Holden, Burt Bacharach, Peter Falk, Gore Vidal, and Carl Reiner. But Young seemed the most meaningful. However, all I could really get out of him were some second thoughts about criticizing Chicago's Mayor Byrne, after she had made a number of uncomplimentary comments about President Carter.

A couple of weightier scoops involved Senator Joe McCarthy and Fidel Castro.

In 1953 a number of papers carried the finale of the long-term "investigation" I had made of McCarthy while he was supposedly making a cataclysmic investigation of Communists in the government. One paper followed up its headline with: "Kup is the newspaperman who called Senator Joe McCarthy's bluff, the night before the election when McCarthy ranted over television and radio, attempting to tie presidential candidate Adlai Stevenson into a gigantic Red conspiracy. . . ."

That story began shortly after the senator from Wisconsin began his tirade, accusing just about everyone and his brother in government of being a Communist. It was the early 1950s, World War II was becoming more of a memory and Russia more of a threat. A moving orator and a consummate user of the media, McCarthy correctly caught the mood of the country. With unsubstantiated charges, he gained followers and momentum. There was even talk of his being a presidential candidate.

I finally caught up with him a few days before the 1952 presidential election. On Monday night, October 27, he stepped farther over the line than ever before, attacking presidential candidate Adlai Stevenson for having Communist ties. Of all the statements hurled by Senator McCarthy in a widely ballyhooed "I'll-tell-all-about-Adlai Stevenson" speech in Chicago Monday night, the one above all he definitely never should have made was his invitation to the press to inspect the documents, pamphlets and photostats he offered as proof of his charge. As McCarthy spoke, he waved these papers for his audience to see and exclaimed in a challenging voice, "I have here in my hand the proof and the press is invited to examine it." Some members of the press (this reporter trying to be first in line) did accept his challenge. What they discovered on close inspection of these documents bore little relation to the charges made by the senator.

One of the major points in McCarthy's speech was when he first held up a picture of a desolate-looking barn, then another photo to show the elaborate furnishings inside the barn. This, according to McCarthy, was the secret headquarters of the Institute of Pacific Relations. Then came a photostat of a letter—a letter, according to McCarthy, which his investigators dug out of the secret files of the IPR. Finally, wildly waving the photostat as proof, McCarthy bellowed: "This shows that Alger Hiss and Frank Coe recommended Adlai Stevenson as a delegate to the Mont Tremblant conference in Canada, called to determine our postwar foreign policy in Asia. Alger Hiss is a convicted traitor and Coe has been named under oath before congressional committees seven times as a member of the Communist Party . . . Why did Hiss and Coe name Adlai Stevenson as the man they want?"

I examined the photostat of that letter supposedly containing such damaging evidence. What did it show? It was a two-page letter, written by a Joseph Lockwood, an official of the IPR, to a man identified only as "Bob," discussing possible speakers for a conference. And the only reference to Stevenson came in a brief paragraph on the second page: "In the field of foreign relations, I understand from Hiss that there are several good assistants working under Navy Sec. Knox, one of them an Adlai

Stevens." This misspelling of Stevenson's name by a person who obviously didn't know him was the *lone* reference to the Democratic candidate in this "devastating" bit of evidence.

But that's not all this "revealing" photostat unveiled. If McCarthy had read the next paragraph of this same letter, he would have noted that the name of one of the nation's most respected publishers was also listed as a possible speaker because of his qualifications in foreign relations— Gardner (Mike) Cowles of the newspaper and magazine chain. Cowles was as far removed from communism as McCarthy was from the facts.

After another of his ranting speeches in Chicago, I managed to corner him for an interview in his hotel suite.

He sat across the room from me, but I had no trouble hearing him. He was making another speech, for an audience of one, me. I listened to his bellowing for some time, remaining only in the hope that I could get a glimpse at the folded sheet of paper which, only a short time before, he held in his hand and proclaimed, "I have here in my hand the proof. . . ." This was the statement he often shouted in claiming he had the names of "communists working in our government." While I kept an eye on the folded paper on the coffee table, McCarthy, an alcoholic, kept drinking. He finally excused himself to go to the bathroom.

The instant I heard him close the door to the john, I moved to the coffee table and seized the paper with the condemning "evidence."

The all important sheet was blank. . . on both sides. He had used it as a prop to "indict" hundreds of persons. And it was blank! That made an interesting column the next day, which other newspaprs picked up.

I also was in Cuba that historic period when Fidel Castro took over in deed but not yet in name. I met with him in February of 1959 in his penthouse suite atop the Havana Hilton Hotel. He was occupying it free, but soon would relinquish it because it was too fancy for his populist blood. I had first been able to contact him 10 days before by phone. It was arranged by an old Chicago friend, Charles Baron, who was running the gambling operation in the Riviera Hotel. Castro came to a reception at the hotel and Baron asked him if he would be gracious enough to talk long distance to a newspaper friend in Chicago. Castro agreed, so a call was put through and in the course of the conversation, Castro said he would be glad to meet me for an interview when I came to Cuba. He told me then that he was serving without portfolio, that his real authority stemmed from popular support, and that he would not shave his beard until the government of Cuba was stabilized. On a more personal note, he also told me he had no intention of marrying again in the future "because I have enough problems now without making a new one."

These were some of the highlights when we later talked in Havana:

K: The press has labeled your government the "Castro regime" and you make many official announcements. Yet you hold no rank as president, cabinet member or minister in the government you serve without portfolio. Doesn't this have the makings of a dictator?

C: Dictator, never. My influence comes from the people, which in turn comes from the success of the revolution. The press calls this the Castro regime, but it isn't. I work outside the government, but in collaboration with it. If I feel certain things should be done, I relay the information to President Urrutia and the cabinet. This, remember, is a provisional government and we are all feeling our way. When I was fighting in the mountains, I promised that, if successful, I would stay out of government as much as the people would permit. That is what I am doing now.

K: You say if you had to do things over, you'd make certain changes. Will you be more specific?

C: I quoted, as best I could remember, from Ben Franklin (another revolutionary figure with some stature). He said, if I had to live my life over again, I'd live it just as I had, with some changes. I was referring to the war trials held in the Sports Palace. That would be one change I would make. We held the trial there because we wanted to show the people—and the world—that we had nothing to hide by letting everybody see the war criminals on trial. We had nothing to fear. But, sadly, it became a circus, as the American press was so quick to point out. If I had to do it over again, I would let television cover the war trials to achieve our purpose of letting the world see our trials are fair and to learn the truth about the Batista brutalities. But no more sports palaces.

K: Next to unemployment [approximately one million of Cuba's six million people were idle], what do you consider your main problem?

C: Oh, we have so many problems. . .so many. . . . But one situation I am dedicated to reform is the health and education of our youngsters. The future must be brighter for them. There is too much sickness among the young in Cuba. Batista killed 20,000 people; we lose more because of poor undeveloped health measures. And the children suffer most.

K: And schools?

C: This is going to be one of our first projects—building new schools throughout Cuba. For Havana alone, I am planning a "school city" for 5,000 students. This will be located where Camp Columbia now stands. (Camp Columbia was the army headquarters and served as the exiled Batista's military fortress.) We will tear down Camp Columbia and in its place will rise this "school city," which we will name "City of Love." Also, we need teachers badly. I just made an appeal for teachers throughout the country and thousands—let's say hundreds—volunteered. They will teach our youngsters any place available, even in the homes, until we get our schools built. And they will teach, for the time being, without salary.

K: Now once again, about your beard.

C: This must be the only beard in the world, judging by the number of questions I answer about it. The beard stays for the time being because it is a symbol—a symbol of the hard fight to free Cuba. I may be putting barbers out of work by saying this, but I won't shave until we have a stabilized government in Cuba. How long that will be, nobody can tell right now. Maybe my Barbudos (bearded ones) will be a good tourist attraction. You tell the Americans that we like them and we want them to come visit us. They will see for themselves how peaceful Cuba now is.

I want to repeat: I wrote in my column that any leader who serves without portfolio and holds no office is undoubtedly a dictator. That prophesy came true.

In February of '85 I was also able to get the first interview with Jeremy (Jerry) Levin, who had been held hostage for eleven months in Lebanon and then managed to escape. Jerry and I had been friends since he was the first producer of my TV talk show 27 years before, a friendship that continued throughout a career that eventually saw him become Cable News Network Bureau Chief in Lebanon. It helps to know people.

I put in a call to Wiesbaden, Germany, where he had undergone a medical examination after his escape. "I've got a lot to tell you," he began, "but first I want to tell you how concerned I am about the four other Americans still being held captive. I'm devoting a lot of my time to trying to help them through my contacts in Lebanon. I know what they're going through and, oh, God, how I wish I could aid in their release."

On the subject of release, there were conflicting stories on whether Jerry had actually escaped or was allowed to go free. "I'm aware of the conflict, but believe me, I escaped! I tied three sheets together to get down to the ground and then ran like hell. I don't mind the other stories that they let me go, though. In fact, I welcome that theory. It could be a signal that they'll do the same for the others they're holding."

How did Jerry keep his sanity during the captivity? "I was determined not to lose hope or sanity. I wouldn't permit it. I kept my mind active by reminiscing about happier moments in my life. As an old baseball fan, I would think of all the trivia I could. Like the names of the original big league teams, then the names of the expansion teams, then the names of the players on my hometown team, the Detroit Tigers. I was even able to finally recall the names of the starting lineup in 1945, when the Tigers beat the Cubs—sorry about that, Kup—in the World Series. My boyhood hero, Hank Greenberg, once promised to hit a home run for me—and he did."

Was he subjected to torture and indoctrination? "Eleven months in virtual solitary confinement might be considered torture. But I was never beaten or harmed physically. And I kept thinking about the people who really were tortured, like the victims of the Holocaust and American prisoners in those tiny Japanese cells during World War II, and kept telling myself, 'This doesn't compare with what they went through.' The worst part was the loneliness and the separation from my family. Far from trying to indoctrinate me, it was rare when they talked to me at all."

Did religion help? "I was never what you might call a religious person. But as a result of this experience, I have had a spiritual awakening. I feel very close to God now. I kept thinking of the old story about the mule. Remember how you get a mule's attention? First, you beat him with a 2-by-4. I kept telling myself that God used the same tactic on me—the kidnaping was the beating with a 2-by-4 to give me the message."

Levin was one of the rare exceptions to the hostage situation. After coming back to the States for some R&R, he and his wife "Sis" went off to a sunny climate. Before he reached Chicago, however, he had his local ophthalmologist express him some new glasses. Levin's had been taken away during the captivity. For all that time he had looked at the world through blurred vision...but with a new vision.

Almost a third of a century before, during the Korean War, I was able to interview Leo Dans, a Chicagoan who was imprisoned by the Communists in North Korea for 34 months. Rather incredibly, he said that Uncle Sam's intelligence officers were unaware of the fact that crucial information they were seeking about Russia was available through Soviet-made movies. Merely by plunking down the price of admission to a theater like the Cinema Annex on West Madison, for example, they could save millions of dollars and many lives.

Dans, of course, was interrogated by the State Department for two weeks after he had been taken from North Korea to Moscow and then brought home. The day Dans returned home and shortly before my meeting with him, he took his family downtown to celebrate. His attention was attracted by a movie advertisement of the Russian film playing at the Cinema. What he saw on the screen startled him. There was a series of shorts on Russia—one dealing with the Trans-Siberian Railroad. Many of the questions asked him in Washington suddenly flashed back into his mind. Here were the answers—right on the screen!

At least, for Dans. With the help of the movie, he was able to recall that the Trans-Siberian was a double-track railroad, employing modern, electric signals, running through a tunnel just before reaching Lake Baikal (which was frozen over at the time of Dan's passing).

Equally as startling to him was the full length color movie *Sadko*. He had seen the very same film a few weeks earlier in Pyongyang, North Korea. He and the other Americans with whom he had been imprisoned had been moved there for a "fattening up" process before being shipped home, the usual Communist propaganda technique. There, the food was plentiful, new clothes were issued and Russian-made movies were shown.

Some of my best stories naturally were right here in town. In '69, I arranged to meet with the Blackstone Rangers—a black militant group. Opinion was explosively divided on whether members of this gang were essentially dedicated do-gooders or violent fanatics and criminals. Since they were an underground group, it was hard to find the truth. I was able to meet personally with the leaders of this "Black P Stone Nation" at their headquarters, and gave them their first—and I think, fair—hearing in the press. The upshot was that the Rangers indeed were comprised in part by an idealistic group, but mostly with members dedicated to terrorism, which was borne out by later events.

In '76, I reported that Hugh Hefner would be stepping *down* as President of the Playboy empire. Unfortunately, other publications picked it up and said he was stepping *out*. The fact was that he was stepping down, not out, to make way for his daughter, Christie, to become president. And in '85, I was able to tell my readers that White Sox owner Jerry Reinsdorf was about to own the Chicago Bulls, too. Speaking of sports, in '67 I persuaded Doug Mills, former University of Illinois Athletic Director, to tell all. He accused President David Dodds Henry of knowing as much as he did about the "slush fund" which gave sub rosa financial aid to athletes. "Let's just say," Mills revealed, "that I and the others at the University simply looked the other way."

I was the first to cover other fights, too—like the one between Arthur Godfrey and Julius LaRosa.

Godrey had made LaRosa a huge star, and then fired him in a characteristic moment of pique. I persuaded LaRosa to write this guest column for me about it:

There have been a lot of stories of how Mr. Godfrey hired me. But I don't think my shipmates on the USS Wright ever were given due credit. They're the ones who really are responsible. Mr. G. was in Pensacola, Florida, to receive his Navy wings. I was a navy air crewman at the time and my shipmates, whom I entertained whenever the occasion permitted, thought I deserved a break. So they managed to sneak a note into Godfrey's barracks during his visit to Pensacola—a note telling him that a certain Julius LaRosa was good enough to sing on his show.

Well, crazier things may have happened in show business. Mr. G. read the note and asked me to appear on the show he was putting on at the Pensacola station for the enlisted men. That's where he first heard me sing. And what happened after that is now history. I only hope I can prove "right" to the men of the USS Wright. And as for Mr. G., sure, things went wrong and we had our big breakup, but he also gave me my first break.

I also like to mention a few show biz stories that come to mind.

Like the time I jabbed Orson Welles by reminding him that it would be a noble gesture if, in divorcing Rita Hayworth, he would remember to repay the ten thousand dollars he borrowed from her during their marriage. (Her lawyer made me do it.)

I wasn't happy to report that the beloved child star of movies, Shirley Temple, would soon end her "perfect marriage" to handsome John Agar. The reason: Mother-in-law trouble. Two of Shirley's dearest friends, told me that the split could have been avoided if Mama (Mrs. George Temple) had relinquished the control she'd exercised over Shirley since childhood. A funny sidelight was that just before we tipped the divorce, Shirley was talking about joining John on a "second honeymoon" to England—to pick up money she'd been awarded in a libel suit against a British newspaper that had claimed she was really a grown midget as a child star. She went—John didn't.

Remember Barbara Payton? She was involved in that three-way thing with Franchot Tone and Tom Neal. She breezed through Chicago for a personal appearance with her movie, *Bride of the Gorilla*, at Minsky's Rialto, and the busty blonde beauty persisted in making statements to reporters that she knew were falsies—such as claiming she didn't know Tom Neal was in town, that she was going to reconcile with Franchot and, most hyperbolic of all, that many Hollywood producers wanted her for important roles. She had troubles enough already, so I didn't want to lay it on her any heavier. But facts are facts. One was that she detested Tone and was planning to beat him to the punch by obtaining a quickie divorce in Mexico. Another was that she not only knew Neal was in town, but

Barb was visiting with him at her sister's home in Evanston (and missed at least one important television show because she couldn't leave the suburbs). Last but not least, she knew she was washed up in movies and was happy to hear she could earn a fast buck by appearing in *Goodnight Ladies* through Chicago producer Jules Feiffer. Maybe you *don't* remember Barbara Payton. I don't blame you.

In '55, I itemed that Dean Martin/Jerry Lewis would split, the breakup of Muhammad Ali's marriage in '65, Joan Baez' goodbye to David Harris in '71, and the parting of Carl Bernstein of Watergate fame and Nora Ephron a few years ago.

One of the saddest stories came when I felt obliged to refute John Wayne's doctors and report the Duke's day's were numbered. Members of the family thought the doctors were issuing erroneous reports needlessly. That wouldn't be in character for Wayne.

On occasion I broke a story too soon. In 1959, Jack Benny mentioned to me that he had lined up Harry Truman to play the piano on his TV show. Jack was bursting with joy. And I promptly used the item. The newspapers started calling Jack before he had a chance to clear the announcement with the former president. "Know what Truman told me?" Benny later related." He said, if Kup says I'm going on the Jack Benny show, and if Jack Benny says I'm going on the Jack Benny show, then I'm going on the Jack Benny show."

Another "Big Story"involved Dick Tracy and Tess Trueheart, who for decades were the most-followed couple in the nation. The comic strip, of course, was "Dick Tracy," and I got the inside that the long-suffering and loyal Tess would finally wed Tracy. In those days, comic strip characters were cultural touchstones. Today, fact continually outdoes fiction.

Like my fellow columnists, I'm often asked why we print items that hurt people. That's when I invoke the standard newspaper adage: If it's our role to comfort the afflicted, it is equally our role to afflict the comfortable.

26

White House Daze

My beat has always included the White House, at least peripher-
ally. And in 45 years I've known presidents and vice presidents
good and bad.

From Truman to Reagan—here are some of my encapsulated memories of the persons who either occupied the White House or were a heart
beat away.

Ronald REAGAN

One story about the President that never saw the light of print occurred when he was courting the beautiful red-haired Rhonda Fleming.
Reagan, then a handsome and romantic bachelor, was mad about the girl.
Rhonda was fond of Ronnie, but not in love. And one night Reagan was
so frustrated that he pulled out a gun and fired a shot at her. I'm sure he
was wide of the mark purposely, but he did scare the romance out of their
idyl. I often have wondered what the course of history might have been
. . .!

Reagan came to the White House with a gung-ho reputation, the
man most likely to push the button, the man who described the Soviet
Union as the "evil empire." His transmogrification was remarkable, as
evinced by his latest summit meeting with Soviet leader Mikhail Gorbachev. His rapprochement with the Soviets will be recognized as momentous as Nixon's opening the door to China. For that alone, he gets high
marks as a president.

George BUSH

He may never live down his flagrant statement in a toast to Ferdinand Marcos on the Phillipines president's re-election in 1981. Lifting his glass Bush intoned, "We love your adherence to *democratic* principles." Marcos, the dictator, an adherent to democratic principles?

Bush immediately was criticized for putting the United States in the same embarrassing position it had been in by supporting the Shah in Iran and Anastasio Somoza in Nicaragua.

It's a comment Bush will have to live with throughout his political career.

Jimmy CARTER

Jimmy became a close friend. I found him highly intelligent—possibly the most intelligent president of the century—and warmhearted. In that respect, you've got to admire a guy who confided that he awakened wife Rosalynn each day at 6:30 with orange juice and the morning paper.

Unfortunately, as superb a husband and governor as Carter was, he often failed as a president because he couldn't make the transition from Georgia to Washington. He brought the modus operandi of the governorship to the White House, did not really delegate responsibility, and failed to master the nuances of dealing with Congress.

Still, I think history will look a bit more kindly on him than we do now.

Jerry FORD

Ford obviously did not distinguish himself as president. But he was an excellent man for a time of transition and healing after Watergate.

I remember in late October of 1976, it was 10 p.m. when the phone rang at my home. "The Chicago White House calling," said the voice at the other end. "The president will be on in a moment." The president was campaigning in the Chicago area, hence the use of the term, "The Chicago White House."

"I just wanted to say hello while I have some free time," I heard the president's voice say a moment later. "Betty and I just finished dinner in our suite (the Arlington Park Hilton), and are watching the 10 o'clock news."

"Funny thing, Mr. President," I said. "I'm watching *you* on the 10 o'clock news. You sound very confident."

"More than confident—we're going to win," he replied. "And Illinois will be the key. This campaign is just like a football game, the competition is good and that makes you work harder."

"I assume you know, Mr. President," I had to add, "that the *Sun-Times* is supporting Jimmy Carter."

"I have no complaints about that, Kup," Ford said. "And you and your wife are invited to come visit us in the White House again after the election!"

Essee and I had been Jerry's guest at the White House the previous year and he was gracious enough to seat me at his table, while Essee had the company of Senator Moynihan at a nearby table. The years have dimmed my memory as to the occasion of the dinner, but I vividly recall that the President, natch, sat at the head of the table, with Carol Burnett on his left and I on her left. And two other guests at the table were Carlton Fisk, then the all-star catcher with the Boston Red Sox (now with the White Sox) and Dallas's reigning football genius, Coach Tom Landry. It was the only time I saw Landry without a hat.

My friendship with Ford goes back to 1935, when we were fellow members of the College All-Star football team. In those days, the All-Star team of college players met the champs of the professional league in a charity game sponsored by the *Chicago Tribune*. I was elected to the squad as a quarterback and Jerry, who had captained the University of Michigan team, was chosen as center. This gave me a different view of the president of the United States. Jerry liked the story so much that he started to tell it on himself.

Richard NIXON

The irony of Richard Nixon was that as untrustworthy as many thought he was, on a personal level he could be warm and genuine. Yet that never came through to the public. The former president, despite his uptight appearance, desperately tried to be "one of the boys." The classic example of this came during his long taping sessions with David Frost for their memorable series of interviews. After one weekend of rest, Nixon greeted the returning crew with what he thought was an appropriate question to prove he was with it. He turned to Frost and his crew and asked, "Well, did you fellows FORNICATE over the weekend?" I was surprised he used the three syllable word when the Watergate tapes proved he used the shorter version so often.

That leads us the controversial passage in *The Final Days*, co-authored by Bob Woodward and Carl Bernstein, that the Nixons had a sexless marriage during their White House days. (How unlike John F. Kennedy!) So many bitter denials were forthcoming over this assertion that I decided to go to the source for verification. I found Woodward at his desk at the *Washington Post.* "You and Bernstein now are known as the Masters & Johnson of Watergate. Why was it necessary to plumb the depths of the Nixons' bedroom behavior?" I asked.

"That was one of the more difficult decisions we had to make," Woodward replied. "We spent considerable time in determining to use that information. We finally decided that a person's private life often explains his professional life. In that context, we thought it was important enough to put into the book."

"How," I asked, "were you able to verify such intimate information?"

"I can't mention names," he replied. "But I can tell you that we adopted the same policy in writing the book that we used in working on the Watergate story for the *Post*—every fact had to have a minimum of two sources."

"What about the many denials now coming forth from the Nixons' sons-in-law, David Eisenhower and Edward Cox, General Alexander Haig, Kissinger, and so forth?"

"Those are largely 'diplomatic denials,' " Bob replied. "We expected them. Sources often tell you things in person, but when they see them in print they get cold feet. Two persons even informed us that they *would* deny having talked to us when the book came out. Look, we collected all this information about one of the most unusual chapters in American history. Do we launder it, or publish it?"

"Dig you later, Watergater."

But I still wasn't convinced that the authors did their homework on the Nixons' homework.

I then asked one of Nixon's longtime associates, Herb Klein, to comment on the report that the Nixons had declared a quarantine on the world's oldest indoor sport. "I consider that a low blow, and I'd challenge it," he replied. "First, because who knows the truth? Only Nixon and Pat, and they certainly wouldn't discuss it. Second, I've spent considerable time with them alone, and they always were a close-knit couple, much friendlier in private than they showed in public. And you don't have to be a psychiatrist to know there would be signals of distress between them if the story were true." That was the end of my investigative reporting on the alleged sterility in the White House.

On a far less sexier note, I recall the time Essee and I were guests at the Nixon White House. As we passed through the reception line, the

President pulled two cigars he had stashed in his pocket for the occasion and said, "You always gave me those cheap cigars when I appeared on your TV show. So now I'm going to reciprocate by giving you two real Cubans." When we got to Pat, who hadn't heard Nixon's comment, she looked at the cigars in my hand and exclaimed, "Oh, did you two have a baby?"

Richard Nixon was the unlikeliest person in the world to turn the White House into a swingin' jazz festival. Yet that's what this unfathomable man did in 1969, when he paid tribute to Duke Ellington on the great star's 70th birthday. Next to the day that Essee and I and our children spent with Harry Truman, this was the most exciting White House visit in our experience. To honor Duke, who incidentally was a native of Washington and whose father had worked as a menial in the White House, Nixon had invited practically every leading jazz artist in the nation to join the celebration. It was Woodstock in black-tie. Seeing so many black artists in a White House not known for its civil rights support was startling enough.

Dave Brubeck, Earl (Fatha) Hines, Hank Jones, Billy Taylor, Ellington, of course, and Nixon—all took turns winging it at the 11½ foot grand piano in a night of musical merriment that turned the White House into a veritable Jazz, Ltd. But the night really belonged to the two men at the top and bottom of the piano-playing scale, Duke and Dick.

Nixon, in a light-hearted mood, turned the evening into a personal triumph with his charm and wit. One of the guests, moviemaker Otto Preminger, summed it up by saying: "I know that half the people here tonight, including me, didn't vote for Mr. Nixon. But after this, we all have a new appreciation of him." The President's toast to Ellington at dinner signaled the mood: "In the many years of White House dinners," he said, "we have toasted kings and queens and princes. But this is the first time we have toasted a Duke."

Later, in presenting the Presidential Medal of Freedom to Ellington, Mr. Nixon got a laugh when he cited Ellington's full name and significantly paused in reading it. "Edward Kennedy . . . Ellington." The obvious reference to his possible Democratic opponent in '72 didn't escape the guests.

Then Nixon made his way to the piano to lead the guests in singing "Happy Birthday" to Duke. Halfway there, the president halted, turned to the audience and said, "I'm going to play—don't anybody leave." Mr. Nixon got through the song without a single clinker, but with no serious challenge to the five other pianists on hand. And the Duke added his own showmanship to the affair by standing and saluting each of the performing jazz stars after they completed their mini-concerts of all-Ellington music. The band, assembled for the occasion, consisted of Lou Bellson on drums, Clark Terry and Billy Berry on trumpet, Paul Desmond and Gerry Mulligan on saxophone, Urbie Green and J. J. Johnson on trombone, Jim Hall on guitar, Milt Hinton on bass and vocalists Joe Williams, Mary Mayo and Lou Rawls.

It was past midnight when Nixon rose to announce the jazz concert was over, but not the evening. "We'll now clear the East Room so it can be set up for a jam session," he declared. And from then, until the wee hours, the room "swang."

Never in the history of the White House had there been such toe-tapping, finger-snapping and wild dancing at a presidential party.

At last, this wonderfully sparkling and simultaneously intimate event came to an end, with Nixon playing a duet with Duke. Duke then bid goodbye to us the way he'd said hello, by saying, "I kiss you on the left cheek. I kiss you on the right cheek. But I won't kiss you on the two other cheeks."

Spiro AGNEW

Vice President Spiro Agnew, who went down in ignomy, further blemishing the Nixon White House, and I tangled on a number of occasions. One resulted when he made one of his outrageous statements, which I answered in the following paragraph:

We trust Spiro Agnew is more accurate in his other charges than he has been in naming the Jews "who control the media in this country." Two glaring errors pop out immediately: Agnew cites Julian Goodman, head of NBC, and Mrs. Katharine Graham, publisher of the *Washington Post,* among the "influential Jews who helped create a disastrous U.S. Middle East policy." Just to set the record straight, Goodman was born a Southern Baptist and now is an elder in the Larchmont (N.Y.) Presbyterian Church. Mrs. Graham, one-fourth Jewish, was reared as an Episcopalian and was married in an Episcopal church, as were her children. So much for a nattering nabob of negativism.

And later, after he had been forced out of office by pleading *nolo contendere* on charges of accepting bribes as governor of Maryland, he appeared on my TV show. By this time Agnew was representing Arab oil interests and defending their cause against Israel. I pointed out that he previously had accepted any number of awards from Jewish organizations and was known as a strong supporter of Israel. But now he was espousing the cause of the Arabs. Money, I indicated, had turned him completely around.

The exchange between us turned acrimonious. He defended his right to pursue whatever course he chose, regardless of what had happened before. The more I pressed him to explain his turnabout, the angrier he got, until he finally refused to discuss the matter and exclaimed, "Let's get onto another subject." After that he remained sullen and quiet. We didn't part too friendly.

Lyndon B. JOHNSON

One of the most controversial presidents, he knew how to handle Congress—but didn't know how to handle the Vietnam War. Probably because of this, L.B.J. received more death threats than any President: 7,000 a month.

He even was given criticism of his Vietnam policy from his own family. Lynda Bird, after seeing husband Captain Charles Robb sent off to Vietnam, returned to the White House and exclaimed to her father: "Why do we have to fight over there when so many people are opposed to the war? Why do we have to send two hundred boys over there in Chuck's company when there is so much opposition here at home? Why?" Shortly thereafter, L.B.J. announced his decision to withdraw as a candidate for re-election.

Through it all, Lady Bird, one of the great first ladies, was the one person who stood behind him. His love letters to her were startlingly romantic. . .as were L.B.J.'s love letters to a "sweet young thing" in Texas.

Hubert HUMPHREY

My relationship with Humphrey, the apostle of political joy, started during the 1948 Democratic convention in Philadelphia and ended with my visit to him at his home three days before he died.

Humphrey had enjoyed some regional popularity as mayor of Minneapolis. But it was the 1948 convention that established him as a national figure. He led the fight for a civil rights plank in the party's platform, a struggle so bitter that it drove southern Senators to leave the party and become anti-Democratic "Dixiecrats." They were one of the two wings of the party that deserted Harry Truman as he sought reelection. The Henry Wallace left-wing action was the other. Truman's victory was all the more remarkable because of the two defections.

Humphrey may have been the most ebullient and eloquent political figure of his time. His love of life and politics was boundless. He could articulate his position with a flood of words that left his adversaries speechless. He charmed friend and foe with a sparkling personality. And with his love of country, he invariably left you humming "God Bless America" to yourself.

Among his many other attributes, Essee considered him one of her finest dancing partners. He could tango and talk at the same time.

Humphrey loved Chicago and made so many visits during his vice-presidency that he became known as "L.B.J.'s ambassador to Chicago."

Yet Chicago was the city that probably cost him his chance to be president. He was nominated during that tumultuous convention of 1968, when the demonstrators and police became embroiled in violence that aroused the nation. I was visiting with Humphrey in his 25th floor Hilton Hotel suite, overlooking Grant Park, where the most bitter uprising took place. The look on his face, as he stared at his TV set and then from the picture window of his suite indicated he realized the election might be lost then and there.

Still, Humphrey, in his uphill campaign against Nixon, might have won had he shed his ties to Johnson and denounced the Vietnam War sooner. He finally did, but too late in the campaign, and that ended his lifelong ambition to be president, an office he would have filled with enthusiasm, energy and a spirit few brought to the White House.

It was Jan. 11, 1978, when I got a call from Jesse Jackson. "Humphrey is terminal at his home and he wants you and me to fly up there and see him." Jackson managed to get a private plane to fly us up to Minneapolis, where the Humphrey family arranged for a car to drive us the 40 miles to their home in Waverly.

Humphrey's wife, Muriel, ushered us into his bedroom and he greeted us in his usual effusive manner. But his wan appearance and barely audible voice confirmed that his days were down to a precious few. Still, he wanted to talk. Jesse and I stood at his bedside, bending over to hear his whisper-like comments. He turned first to Jesse, with whom he obviously had been impressed.

But what impressed me was the more Humphrey talked, slowly at first, the more he began to recapture his enthusiasm of old. He told Jackson, in some detail, how to obtain federal funding for his causes in Chicago, who to see, and what to say. He had an exact, if brief, answer for each of Jackson's questions. He was mentally alert even if death was just days away.

To me he talked about his lifelong effort to make public service an honorable profession and how to encourage young people to become involved. I thought of his eulogy as he added, softly, "I'd like to be remembered as a man who really gave of himself to his country."

It was time to leave and Jesse and I agreed, ever so sadly, that much of the joy of politics was gone.

I must add one footnote to the 1948 Democratic convention. All of us assigned to the story, obviously, reported that this was the first political convention covered by television. But none of us realized at that time how tremendous was the impact of TV. Little did we know that the face of politics would be forever changed.

27

The World's Longest Column

There's so much more. After 45 years of columning, there would have to be. And there's no way to wrap it in a neat package and tie it up with a bow.

So at this point, after some 13,000 columns, I'm going to claim a columnist's privilege and simply "item" some of the happenings and people who made things happen on my beat from 1943 through 1988. Here, in alphabetical order, is the world's longest column:

AIDS

Who would have thought the slogan, "Make love, not war" would be outdated so soon?

Ed ASNER

Though he made his name as a hard-boiled TV exec on the "Mary Tyler Moore Show" and a tough editor on his own "Lou Grant Show"—and fought unstintingly for causes in which he believed—Asner admits to being a coward. It even drove this winner of more than half a dozen Emmys to a psychiatrist at the height of his success. Asner reminds me of the "cowardly" lion in the *Wizard of Oz*—a brave man.

Lauren BACALL

A fine actress and interesting woman, the most interesting thing

to me about Lauren is the men she chose. What four could be more different than Humphrey Bogart, Adlai Stevenson and Frank Sinatra and Jason
Robards? Ms. Bacall carried on an intense flirtation with Stevenson while
campaigning for him, but the relationship was never more than that. On
the other hand, she was euphoric when Sinatra swept her off her feet. . .
and turned bitter when he jilted her with no warning. She could whistle
for me any time.

Ernie BANKS

The most famous and beloved modern Chicago Cub baseball
player, like so many athletes who reached the top, Ernie had to make a difficult adjustment when his playing career was over. His marriage crum-
bled and jobs in keeping with his stature were rare. He did continue with
the Cubs in a public relations capacity, making appearances, signing autographs, delivering speeches and bringing his indomitable "Let's Play Two"
today spirit to Wrigley Field.

But one chapter in Ernie's life made him something special for me
and countless others who were aware of the situation. Leo Durocher, then
managing the Cubs, detested Ernie. He was jealous of Ernie's popularity,
which overshadowed his. And The Lip did whatever he could to down-
grade and even embarrass Ernie on the field. But Banks never complained
and never cracked under pressure. He remained No. 1 and never went
public with his problem. He was a class act at all times. And, of course,
he outlasted Durocher.

The BEATLES

Probably the most popular singing group of this century, the Beatles
once claimed they were more popular than Jesus. Hardly anyone made a
stink (though when they said they were more popular than Frank Sinatra,
they got flak).

Paul McCartney was really the musical leader of the group and, underneath it all, rather conventional. When he married Linda, he was worried that the groupies who followed him everywhere would think he'd
gone square "because I'm a married man now and my wife is in the act."

I was closest to Yoko and John—who was really the ideological leader
of the group. I took them to task for castigating this country, then suddenly loving it when they faced deportation. But they called on me when
Yoko's daughter disappeared and they thought she might be in the Chicago area. They asked if I would print this message in the column:
"Happy birthday, Kyoko, wherever you are. Please get in touch with us

through the media. We miss you very much." And another message to Tony Cox, Kyoko's father who had disappeared with her, despite a court order granting custody to Yoko: "Give us a chance. The war's over, if you so want it."

Saul BELLOW

After he won the Nobel prize for literature in 1976, I asked this leading Chicago author whether it meant more than all the other awards he'd received. "I can answer that by citing the experience I had with my young son," he answered. "I took him on a tour of Europe, during which we visited dozens of museums and churches. We finally came to St. Peter's Basilica in Rome. I told him this was the largest church in the world. 'Good,' he told me, 'Now we don't have to see any more.' " That was Bellow's way of indicating he'd had enough awards, a reaction I can understand. But Bellow and I were never close. In fact, in one of his books he invented a character who was a caricature of me. And most unflattering. I never mentioned the book to him, nor did I give him the satisfaction of knowing I was aware of his backstabbing. Let's say our personal relationship cooled.

Yogi BERRA

Along with Yankee manager Casey Stengel, under whom Berra played, Yogi is the king of the malaprop. Of the many Yogi anecdotes in circulation, the one which broke me up most was when in 1962 I told Yogi that the Russians were thinking of trading captured spy pilot Gary Powers for Rudolph Abel. Yogi observed, "It figures to help both clubs." Yogi developed an image like Samuel Goldwyn, famous for his malapropisms, most of which were concocted by others. The same was true for Yogi. Still, the one I know Yogi did utter concerned the most popular New York restaurant of the day: "It's so crowded, that nobody goes there anymore."

BULLFIGHTS

If you're ever tempted to see one...don't. Or maybe you should, so that you'd never want to see another. I witnessed my first—and last—corrida in Palma de Mallorca while Essee and I were on our usual vacation in London and Europe. I'd seen animals accorded more merciful treatment in the slaughterhouses of the old Chicago Stockyards. There, at least they were put to death with one powerful blow. In the so-called sports arena of the corrida, the bull was tortured with a series of stabbings that caused him slowly to bleed to death before the "brave" matador delivered the coup de grace. First, the picadores came on horseback and drove javelin-like sticks into the bull's neck and shoulders. Then came the banderilleros who stabbed the bull with small swords. Finally, with blood gushing from the plethora of wounds and the bull's life ebbing, the grand matador entered the ring and tormented him with red cape and fancy footwork. Better Mike Tyson should take on Woody Allen.

Jane BYRNE

Chicago's first female mayor wasn't a credit to the women's movement with her bizarre conduct, but she was a newspaperman's delight. She was feisty, alternately vicious and gracious and set a record for flip-flopping. *Time* magazine called her "Calamity Jane." I called her "Ayatollah Jane," and previously, when she was serving as the city's consumer chief and was locked in battle over taxi rates, I referred to her as "My Fare Lady."

Our bittersweet relationship was somewhat difficult because Jane was very fond of Essee and often gave her civic assignments, one of which was to serve as hostess for the visit of Queen Beatrice of the Netherlands. Essee was honored by Beatrice with a medal and the title of Dame. I spared Essee the comment that she was a helluva dame long before she met Queen Beatrice.

Ayatollah Jane was an item in the column almost every day. Essee flinched, but she never asked me to let up. I merely was calling 'em as I saw 'em.

There was the time I received a call from the White House about Jane. A top aide to President Carter asked with more than a little consternation: "Less than two weeks ago, your mayor declared at the dinner which the President attended that if the election were that night, she'd vote for Jimmy Carter. What did Carter do in the last 11 days to make her change her mind? We don't understand that kind of politics." Janie, of course, had done her 1,001st flip-flop, endorsing Carter for president in 1980 one night, and 11 days later switching to Ted Kennedy.

Her moods spared no one, including husband Jay McMullen. Often, she made him go under wraps so that there wouldn't be problems. But frequently he did travel with her, and what happened when Jane was about to make a speech in San Antonio was typical. McMullen, a former newspaperman and speech writer, had prepared Jane's address. In a public scene worthy of Virginia Woolf, she looked over the speech and shouted at him: "Why don't you just throw it in the trash!"

And I took delight in repeating from time to time a quote attributed to Jay, who in a moment of exhiliration, told a magazine writer, "My wife has the niftiest pair of legs and the cutest ass."

Yet the time that Jane and I got into it most warmly was when she called me a "freeloader." Her Honor made that "freeloading" charge, among others, on her return from a vacation in the sun in Puerto Rico. Too much sun has been known to have a deleterious effect on people. The mayor's effort to besmirch this reporter, along with the *Tribune's* Bob Wiedrich, wasn't consequential. She publicly labeled Wiedrich and myself as "two of the greatest freeloaders in the city," adding that restaurant owners around town invariably picked up our tabs. I asked my lawyer/accountant, Marshall Harris, to round up all my receipts for restaurant bills and delivered them to Jane. End of accusation.

And I'm sure Lady Jane was embarrassed when I printed how many traffic tickets she received for illegally parking her car near 111 E. Chestnut Street, where Jay lived. That was in her pre-mayoral days when she was serving as the city's consumer chief and was dating Jay. Many of the tickets, I pointed out, indicated her car was parked there long past midnight and the inference was obvious. But Jane maintained, with a straight face, that it was all in the line of duty because she was making speeches in that area. And she said it without cracking a smile. "If you believe that," I wrote, "Boy, have I got a bridge for you...."

For all her irrational behavior as mayor, I still had a soft spot for Jane. Her bizarre conduct helped fill many a column.

Truman CAPOTE

It's a scene still fresh in my memory: Truman Capote sobbing uncontrollably.

Let me set the stage. Capote happened to be in town on the night Larry Adler, the harmonica virtuoso, was opening at the Tango restaurant. We invited Truman to join our party, which also included two outstanding drama critics, Glenna Syse of the *Sun-Times* and Richard Christiansen of the *Tribune*.

Shortly before, the first chapter of Capote's *Answered Prayers*, a book he never finished, appeared in *Esquire* magazine. The reaction to the chapter was cataclysmic, especially among his New York friends. He had revealed some of their deepest secrets, all told to him, they thought, off the record. But Truman took the position that "everybody knows I'm a writer and they should have known that I would use those stories."

Many a friend denounced him, but only one really hurt. That was "Babe" Paley, wife of the chairman of CBS and a leader in New York society. She had been one of his dearest companions.

With that background, shift back to the Tango. Adler played a tune that obviously reminded Truman of Mrs. Paley. He burst into tears. His sobbing shook the table, as well as the rest of us. Between his flood of tears, he moaned, "I've lost her, I've lost her." Capote was hunched over the table, sobbing and shaking. And in his shaking, he knocked over a glass of water that sent the rest of us scrambling. Adler, still playing, looked at Truman aghast. The other patrons also were staring at our table, wondering what was going on.

Truman finally gained control of himself, straightened up and watched, red-eyed, as Adler completed his performance.

His sobbing was justified. Babe Paley never talked to him again.

Johnny CARSON

Probably the most private person in show biz, I was still able to gain a scoop on one of his divorces.

William (Billy) CARTER

Billy gave a new meaning to the phrase "brotherly love." Though two recent presidents, Richard Nixon and Lyndon Johnson, had to bear the burden of wayward brothers, Billy's loose-lipped litany of loathing blew the Nixon and Johnson kin out of the water. An example: Billy, right after making some anti-Semitic statements, called Jimmy's dearest friend, Atlanta attorney Charles Kirbo, "about the dumbest bastard I ever met."

Billy's motive was simple: Jealousy. And the moral is that the thoughtless seldom are wordless.

Chevy CHASE

One of the most creative comedians, he had the balls to stand up to network bosses. Chase once told me that the TV execs were "killing comedy on TV," especially by censoring comedians' ad libs, so that "the best jokes are never heard by the audience."

CHICAGO

If they asked me, I could write a book. . . .

However, I will simply quote from Le Figaro, a leading Paris daily: "Chicago is now the primary city in the United States." To which I add, "Amen."

However, primary does not mean perfect. *Le Figaro* added: "Il estime que la place des Noirs est dans leurs ghettos." Loosely translated: "I believe that the place of the Blacks is in the ghetto."

Bill COSBY

An enduring comedian because, like Bob Hope before him, Cos' humor is rooted in unchanging values. When Bob Culp, with whom Cosby soared to fame in the TV series "I Spy," wrote a script and asked Bill to do it with him, there was nothing in show business at the time that Cosby wanted more. But he was serving as an Adjunct Professor at the University of Massachusetts and *that* he wanted more.

When in Chicago, he spends most of his spare time playing tennis at the McClurg Sports Arena or slot machines with his friend, restaurateur Jimmy Rittenberg.

CRITICS

Essee says that I'm the only person she knows who doesn't have an enemy in the world—but it isn't quite true. Every week, hate mail comes across my desk. I have frequently received threatening letters from Let Freedom Ring, an ultra-right-wing organization which has long promised to "zero in" on this reporter for an exposé. When I supported Uncle Sam's stand on Lieutenant William Calley, Jr.'s, court-martial, I got a bomb threat or two. I hardly ever answer any of them in print.

But in December of 1976, the tedious TV critic of the *Chicago Tribune*, Gary Deeb—who had almost made a career of criticizing me—also made no fewer than five errors in his column, and I couldn't resist pointing it out. Carroll O'Connor had previously written Deeb's editor saying that Gary was not above pilfering ideas and items from the Hollywood trade papers. Unfortunately, he didn't pilfer accuracy.

When I questioned Deeb's inaccuracies, I didn't want to keep repeating his name, so referred to him as "he of the prickly personality." You get the inference.

Deeb and I eventually patched it up and now we're nodding acquaintances.

Richard J. DALEY

He generally was regarded as the greatest mayor in the world during most of his adminstration. He was the master technician, who knew every facet of city government and spared no effort for the city he truly loved. His blind spot, however, came in race relations and his popularity started to dwindle with the arrival of the civil rights movement, when he lost the black community. It was during his administration that Chicago became known as "the city that works." And he died as would have wanted—in office.

Daley had the reputation of governing with an iron hand, but little known is the fact that he accomplished as much with his art of persuasion as he did with his velvet glove. One of his shortcomings was the inability, at times, to express himself clearly. This led to a classic statement by his press secretary, Earl Bush, who once castigated the press with, "Don't print what he says—print what he means."

But actions speak louder than words and Daley was able to accomplish wonders in office.

Sammy DAVIS, JR.

Sammy once kidded about himself: "I've been on the cover of *Ebony* twice—once with Frank Sinatra, a Gentile, and once with my wife, who's white [Mai Britt at the time]. I still have hopes of making *Ebony* as just an ordinary Jewish black."

The years have dimmed this story, but it will remain ever fresh in my memory—the story linking Kim Novak, then the blonde and beautiful Hollywood queen and Sammy Davis, Jr., then as now "Mr. Talent."

Let me set the stage: Kim Novak, born Marilyn Pauline Novak in Chicago, was "discovered" after she won a beauty pageant with a unique name, "Miss Deep Freeze," sponsored obviously by a home appliance firm. Nothing could be further from Kim's persona than "deep freeze," as her many Hollywood romances later proved.

She came on the scene in 1957 just as Harry Cohn, the despotic ruler of Columbia Pictures, was having contract trouble with Rita Hayworth. He quickly signed Kim as a threat to Rita and then started pushing her into stardom. Boasted Cohn at the time, "I'm going to manufacture a star to replace Hayworth." And he made good on his promise. In three years, Kim was among Hollywood's leading box office attractions. But the critics still reported Kim wasn't an actress in the true sense of the word. To which Harry screamed, "After eight pictures, what do you expect, Greta Garbo?"

It was at this time that I got a tip from Hollyweird: Novak and Sammy Davis had fallen in love and they were Chicago-bound, by train, so that Kim could introduce him to her parents, Mr. and Mrs. Joe Novak. I broke the story and Cohn promptly threw a fit. His "star" marrying a black! That was preposterous in those days. Her career would be ruined and his "manufactured" star could forget Hollywood. More, he had three Kim Novak films in the can and he visualized millions of dollars going down the drain.

Cohn didn't wait long to act. He called on some of the "boys" to warn Sammy. Either break it off with Novak or you'll lose your other eye.

Sammy could read the fine print. Cohn was playing hard ball. Not only was Davis warned to end his affair with Novak, but he also had to marry a black woman to prove his fling with Kim was meaningless. A short time later, Davis made a surprising announcement. He would marry an unknown dancer, Loray White, of his own race and "live happily ever after." The shotgun marriage was just for show...Harry Cohn's show. Within a few weeks the marriage was dissolved. I doubt if Sammy ever saw Kim again. And Cohn had his "manufactured" star to keep the box office jingling for a few more movies.

Walt DISNEY

When this genius (natch, he was a Chicagoan) died at the end of 1966, it was the first Disney story without a happy ending.

Phil DONAHUE

Though Erma Bombeck calls him, "Every wife's replacement for the husband who doesn't talk to her," off-camera the perfectionistic Phil can throw a temper tantrum over the slightest slip by his staff. Because Donahue's wife Marlo is the daughter of Danny Thomas, it was natural that we should all be close. His book, My Own Story, bears this inscription: "To Kup and Essee, with gratitude for their kindness and relief that they didn't report all the items in this book before I did. Love, Phil."

DOONESBURY

This famed cartoon by Garry Trudeau in 1979 depicted leading Chicago attorney Sid Korshak in such deprecatory and libelous terms that many editors refused to run the strip. As a result, a rival cartoonist (using Trudeau's style) did a cartoon with what was obviously Trudeau talking to his lawyer, who asked: "Do you have any proof?" and "Trudeau" replies: "Hell, I don't need any proof. This is just a cartoon!"

Clint EASTWOOD

Today's John Wayne, Clint is what he seems to be, a straight-shooter. However, he isn't the "Dirty Harry" he became famous for on the screen. Clint once ran afoul of Barbara Walters, for example, when he accepted an invitation to attend a Hugh Hefner party in 1980 to watch the closed circuit telecast of the Ali–Holmes fight at the West Coast Playboy mansion. Barbara, a late arrival, spotted Eastwood...whom she'd interviewed on TV just hours earlier, and exclaimed: "What are *you* doing here? You just told me in our interview, Clint, that you never—but *never*—attended Hollywood parties!"

Jane FONDA

"Causes," from politics to shaping up notwithstanding, Jane Fonda is simply...real showbiz. She appeared at Notre Dame in the fall of 1970 and was asked if she ever won an Oscar whether she would accept it. Jane replied that she despised the Academy Awards and would *not* accept an Oscar. Fade into April 10, 1972...and Jane on stage...to accept her Oscar.

More recently, Jane ran afoul of Vietnam veterans, who threatened to prevent her from starring in a film shot in New England. She had long been criticized by veterans for coddling up to the Vietnamese during the war. But now her career was being hampered. So Jane asked for time on Barbara Walter's "20/20" TV show for a *mea culpa* speech. She satisfied many Vietnam vets, but some American citizens still have trouble forgiving "Hanoi Jane."

William FRIEDKIN

A Chicagoan, who gets my vote as Hollywood's top director (beginning with *The French Connection* in the 1970s and later, *The Exorcist*), he has spent more time trying to save the life of Paul Crump, a convicted murderer on Death Row, than on any of his marvelous movies.

Friedkin enjoyed a meteoric rise, from menial worker at WGN-TV in Chicago to Oscar winner for *The French Connection*. He oft describes himself as my "protege." But not true. Talent won out and he has a surplus.

Cary GRANT

As classy an actor—and a man—who ever put his footprints in Grauman's Chinese Theatre...but also known as "the first of the nonspenders." In 1968 when Dyan Cannon won a divorce from Cary, she was bitterly disappointed at the court's financial arrangement. Her attorney termed it "peanuts" in view of the actor's multi-million dollar fortune. However, Cary had given Dyan several expensive gifts of jewelry—so expensive that Hollywood was amazed. It was later learned that Grant had not purchased the gems, but had taken them out of his vault. . . where he kept a collection of jewelry "repossessed" from previous wives.

Paul HARVEY

One of a handful of commentators who has endured and has such a large following that in a recent radio rating, his five ABC news shows were listed 1-2-3-4-5. Nobody can touch that. He also commands one of the largest fees for speeches, an estimated $20,000. And I know him well enough to state that the brains behind the Harvey empire is his wife, Angel. She handles the money.

Hugh HEFNER

Essee doesn't give him a "10" when it comes to personality. And there's no doubt Hef isn't personally as exciting as the pages of *Playboy* are—or *were*. . . but none can deny he was an innovator in magazine publishing and played a major role in the sexual revolution.

I recall a quarter of a century ago Hefner had his own scoop in the making by paying a then record sum of $25,000 for revealing photographs of Marilyn Monroe (taken while she was filming *Something's Got To Give*). The photos were to be featured in his December 1962 issue to commemorate the ninth anniversary of *Playboy* and of Marilyn's famous calendar nude. When M.M. died, H.H. simply tossed out the photos.

Ernest HEMINGWAY

Hemingway was the embodiment of a writer who lived what he wrote. Because of that, he had innumerable brushes with death. Each time, "the legendary luck of Hemingway" pulled him through. When Hemingway reached the point when he could no longer be the man he wanted to be, he ended his life.

One time, it seemed certain he had died in an African air crash. A few of us, including the famed critic and authority on Hemingway, Malcolm Cowley, and well-known Michigan Avenue bookseller Stuart Brent, gathered to reminisce. No longer, we sadly agreed, would visitors to Havana drop into the "Florida" restaurant on the chance of seeing Hemingway holding court in his favorite haunt. And no longer would Hemingway's pals phone the owner of the Hotel Ambos Mundos in Havana to make an appointment with the author. (The hotel owner was the contact through whom you reached Hemingway when he was "hiding out" and inaccessible.)

Another Hemingway brush with death, Cowley recalled, was the time in World War I when Ernest was serving with the U.S. Red Cross ambulance corps in Italy. As usual, he sought and found danger. In this instance, he accompanied three Italian soldiers to a point so close to the lines of the enemy, Austria, that they were easy targets for a grenade. Two of the Italians were killed immediately. The third lost a leg. Hemingway was hit hard by shrapnel. Despite his wounds, "Papa" put the surviving Italian on his back and started for safety. They were near the Italian lines when the enemy's searchlight caught Hemingway in its glare. A burst of machine gun fire hit him in the leg and foot and, as he later recounted, "I was sure I was a goner." The Italian he was carrying on his back had died and the soldiers who retrieved Hemingway were sure he was dead, too. Ernest wore the look of death as he was hauled back to safety. But his amazing resistance pulled him through with nothing more serious than a game leg he was to carry through life.

In World War II, there was "Task Force Hemingway." It consisted of five or six unemployed soldiers of fortune who managed to keep ahead of the U.S. forces advancing on Paris. Hemingway's "task force" joined up with the French resistance group, the Maqui, to capture a Nazi-held town near Paris. There they sat and waited for Uncle Sam's troops to catch up with them for the grand march into Paree. For reportedly carrying arms in this military maneuver, Hemingway was court-martialed. He had violated the military order that war correspondents were not to bear weapons. But Hemingway's fellow correspondents came to his rescue and testified, undoubtedly with tongue in cheek, that they never saw him committing such a dastardly deed. He was acquitted, one of the few times the brass ever winked at an obvious violation of military law.

And in the midst of our reminiscing came the good news—Hemingway's downed plane was located and he was alive. Once again, the "Hemingway Luck" prevailed.

My one in-depth meeting with Hemingway will always be vivid. I was struck first by his physical persona, then by the meticulous perfectionism in everything he did and said. But, most of all, I will never forget the way this great storyteller listened. He was capable of marshalling his complete attention on the person speaking, his eyes wide open and yet boring into you. He dominated our conversation completely, not by what he said . . . but by how he *listened*.

Rock HUDSON

At the end, this native of north suburban Chicago gave me one of the most horrifying sights I've seen. Rock looked so bad that many of his friends actually failed to recognize him in the final months.

Hollywood and those who covered it had always known of his homosexuality, of course. But Rock was discreet and for awhile no problems arose. When the talk inevitably got to a point which worried Rock's agent, Hudson agreed to marry the agent's secretary, Phyllis Gates, in an effort to end the rumors. They never spent a night together, Gates confided, and were soon separated and quietly divorced two years later.

"Dynasty's" Linda Evans, despite reports to the contrary, bore him no ill will for kissing her on the mouth when he appeared on that show during his illness. A decent human being with deep problems, Rock's sometimes sparkling and yet largely tragic life might have been summed up when he told me: "I really wanted to be a singer."

Howard HUGHES

An enigma—with an unparalleled predilection for privacy.

Though paranoid about his privacy, Hughes was sensitive to everything going on in the world, particularly what was written about him. Periodically, while he was ensconced in hideouts from London to Acapulco, I received calls from his long-time confidant Perry Lieber, who would report, "The boss asked me to tell you that he liked what you wrote about him" or "The boss is mad as hell at you, and wants you to call so-and-so to get more details on your story."

Lieber, one of the giants among movie publicists, had an unusual role in working for Hughes. He was the only press agent paid a fabulous fee to keep his client's name *out* of the press.

Mahalia JACKSON

She had a heart as big as her voice.

I worked with Mahalia on dozens of benefits to raise scholarship funds for ghetto youngsters. To Mahalia, money was only something to give others. Typically, she made a most generous provision in her will for her first husband, a post office clerk, though their marriage was very brief.

True to her religious beliefs, Mahalia never played Las Vegas despite huge financial offers. Nor would she appear anywhere if liquor was served. I may have been responsible for Mahalia's only violation of that strict adherence. It happened when I invited her to join the array of stars who appeared annually at the Harvest Moon Festival. She was, of course, the star of the evening. And after the performance, Mahalia was invited to join the cast party, held traditionally in the swank Ambassador East. "Oh, no," she replied. "I don't belong there," apparently believing a black wouldn't be welcome. But I pleaded and insisted. And finally Mahalia, reluctantly, did agree to attend the party. And, as you might expect, when she walked into the room she received a standing ovation from all the other stars.

But I turned red during the ovation. I suddenly remembered alcohol was being served and many of the artists had drinks in their hands. Had Mahalia known this beforehand, no way would she have attended. But she was courteous enough to ignore the drinks being served and enjoyed the adulation to the fullest. She was, however, the first to leave.

At the hundredth anniversary of the Civil War in Washington, D.C., a slew of notables, from Bruce Catton to Arthur Schlesinger, attended. But Mahalia stole the show with these words: "I can understand how you experts feel about the Civil War. But this occasion has a deeper and more personal feeling for me—for the granddaughter of a slave to sing at the Lincoln Memorial."

Jackie KENNEDY

Jackie's half-sister, Lee Radziwill, once told me that their mother urged the two girls to "be more like Julie Andrews." And, in an essential sense, Jackie was more like Julie Andrews than Julie Andrews was. In her marriage to J.F.K., she had to endure his infidelities and his early death which left her with two children to raise. In her marriage to Aristotle Onassis, she was really more of a pawn in the intense rivalry between multimillionaire shipowners Onassis and Stavros Spiros Niarchos, each trying to outdo the other in seeking respectability. Moreover, Ari still visited his true love in Paris, Maria Callas, during his union to Jackie. Yet, through these and other trials and tribulations, Jackie never lost her dignity.

Onassis, by the way, was a hamburger freak. Jack Benny once told me of a night in Monaco in the wee hours when the two decided to have a snack. Onassis ordered a hamburger, and then slammed it down in disgust. "Look how big this hamburger is," he exclaimed. "I keep telling them to make thin ones. I own this stand. I own the gambling casino, I own the hotels—but I can't get a decent hamburger!"

In Jackie, he had filet mignon.

Henry KISSINGER

Sharp-tongued, with an equally sharp intellect, Kissinger is typified by a remark he made at the world premiere of the movie *Superman* in 1979: "I want to thank Warner Brothers for making the story of my life." Some years before, when he was dating the gorgeous Jill St. John, Kissinger was in the news because of kidnap threats. I could never understand why anyone would want to kidnap Kissinger when Jill was around.

Robin LEACH

Rich and famous because of his "Lifestyles of the Rich and Famous," I recently asked Robin which rich-and-famous person was the most unusual of them all. Without hesitation, he named Japan's Yoshiek Tsutsumi (who *Forbes* magazine reported was the richest man in the world with over $20 billion). "Tsutsumi was undoubtedly the cheapest man I ever met," confided Robin. "He would use Scotch tape to keep his shoes together. He would have the used sheets in the hotels he owned cut up into towels for his offices." Tsutsumi earns half a million dollars an hour in interest alone.

Jerry LEWIS

Jerry, of course, is noted for his indefatigable efforts on behalf of muscular dystrophy. Little known is the fact that an extemporaneous remark cost him one of the major supporters of his annual telethon. While ad libbing with Ed McMahon, Lewis blurted out that Budweiser (McMahon's sponsor) "is my brand and the best." This pleased Ed, but not Olympia Brewing Company, the sole sponsor of that telethon, which had pledged $618,000 and promptly withdrew its support (although continuing to raise funds for the Muscular Dystrophy Association in other ways). . . .

LIBERACE

I got credit for breaking the news that the famed entertainer was dying of AIDS. But actually the *Las Vegas Sun* was first to indicate he was a victim of the terminal illness. As soon as the *Sun* story was relayed to me by a friend in Las Vegas, I got on the phone. I reached out for a number of contacts in Las Vegas, one of whom managed to talk to Liberace's doctor. He confirmed the story. I tried reaching Liberace's manager, Seymour Heller, a long time friend, but he was taking no calls. I decided I had enough verification to go with the story.

Essee had seen Lee some months before when he came to Chicago and appeared on my TV show. She was startled by his appearance and asked if he had had a "face job." He covered up by saying "Yes, but it was a terrible job." The AIDS signs were all there at that time.

Though Liberace's homosexuality was obvious, he made every effort to hide it. Many years ago, a London paper described him as a homosexual. He sued and won, but the verdict later was reversed.

Like many gays in show business who sought desperately to remain in
the closet, Liberace paid dearly. The first incident involving Liberace that
came to my attention occurred while he was on tour for his movie, *Sincerely Yours*. Warner Brothers assigned two press agents, Frank Casey and
Joe Friedman, to accompany him with strict instructions, "Don't let anything happen." The warning said it all. But in New Orleans, Lee managed
to elude the two publicists for an hour or two. And they eventually found
him in a hotel room, with another male. Lee avoided publicity over the
affair, but he paid off handsomely.

Joe LOUIS

A beautiful human being and possibly the greatest heavyweight who
ever laced on gloves.

And Joe was no slouch when it came to words. There was the time he
was preparing to fight Billy Conn and the press kept reminding him that
Conn was so fleet of foot that Louis may never catch him. To which Louis
riposted, "He can run, but he can't hide." That classic has been used
many times, especially by President Reagan (without attribution).

And Conn did come close to using his speed to defeat Louis. For 13
rounds, he stayed clear of Joe's devastating punches and outboxed him. He
was well ahead on points when he made the fatal decision to go for a
knockout. But trading punches with Joe was not the smartest strategy.
Louis finally scored a knockout.

Before their second fight, Conn told me "I can outbox Louis for 50
rounds and that's what I'll do this time." but there's many a slip between
cup and lip. Conn was kayoed in eight. This one was comparatively dull
until the knockout...so much so that a famous ringsider, President Truman, dozed off in the early rounds.

Conn and Jim Braddock, from whom Joe won the heavyweight championship in Comiskey Park, had something in common. Neither feared
Louis, which was a rarity among his opponents. Many were defeated before they stepped foot in ring. Few persons remember that Braddock, the
"Cinderella Man" of the ring, came close to knocking out Joe in the first
round. He caught Louis with a devastating right that rocked the Brown
Bomber. But then, in his eagerness to finish him off, Braddock threw
punches carelessly and wildly. That gave Joe time to hold on and regain
his poise. And the end then became apparent, Joe by a kayo and the new
"champeen" of the world.

Joe was as gentle outside the ring as he was deadly inside. But he had
two overwhelming flaws. He had no sense of money. He squandered it ev-

ery which way and fell so far behind in his income tax that Uncle Sam, generously, gave him a pass as an "uncollectable case." And he fell on such evil times that his last job, provided by friends who still worshipped him, was as a shill in a Las Vegas casino.

And women. Any gal with good moves would put Louis down for the count. This caused the rupture in his marriage to the lovely Marva Spaulding. The marriage was on the rocks in the late 1940s, when Chicago Judge John Sbarbaro, in an attempt at reconciliation, had a heart-to-heart talk with the couple in his chambers. He pointed out to Louis that he was the idol of millions of youngsters who might be influenced by his actions. And the judge suggested to Marva that her singing career might best be discarded in order to remain wife of the world champion. Sbarbaro thought he had the couple convinced until the champ spoke up: "Judge, it's just no use. You've seen my fights. Let me tell you, I've had tougher ones with her than in the ring." The judge granted the divorce.

When Joe went after a woman, it was with the same persistence that he stalked a foe in the ring. I remember when Lena Horne was appearing at the Blackstone Hotel in Chicago. Joe was a nightly visitor and filled her suite with unmatchable gifts and flowers. The idyl didn't last long, but it was intense for its short duration. Just in passing, if you've seen Lena perform, you know she prances about the stage like a tigress, with the very same moves Joe used in the ring.

As they earlier said about John Barrymore, "Good night, sweet prince."

Dean MARTIN

Much funnier in person than his former sidekick, Jerry Lewis. One of the funniest remarks he ever made was in '64 when Sammy Davis, Jr., was panicky about a Goldwater victory. "Don't worry, Sammy," Dean soothed. "If Goldwater wins, I'll buy you!"

For every Martin bon mot, there are a dozen hilarious stories about Dino. The line that broke me up the most was Shecky Greene's: "Dean drinks so much that he doesn't even know that Jerry Lewis left him."

Willard MOTLEY

One of the first black authors to achieve national prominence in this era, he quickly learned that his popular book, *Knock On Any Door*, would be costly to him. It was 1947, and the landlord of Motley's half-unfurnished house in the slum area of North Wells heard about the book, knocked on the author's door and raised Motley's rent 50 percent!

Pablo PICASSO

I really think Chicago became his favorite American city because of the incredible amount of fan mail Picasso received from admirers of the huge sculpture that bears his name in the Loop. And, with his characteristic indefatigability, Picasso answered virtually every letter. A Chicago photographer, for example, took a color photograph of the sculpture and sent it to Pablo for an autograph. Nineteen months later, the photograph, with Picasso's autograph, was returned. . . .

PRINCE

Actually, a prince of a fellow. Teaching star, Marva Collins, head of Westside Prep School, received a half-million dollar contribution from the rock star, which enabled her to purchase the huge building across from her school on West Chicago Avenue to establish a national teacher training institute. This fulfilled Collins' dream of training more than a thousand teachers. Prince's interest in Marva began when he paid a visit to the school in 1983. He had come under criticism, by the way, for declining to join two dozen singing stars who in 1985 recorded an album in Hollywood to benefit famine-stricken Ethiopia. When I asked him about that, Prince said, "I prefer to do things myself, rather than with groups," and then reluctantly revealed that all the proceeds of his record, "Tears in Your Eyes," would be donated to Ethiopian relief.

Burt REYNOLDS

Burt's keen and mischievous sense of humor enables him to rise to almost any occasion. As a for instance, when he appeared in *The Rainmaker* with Lois Nettleton in Chicago, they were playing the key scene where con-man Burt is trying to convince Lois that he really *can* make rain and end the drought that imperils the farm area. At that precise moment, a typhoon-like rainstorm swept through the Chicago area, permeating the theater.

Burt, ever equal to the situation, simply stepped forward and said to the audience, "*See?*"

Paul ("The Waiter") RICCA

One of the central figures in Chicago crime for two generations, Ricca was finally laid to rest in fall of 1972 with his expensive sapphire ring on his pinky, and with matching sapphire cufflinks—just as he would have wanted it. Unfortunately, a mysterious couple knocked on the door of the Galewood Funeral Chapel late on the night before the funeral after all mourners had departed, pleading for admission because they had been delayed by traffic and simply "*had*" to pay their respects to a dear, *dear* friend.

The lone attendant allowed them to view the body of the beloved for a few minutes. When they left, the priceless ring was gone.

Jackie ROBINSON

A gutsy guy who broke the color line in baseball, but otherwise had too many bad breaks. Long before it became public, Jackie confided that he had failed to spend enough time with his son, Jackie, Jr. It wasn't until the boy was hooked on drugs that Robinson realized his shortcomings as a parent and helped his son get the monkey off his back. But Jackie, Jr., was killed shortly thereafter in an auto crash.

Robinson's baseball career was historic, but too brief. He was never in good health after he left the game, having developed diabetes, and he succumbed to a heart attack on the eve of the publication of his autobiography: *I Never Had It Made.*

Cybill SHEPHERD

Much has been made of the recent birth of twins to this former model, and forgotten is this statement she once made to me: "I'd rather be dead than wed."

Mr. T

This fierce-faced TV hero, who rose from Chicago night club bouncer to movie and TV stardom, was not always a hero to his family. He had severe problems with his brother, Gus Tero, a fireman, and his mother. But Mr. T made amends eventually. He bought a home in one of Chicago's most exclusive suburbs, Lake Forest, and then an adjacent one for his mother. And you remember the headlines when he chopped down the lovely oak trees on his estate, forgetting that "Only God can make a tree." We have patched up our differences (stemming from my column items about his family difficulties) and now he graciously responds when I call on him for benefit performances. He's a show-stopper with his eloquent, heart-felt speeches to youngsters about staying in school.

Elizabeth TAYLOR

One of the rare "child" stars who has survived—and whose beauty has survived—Elizabeth Taylor has countered criticism of her private life and multiple marriages by saying, "I never slept with a man unless I intended to marry him." In any case, she did get an early start on both. At the age of 17, Elizabeth had already been engaged and dis-engaged twice, to former Army football star Glenn Davis and millionaire William D. Pawley, Jr. Just before breaking her engagement to Pawley, she was called on the carpet by the boss of her studio, L. B. Mayer, who warned Liz that being linked with so many men in the gossip columns could hurt her career. "You shouldn't have so many boyfriends," he commented, "especially when you're engaged."

Liz found true love with producer Mike Todd, as flamboyant as he was street wise. The marriage was stormy, but love conquered all. Their frequent battles were page one news; their reconciliations were tender whispers in the night. One of the most poignant memories I have of Todd concerned the time I was in New York to cover a dinner honoring him. Flying from California to New York that day for the occasion, his plane crashed and the life of the colorful Mike Todd was snuffed out. Among the mourners that night were the cynics who exclaimed, "A finish only Mike Todd could arrange."

In the summer of 1965, Liz and Richard Burton played "true confessions" with Essee and me over an unforgettable two-hour luncheon in the Pump Room. Liz confided that only two of her marriages were really happy ones—to Mike Todd and, now, to Burton. "And you better believe that, Charlie," she added, looking directly into Burton's baby blues.

Richard confided that he was so happily married that he was no longer a "chaser." He admitted he had spent a good deal of his earlier life chasing pretty girls. "But no more, Luv," he exclaimed, looking directly into Liz's violet orbs. "Yes," deadpanned Liz, "no more—but no less, too?"

That's the way the conversation went with "Charlie" and "Luv," the pet names Burton and Liz used for each other. When the Burtons explained they'd finally found real happiness together, I believed it because of that good-natured ribbing and candor they enjoyed. "Everybody knew you were one of the world's greatest chasers," said Liz, getting in the needle again. "Maybe that's because I matured late in life, Luv," Richard philosophized. "I didn't discover girls until much later than most boys. So I tried to make up for lost time."

"But you didn't have to work *overtime* at it, Charlie," Liz shot back.

Most people believed Liz and Richard first met during those torrid *Cleopatra* love scenes, on and off camera, while she was married to Eddie Fisher and Richard to Sybil. But Burton set the facts straight that day. "We first met some 13 years ago, when Luv here was married to Michael

Wilding. She wouldn't give me the right time of day then. She completely ignored me."

"For some inexplicable reason," chimed in Liz, "I didn't like Richard then. Did I, Charlie? I don't know why, unless some kind of reverse chemistry was at work. I was rude to him. Now I realize that subconsciously that meant I must have liked him very much."

The subject of Mike Todd came up and I suggested that the Burtons' marriage must be very solid indeed to allow talk of previous husbands. "Only Mike Todd," replied Burton. "I knew and liked Mike. I can't say the same for her other husbands."

"And we both are very fond of Richard's ex-wife, Sybil, aren't we, Charlie?" interjected Liz, evening the score.

"I understand the young man she married, Jordan Christopher, is very quiet. He seldom speaks," Essee offered.

"That would be a natural next choice for her," said Burton.

And on that hint, Essee and your reporter departed, while Luv and Charlie prepared to entrain for Hollywood and the filming of *Who's Afraid of Virginia Woolf?*. . . in which they jabbed and screamed at each other as the screen has seldom seen.

Once before, Essee and I sat with Liz and Burton, but on a much sadder occasion. Es and I were dining at Chasens, the famed Hollywood restaurant. It was shortly after our beloved Cookie's death. Elizabeth and Richard were alone at an adjoining booth. They summoned us to join them because, as Liz declared, "I know how you feel and we'd like to commiserate with you." They did help lift our spirits.

Burton is gone, but in her fifties Liz is still on as many magazine covers as Madonna, Cher and the latest female TV rage. She is a true survivor. Not long ago I asked her about all the weight she'd lost. This was her answer: "I'm teed off at people constantly asking me if I had surgery to lose weight. The next time I'm asked that question, I think I'll take off my clothes to show there are no scars!"

And she might.

THANKSGIVING

Thanksgiving Day, for many of us, means turkey on the table and football on TV. That's not bad, and I'm not knocking it. But sometime between the drumstick and the drum major, call time out to count your blessings. That's what Thanksgiving Day is all about.

It is the day to remember that too many of our fellow citizens do not share fairly with some of the rest of us, and to ask, "Why not?" Of all the people in our nation, the Indian especially comes to mind on this day. Thanksgiving, for all its blessings, also represents a grievous era in our history, an era during which the Indian was dispossessed of his land and relegated to a substandard existence from which few have emerged.

Thanksgiving Day remains, as it was in the days of the pilgrims, essentially a family day. It is celebrated in comparative simplicity and privacy, with the entire family gathered around the groaning board and stuffing itself with turkey stuffing. It's a day to give thanks for our well-being, whatever the current economic or national problems, and for living in one of the world's most affluent nations. Sometime on that day it is crucial to remember that there is more to the good life than food and pleasure. There are the aspirations and ideals that nurture our quest for the impossible dream and for the day when bigotry and discrimination and poverty will vanish, along with the violence that has become so rampant. On this day, we can all bend the knee symbolically and give thanks that the freedom of spirit and mind is still ours to make that dream come true.

Robin WILLIAMS

He has the potential for being one of the great funnymen of our time. I knew it when I caught his nightclub act several years ago and watched him deal with a heckler as adroitly as a Bob Hope or Henny Youngman. A young lady in the audience wanted badly to get into Robin's act (or perform a more personal act with Robin), and yelled out, "Robin—I'm free! I'm free!"

Coolly riposted Robin, "I know—I saw your name on the bathroom wall."

Oprah WINFREY

The female Johnny Carson.

Oprah combines an array of qualities that should keep her at the very top. The most important is that, like Johnny, she simply has control of things.

When Deejay Warren Freiberg of Lansing's WLNR-FM sprayed one of the other guests with liquid soap on Winfrey's show, suggested a firebomb be dropped on Cabrini Green, and labeled Mayors Washington and Gary's Richard Hatcher "garbage," Winfrey immediately told him to go out with the garbage. Oprah also asked Brooke Shields whether it was true that she had signed a contract to remain a virgin until her book, *On Your Own*, was published. (Brooke wouldn't commit herself about the contract, but she did admit to being a virgin.)

Not that Winfrey doesn't commit an occasional gaffe herself. When she conducted a "Best Chicago Husband" contest on her show, the winner was Sam Boyd, who delivered an endearing story of his 50 happy years of marriage to Claire (and won an all-expense trip to Paris). We hated to tell Oprah that Boyd could have won the prize as "Best Fibbing Husband." No sooner was the show off the air than our office and Channel 7 were besieged by calls from "friends" of Sam, saying he had missed the length of his marriage by more than 48 years.

Maybe it *seemed* like 50. . . .

The WORLD

Two quotes stand out:

It is a gloomy moment in history. Never has there been so much apprehension. Never has the future seemed so incalculable. In France the political cauldron seethes. Russia hangs like a cloud on the horizon. All the resources of the British are sorely tried. Of our own troubles in the U.S., no man can see the end.

Our earth is degenerate in these latter days. Bribery and corruption are common. Children no longer obey their parents. Every man wants to write a book. The end of the world is evidently approaching.

Yesterday's newspaper? Next week's *Time*?

No, the first was a quote from *Harper's Weekly*. . .Oct. 10, 1857. The second quote was inscribed on a slab of stone in Assyria. The year was 2800 B.C.

Frank Lloyd WRIGHT

He strode majestically to the Chicago witness stand and took the oath. He wore his white hair long and flowing, and was as smartly and fundamentally dressed as his structures dress the earth. The prosecuting attorney began the examination.

"Your name?"

"Frank Lloyd Wright."

"Your occupation?"

He fixed a silk handkerchief in his suit pocket and rapped his elegant malacca cane against the floor. "I am the world's greatest living architect," he answered.

Later, I asked Wright how even he could say such a thing. "I had to," he said ingenuously. "I was under oath."

28

The Weekend

I t's Saturday—about 10:30 a.m.

This is the one day that the column doesn't appear in the paper and I don't have to write one because the Sunday column, written late Friday night, is already on the street. If something big breaks this morning, I'll get it into the late edition.

Saturday, I always make a couple of stops on the way to the office. Usually, one is the barber shop. Today, I got a lead there for a possible item. Through the years, as many good stories have come to me from barbers, cab drivers and doormen as from VIPs.

Before I leave home, I read the competition—the *Tribune*—while I'm having breakfast and getting dressed, making some notes on stories I want to pursue. I read Page One first, then Sports and the columns, and glance at the editorial pages. I miss Mike Royko's column on Saturday when he doesn't appear and make a mental note that I envy his weekend off. I should point out that the first edition of the *Sun-Times* is delivered to my home at midnight. Reading it cover to cover keeps me up to at least 1 a.m. And I'm up for the day at 6 a.m. I don't get much sleep, but who's complaining.

I walk into the office and greet my Saturday assistant April Branch. The office looks like a museum now—with photos of the famous, awards, the sailfish that didn't get away hanging on the south wall, hundreds of books, bound copies of the column since it began, gifts that mean something to me, and much more.

I check the column in the early Sunday edition one more time and make any corrections I deem necessary for the later edition, insert one more item, brush it up a bit. I make a note to send clips to all out-of-towners mentioned in the column, with this line: "It's a pleasure to mention your name—it gives the column some class."

Then I start going through the mail. There are dozens of requests for contributions, some bills, too many invitations, and a slew of items people would like to get in the column. I go through them, see if there are any fit to print. Usually, there are a couple which I tab for future use. Once in a while, I'll find something worth following up for the very next day. If an item says "Exclusive to Kup," I get interested.

I begin as always by making an outline for the next column and making a few phone calls. The TV is on in the background in case anything might be happening on one of the interview or news shows, and particularly if there is a football game. Weekdays, by the time Stella Foster comes in at 9:30, I'm usually pretty well organized.

This is the perfect junction to tell you about Stella. As I write this, I think of all the secretaries I've had since 1943—Anne Emme, Frances Gray, Connie Chancellor, Jean Krueger, Raeona Jordan, each invaluable in her own way. But there's only one Stella. She performs the duties of assistant as well as secretary. She's now in her 18th year with me and is as much a part of the column as I am. She's masterful in handling phone calls, oft times two or three at the same time in the course of answering or making a minimum of 75 calls a day. She has developed a practiced eye in recognizing a newsy item or a phone pest. She knows who to put through and who to put off. And through osmosis, she has become as well known around town as her boss.

And like Essee, she does a lot of the reading I don't have time to do. That includes out-of-town newspapers and magazines, which often provide clues to stories for the column. I've never had a leg man, as have so many other columnists. In the office, it's just Stella and me against the world in turning out six columns a week.

You may have wondered about the location of Kup's Column in the Sun-Times. It's the worst location of any column in the nation, far back among the ads. The previously mentioned Russ Stewart, former managing editor of the paper, was responsible for the placement. He reasoned that the column would attract advertisers to the back of the paper, whereas most advertisers want to be up front. He proved right. Advertisers eventually sought "adjacencies," a location near the column. I was stuck. Whenever I complained about my location, editors pointed to the newspaper readership surveys which showed the column as one of the paper's most popular features. Who could fight that? In recent years, my Sunday column was moved to the high rent district—page 14. But with the move came more work. The Sunday column now consists of a full page, two-thirds type, one-third photographs of persons on my beat, with captions that are news items.

Back to Saturdays, when I operate at a more leisurely pace than the frantic Monday-through-Friday madness.

About 12:30 I have lunch with a regular group, usually at Cricket's or Ditka's. During the week it's Eli's, Arnie's, P.J. Clarke's, Gene & Georgetti's, the Pump Room or the Tavern Club. Lunch is light, usually a salad. Once I was a steak-and-potato guy, but now meat is largely verboten. That's a price you have to pay. It isn't that high a price.

About 2:30, I'm back in the office. The phone rings. Someone wants tickets. Writing the column is just one of my responsibilities. I also run a ticket agency. I'm constantly called on to make hotel reservations, dinner reservations, airline reservations, theater reservations—for friends who are not shy about calling for such help. One typical incident along this line came up some years ago when Sammy Davis, Jr., was headlining at the old Copacabana Night Club in New York. Friends of mine were in New York at the time and couldn't get reservations to see Sammy, so they called me in Chicago. I then phoned Sammy in New York at his hotel and arranged for them to catch his performance.

I put a sheet of paper into the Remington I've used for 25 years, and rough out a few items I plan to transfer to my word processor later. If they don't play well, I do it over until I'm satisfied.

I take a pipe from the rack of a dozen or so, fill it and light it, while playing with the items. The pipe goes out again and again while I rework the words. Really, I smoke the matches, not the pipe. When I was a sportswriter, it was cigarettes, but I quickly changed to cigars because I realized that very few cigarette smokers would write columns for 45 years. The cigar became one of my trademarks, but I gave that up—another small price to pay.

Finally, I get the items right. I make a few more calls, organize a bit more, wrap up some loose ends, turn off the TV and the lights and leave the building. My medical resume for the last seven years may be as long as my Sunday column, but I feel great now. I decide to walk across the Wabash Avenue Bridge, now named the Irv Kupcinet Bridge, before catching a cab. It was a thrill when they named that bridge after me. I wish my parents could have been there to hear the laudatory remarks. My father would have loved it. And my mother would have believed it.

Some of the things said, though, when the bridge was dedicated in June of '86 were a bit much. The headline in our paper ran NOW IT'S KUP'S BRIDGE and the story began:

> The Irv Kupcinet Bridge went up for the first time yesterday, stopping traffic with style and class the way Kup has for years. By unanimous decree of the Chicago City Council and Mayor Washington, the Wabash Avenue Bridge was renamed for Kup in a noontime ceremony next to the *Chicago Sun-Times* building. The four-lane bridge that spans the Chicago River was renamed in honor of Kup's 50th anniversary as a journalist. "He has been a bridge in our community," Mayor Harold Washington said.

I thought of asking, since the bridge now bore my name, if I could erect toll booths at each end. And when the late Harry Golden wrote, "The Wabash Avenue Bridge, one of the most beautiful in the nation, now bears the name of Irv Kupcinet," I commented in the column that it seemed fitting. . . since opposites attract.

I catch a cab and a few minutes later reach our apartment overlooking my favorite lake. Two thoughts invariably come to mind. One is the beauty of Chicago's lakefront, especially in the summer when hundreds of sail boats add to the majesty of the scene. It's as beautiful as the French Riviera, only cleaner. The other thought is how fortunate I am to reside only a few minutes from the office. Suburban living never attracted Essee or me. Now I'm able to go back and forth in no time. And on our frequent evenings out, I'm able to get home to change clothes, often into a tuxedo, and then make the rounds. Living in the suburbs with my schedule would be panicville for putting the words together for a daily column.

Words—the power of words. In 1952, *Look* Magazine summed it up best with a commentary that stuck in my mind:

> They sing. They hurt. They sanctify. They were man's first, immeasurable feat of magic. They liberated us from ignorance and our barbarous past. For without those marvelous scribbles which build letters into words, words into sentences, sentences into systems and sciences and creeds, man would be forever confined to the self-isolated prison of the cuttlefish or the chimpanzee.

> We live by words: Love, Truth, God. We fight for words: Freedom. Country. Fame. We die for words: Liberty, Glory, Honor. They bestow the priceless gift of articulacy on our minds and hearts. And the men who truly shape our destiny, the giants who teach us, inspire us, lead us to deeds of immortality are those who use words with clarity, grandeur and passion. . ."

I don't know how much that applies to Kup's Column, but to me it's always been an awesome responsibility, and no doubt the biggest reason for all the multi-hour days in trying to do it right. I've often been asked about the art of writing a column. There's not much I can add to what's been said—or shown—on all the previous pages. To sum it up, I'd say that my first rule is to get it first—but get it right. Second, be as visible as possible, which means attending dozens of functions and events, and be available to everybody, big or small. It's also been my policy not to hurt people needlessly. But if their knuckles deserve to be rapped, let 'em have it.

Essee isn't home yet.

Most Saturday nights, there's something we have to do, so ordinarily I take a nap now. Tonight, happily, we simply collapse and lie around the house, talking, reading, watching TV. Inevitably, there are a few phone calls. We never turn off the phone. I fall asleep early tonight, shortly after midnight, and awaken a little after dawn Sunday morning. I awaken with the same thought every day: There's so much to do. And today it includes going to the office to knock out a Monday column.

Essee is still sleeping. When we took out our marriage license, we were interviewed and she said she would be sleeping till noon and would never make breakfast. Since we stopped staying out into the wee hours, she doesn't sleep till noon anymore. But she's made good on the breakfast vow.

Breakfast is pretty ritual. Grapefruit juice, cereal with skim milk, toast and coffee. Yes, one more small price to pay, but well worth it to be 76 and about to go to the office again.

I look at Essee before leaving. She's an amazing human being. What a survivor. Before leaving the apartment, my eyes go to the portrait of Cookie, and I quietly sigh over what might have been. I still can't believe she's gone. My parents, of course, are gone too. My only sister, Sophie, and my two brothers, Ben and Joe, are gone.

Everyone's life has some beauty in it. Yet frequently, suddenly and for no reason, life takes back what it has given. Then, you must make the pain a part of you—and continue doing what you do.

What I do is write a newspaper column.

It's time to start on the one for tomorrow.

Index